Me and MURDER, SHE WROTE

My Adventures in Television with Angela Lansbury,
Peter Falk and Jerry Orbach...among others

An Unauthorized Autobiography by
PETER S. FISCHER

GROVE
POINT
P R E S S

Pacific Grove California

BOOKS BY PETER S. FISCHER

The Blood of Tyrants
The Terror of Tyrants

The Hollywood Murder Mysteries

Jezebel in Blue Satin
We Don't Need No Stinking Badges
Love Has Nothing to Do With It
Everybody Wants An Oscar
The Unkindness of Strangers
Nice Guys Finish Dead
Pray For Us Sinners
Has Anybody Here Seen Wyckham?
Eyewitness to Murder
A Deadly Shoot in Texas

Me and Murder, She Wrote

ISBN 978-0-9886571-3-7

For Lucille…who was with me all the Way

and for Geoff—without whom there
would have been no Way

·········· Trivia Teasers ··········

At the end of each chapter you will find a
fun trivia question. See how well you do
and no peeking at the answers which you
will find on page 230.

CONTENTS

PREFACE

THIS BOOK is dedicated to the dreamers, to those who, as a child, had a secret ambition, a deeply buried desire they may have shared with no one. We are all dreamers to a certain extent. We all have ambitions for a good life, a good marriage, perhaps children, good health, good friends and, if possible, tranquility. I'm not talking about that. I'm talking about "the dream". I'm talking about the freckle-faced kid in Pop Warner who wants to be the next Tom Brady. Or the lanky 12 year old taking his first lesson who suddenly wants to be a right-handed Phil Mickelson. Or the little girl in pigtails and braces on her teeth who dreams of standing on the stage at the Oscars clutching her award, tears streaming down her face. I'm talking about the so-called "impossible" dream.

Maybe it's something very ordinary. Would you like to be a five-star chef, perhaps not famous, but working at something you love? How about an illustrator of children's books? A photographer? An architect? Would you feel fulfilled as a veterinarian, caring for sick and injured animals? Maybe a lumberjack out in the sun and fresh air instead of being cooped up in a stuffy office nine hours a day.

Many people in this world, far too many, settle for what they believe is attainable without testing the limits of their ability. Many choose a humdrum job because it provides security. Or a pressure cooker job which provides wealth while tearing away at body and soul. Did you ever stop to think that maybe Mike, your mail carrier, might have once dreamed of owning a small dairy farm somewhere, of being his own boss and enjoying the freedom that comes with it? Be honest. How many people do you know that get up in the morning, smiling, ready to take on the world, because they are working at something they love? And how many do you know who are merely going through the motions?

When I was five years old, I had a dream. I wanted to tell stories. I wanted to be a writer. I had learned to read when I was three. I went through kiddie books voraciously. Nothing made me happier. As soon as I could put words together semi-coherently I started writing little stories. One page. A half-page. Maybe even a novel-sized two pages. As I grew older I discovered radio and movies, scenes and dialogue. Prose was okay, drama was even better. I attended The Johns Hopkins University because they had a department devoted to Writing, Speech & Drama.

But fate took a hand. I got married at a young age to a lovely young lady who stole my heart and we had three beautiful children in three years. Given that, I needed to make a living. The dream, though not forgotten, was shoved to one side. The years slid by. I kept writing at my desk in my den but time was always in short supply. I was writing and writing and I think, getting better and better. I refused to abandon hope. I knew if I did, as much as I loved my family, the rest of my life would become a dreary journey to the coffin.

At the age of 35, my life turned around and through a fortuitous set of circumstances, I was given the chance to pursue that childhood dream. Yes, luck had a lot to do with it but when my break came, I was ready to take advantage of it. I spent the next thirty years living a life I never would have thought possible.

So all you dreamers out there, this book is for you, and particularly those of you who may have given up and settled for a great deal less. Never got to play shortstop for the Dodgers? How about opening a sporting goods store and spending your free time coaching Little League or working as an umpire. Failed to hit it big on Broadway? There are little theater groups in every town in America. High schools and junior colleges need drama teachers and coaches. Do you shoot golf in the low 70's but never got good enough to make the tour, even a local one. I know an avid golfer who spent a year learning how to make custom golf clubs. Now he earns his living at it.

Whatever that dream was, if you are stuck in a boring, humdrum job you hate, reconsider your options. You get one whirl around this planet. Don't toss it away. If you care enough and work hard enough, anything is possible.

A word of warning. I am not an archivist. I do not save letters and I have never kept a journal or any sort of diary. What you will read in these pages is totally dependent upon my memory which has not yet deteriorated into porridge. Nonetheless, while I promise you that my reminiscences are 99% accurate, there may be places where I have included the wrong person in a meeting or my chronology is slightly bollixed. This is the way I remember it and it is pretty damn close to the truth, the whole truth and nothing but the truth.

If You Are A Writer, Then Write

Someone recently asked me if I was ever going to write my autobiography and I said, no, I wasn't. First of all, no one is going to care and secondly, it's a lot like work. Thirdly, my life is jam-packed with many incidents and personal things I would just as soon keep private besides the fact that they would probably bore you to tears. But it did occur to me that I might have a couple of experiences worth relating to would-be writers, especially those who might be on the brink of giving up. Bad idea, and if you really are a writer, totally incomprehensible. If you have paper, pen and a brain, you write. Everything else is immaterial. Now, if you are talking about writing professionally, that is something else again. That will require not only talent but a certain amount of luck.

I have been a writer all of my life. Even now while I collect my social security checks, I am still deeply immersed in writing, having created a series of novels collectively titled "The Hollywood Murder Mysteries". They are a fun-filled parade of classic whodunit mysteries set against the background of post-WWII Hollywood and the era of actors like Bogart, Cagney, Wayne, and Brando and directors like John Huston and Bill Wellman. There are ten so far with more to come. I'm not getting rich but they are selling well enough to keep me interested and even more than that, the critical response from everyday readers as well as highly respected critics has been universally positive. So instead of growing roses or dabbling in pork bellies, I'll keep at it. Why? Because I am a writer and have been since I was five years old.

But as to writing professionally and making a living at it, that is indeed a different story and one that begs recounting for all you talented would-bes and wanna-bes out there.

For the first 34 years of my life I was a dabbler. In high school and college

I wrote plays that were produced but these were the tiniest of ponds. In those days, I never gave a thought to being paid for my work with one notable exception. And I am going to tell you about it because it was a watershed moment in my life. It happened between my sophomore and junior years in high school. I was fourteen years old and mowing lawns and washing cars to make spending money and in the afternoon I would watch Matinee Theater which was on every afternoon. These were one hour live dramas, some adapted, but many originals. I sensed I was learning by osmosis and on that basis I had the temerity to think I could write one of these.

Two weeks at the typewriter and I came up with something that I thought (at the time) was pretty good. With unbridled hubris, without an agent, without any sort of credential, I mailed it off to NBC where most likely it would end up in a pile of other unsolicited scripts, the lowest of the low in literary circles. Well, of course, they turned me down. Yes, I got rejected. I got rejected with a two page single spaced personal letter from one of their producers who used words like "intriguing", "different", "well-thought out" as well as other words like "mawkish", "stilted dialog", "amateurish". Amateurish?? I was fourteen years old! I treasured that letter for years. Somewhere along the way it got lost. I wish I had it back because more than any one single event in my life, this is the one I would hang onto when the going got tough.

After college and a stint in the Army I got married to the girl of my dreams which meant that employment came ahead of pipe dreams. These were what I call the "lost years" between 22 and 34 when I worked hard for a living at jobs that had nothing to do with my deep seated ambition to succeed at writing. Insurance investigator, trade magazine editor, and finally editor-publisher of my own small magazine. And all the while I was spending time writing short stories or fanciful scripts, one act plays, just about anything to keep my hand in. All of these remained in my file cabinet. No one saw them. They weren't good enough.

I don't know whether it was fear of rejection that made me keep my work to myself throughout those years. I suspect it was. On the one hand, I had to steal the writing time in dribs and drabs and it was an awkward way to write.

It wasn't and couldn't be my best work. That's what I told myself. But beyond that lurked the terror that every writer faces (and painters and poets and musicians), that if I put myself out there and the world says no thanks, I will have to face up to the fact that my dream was just that, childish nonsense without substance in the real world. Deep down I believe I was paralyzed by that fear.

I was 34 years old when I finally decided to face my demons. If I were to become a professional writer I would have to give it everything I had. I could no longer blame the world for my failure. If I wasn't good enough, so be it. Better to find out right away than to spend the rest of my life deluding myself that the fates had conspired against me and that "if only...." "If only" is a crutch used by those who never entered the race or stayed the course. It is a phrase cherished by life's losers and I was determined not to be one of them.

Somewhere around my 30th birthday I quit my job as the editor of the trade magazine. It didn't pay a lot, I was bored and the owner's son would soon be graduating college and I was beginning to feel dispensable. I was also toying with the idea of starting a local sports car magazine to deal with the activities in and around the New York metropolitan area. I decided to give it a shot. It started out small and grew but not very fast and it was wasn't making me all that rich. After three years I was earning about 80% of what I had walked away from but with my wife Lu teaching, we were managing just fine.

And then two things hit me. One, my little magazine wasn't going to grow much beyond what I already had and two, despite being the chief cook and bottle washer, the entire operation only took two weeks in every month where, if I had the drive, I could sit down at the typewriter and get serious about my writing.

I decided to get serious.

> After several years of writing for live television in virtual anonymity, Rod Serling became an "overnight success" with 'Patterns'. Which script was it?
> a) His 31st
> b) His 40th
> c) His 55th
> d) His 72nd

The luckiest guy in the world in a big hug with the loveliest
and warmest star on television.

Please, Call Me Angie

I WAS SITTING IN MY OFFICE on a beautiful day in late February, 1983. I was a reasonably successful television writer-producer. My work on "Columbo" had given me credibility and even some name recognition. In the past eleven years at Universal Studios I had been entrusted with writing and producing several movies of the week, a couple of mini-series, several pilots and four series as well as a dozen or so scripts. My position with the studio was secure. I was well-paid and yet as I glanced at my wrist watch I was a little ill at ease.

It was shortly past one o'clock. At two o'clock, Dick Levinson and Bill Link and I were scheduled for a meeting in the office of Robert Harris, president of Universal's Television arm. At this meeting we were going to meet Angela Lansbury, movie star and Broadway icon, who had read a script I had written and expressed some interest in playing the lead role.

Angela Lansbury? What did I know about Angela Lansbury that had anything to do with the bright and charming, delightfully down home character I had recently committed to paper? Oh, sure. She was a good actress, no question about that. She was also that snippy little tart in Gaslight that bedeviled Ingrid Bergman and shamelessly batted her baby blues at Charles Boyer. She was the saloon girl in The Harvey Girls who made life miserable for lovely Judy Garland. She was the hard-nosed publisher in State of the Union who caused frostbite to afflict anyone she came near. And worst of all, she was the harridan of a mother to Laurence Harvey in The Manchurian Candidate whose onscreen presence made Eva Braun seem like Mary Poppins.

Oh, yes, I knew all about Mame. In fact I'd seen Miss Lansbury perform it live on Broadway. Riveting. Spectacular. Funny. All those things. But also flamboyant, theatrical, larger than life. Nothing like my character. And there was Mrs. Lovett, the murderous pie lady in Sweeney Todd. No, no, no. This star, this actress of many talents, would never do.

All these things were floating around in the back of my mind, unvoiced to anyone. What if she said yes? Well, if she said yes, our pilot was a go-project. That would be good. But how would I rewrite the script? How would Shakespeare rewrite Macbeth to star Billy Crystal? All these misgivings plagued me as I broke one of the fundamental rules of my life. Something to do with crossing bridges. Well, the bridge was looming ever closer.

At ten minutes to two my b.e.a. (beautiful executive assistant) Sandy Quinn warned me it was time to go. Dick and Bill and I met downstairs and together we trudged toward the ominous Black Tower, the fourteen story executive building where careers were made or destroyed on the turn of a rating point or the whim of an executive who'd had a bad hair day or a three martini lunch or something that had been wheezed up his or her nose.

The moment of truth was at hand.

But let's go back a couple of months. It was late '83. CBS had let it be known through the tower executives that they would be very open to the idea of a new murder mystery from Dick and Bill and since these two gentlemen had long ago given up the ordeal of actually having to write a script for episodic television, I was thrown into the mix as the grunt who would end up doing the actual work. The truth is, I was really excited by the idea. Forget the fact that Dick and Bill and I had been involved with a misbegotten project called "Hellinger's Law" which we rightly disowned in fear of our careers. This time we'd get it right.

It didn't take long to come up with an idea. Dick had always wanted to do a series about a retired magician who uses magic and illusion to solve difficult cases. Bill had no problem with it. Neither did I. So we started putting together some thoughts on a series we thought should be titled "Blacke's Magic". In Dick's view the hero was an older man, mid fifties maybe, who had just gotten tired of the grind. Possible problem: networks like younger demographics. Maybe there was compromise in there somewhere. In any case CBS knew what we had done with Ellery Queen. The fact that we had failed to get to a second season didn't seem to bother them. If the idea of magic appealed, we might get a go ahead to pilot story or maybe even pilot script.

We took a meeting at CBS with Carla Singer, a senior development executive and from moment one, we could see we were on the wrong page. What we were really hoping for, Carla told us, was a mystery with a strong female lead. She also needn't be particularly young. Yikes! I said to myself. Except for Angie Dickinson (Policewoman), Lynda Carter (Wonder Woman), and Anne Francis (Honey West), the history of prime time television was littered with the bodies of talented actresses in one-hour dramas machine gunned to death by A.C. Neilsen's assassins. Worse, the above named ladies, all excellent in their roles, also had obvious sex appeal which could only help when competing with the likes of Ward Bond or Ernie Borgnine.

Both chastened and encouraged, we took our leave, determined to see if we could come up with something that would please CBS as well as ourselves. That last requirement was important. We weren't interested in getting a show on the air unless it had a fighting chance to be a success, even a modest one. In short we were no longer in the valiant-effort, good-try, too-bad-it-failed game. If what we came up with didn't look promising we were prepared to walk away.

After a couple of days I devised something I thought would be a natural, given the parameters CBS had set. It seemed a little simple. Maybe too simple. Maybe too obvious. On a Saturday evening at nine o'clock CBS had aired a TV Movie "A Caribbean Mystery" starring Helen Hayes as Miss Marple, Agatha Christie's buoyant outgoing armchair detective. It had a cast of well-known television personalities and former movie stars, much as we had done with Ellery Queen in 1975. The movie was scheduled against 'The Love Boat' which used the same guest star format but was beginning to show its age and Miss Hayes and the movie did respectably well.

All right, I thought. *Why don't we meld Miss Marple and Miss Christie into one character, a mystery writer who actually solves murder mysteries using logic, good sense, observation, and a twinkly sense of humor that masks the sharp brain lurking beneath a very attractive hair do.* Another requirement. While Miss Marple and Miss Christie are British through and through, our heroine had to be one hundred percent American, middle class, with Yankee forth-rightness and integrity. And what better place to set her down than the rock-ribbed coast of Maine. She's a voracious reader. Make her an English teacher who secretly writes murder mysteries for her own amusement, never dreaming that she would ever show one of her manuscripts to anyone. We want her as a stand alone character, free to move about unencumbered by children or a husband so we make her a widow who had a wonderful marriage and now has been alone for several years. Her hometown would be the scene of some of these mysteries but we would put her on the road to exciting locales both in the States and overseas. As a successful author (which she would become in the pilot episode) her travels would be natural.

Dick and Bill and I got together and kicked it around. I gave her a name and a hometown. Jessica Fletcher sounded very sturdy and Yankeeish and as for Cabot Cove, well, who's to say that John Cabot, the explorer, didn't stop by at her little cove for a night or two of revelry or other diversions.

We decided to toss this fluffy souffle at CBS and see what they thought. We needn't have worried. They loved the idea, especially Harvey Shepherd, head of programming who was, at all times, our staunchest champion in this enterprise, even in its darkest hour which, unbeknownst to us, would be coming up soon.

It didn't take long to bang out a broad outline of a story. Dick came up with the gimmick of killing off Sherlock Holmes, a sure attention getter, and we used a few time tested twists (mainly mistaken identity) to make it work. A world famous fast food fish mogul tosses a costume party at his posh suburban estate. A private detective is caught rifling one of the rooms and gets tossed out on his rear end. The next morning the fish king is found floating face down in the swimming pool. Horrors! Who could have had a motive to kill this philandering, dishonest, dislikable imperious mogul? Why just about everybody. But wait! The body is fished from the pool. It is not the fish king, it's the private detective wearing the Sherlock Holmes costume.

Dick and Bill smiled at me. Well, there you go, pal. There's your story. Just fill in the blanks. Hah, I laughed. Thanks, fellas. All you've left me with are acts two through eight, inventing characters, developing twists, creating red herrings, figuring out who the killer is and why and finally working up a believable clue that Jessica can use to nail the perp to the cottage door. Piece of cake, says Dick as he and Bill exit my office leaving me to eye my two pages of notes with great skepticism.

Well, I got started arranging the puzzle and creating the narrative and bless them, the boys were a great help when I got stuck now and then and had to zig zag my way out. Now for those of you who haven't yet seen the pilot (and I can't believe you haven't if you have bought this book) I'm not going into any more of the plot. But after a week or so, we had the story outlined, shipped off to CBS and almost immediately got a response. "Love story, please write script." Which I did.

Writing the script was easy because the story structure was sound and I rarely had to deviate from it. Here and there a grace note, or a humorous scene. As I recall the bus chase wasn't in the story outline. Suspect boards bus. Jessica looks for cab to follow. No cab. Second bus pulls up. Jessica boards and while she didn't say "Follow that bus!", that's what it was all about.

A couple of weeks later, the script was finished to our satisfaction and off it went to CBS. Back came their response. A commitment to film the two hour pilot with only one caveat and it was a beauty. The commitment would be cancelled if we couldn't come up with the right actress to play Jessica.

We already knew this was going to be the key to a successful pilot (and the series, if we did it right) and we had been noodling with all the possibilities. To be sure, there were dozens of candidates available, maybe more. After a certain age in television (true of the movies as well) actresses find it harder and harder to find work. Not fair, but a reality of the business. We considered and discarded many former movie stars, some because they had no interest in doing television, others who were retired, others because they didn't project the quality we were looking for. Number one, this lady had to be instantly likable and not just "act" likable. That eliminated a lot of contenders. She had to exude intelligence. There go some more. She had to be down to earth and not reek of big city sophistication. Bye bye to another bunch. We thought about television names but there were only a few and almost all had achieved popularity in comedy. And finally, in line with television exposure, there was the dreaded "Q rating" which everyone in management insisted did not exist but certainly did. A performer's Q was based on recognizability and likability. (In one of the Q's earlier surveys, it was found that John Wayne had a Q of 5 out of 100 whereas Michael Cole of "The Mod Squad" was somewhere up in the 70's.)

So the problem was pretty well defined. Get ourselves an actress who would be right for the part and could score a Q that would meet with network approval. I forget who said it first but I do know we all nodded in agreement: Jean Stapleton, Archie Bunker's long suffering wife Edith who had recently left the show to pursue other challenges. She certainly was a warm and likable on-screen presence and as for her acting chops, she had plenty. She had played many more parts than Edith and we were sure she could handle whatever we threw at her.

Harvey Shepherd concurred. Great idea. Go get her and the pilot is a go-project. So we went after Miss Stapleton. A luncheon was set up at the Bel Air Country Club. The three of us were there along with Robert Harris and Miss Stapleton, accompanied by either her agent or her manager, can't remember which. It was a lovely luncheon, full of bonhommie. Miss Stapleton was gracious. Dick, always the mouthpiece for our little triad, sold the concept brilliantly. Miss Stapleton smiled. It sounded delightful. Of course, it would depend on the script and beyond that, she had other factors to consider. She had just lost her husband of many years and we knew she was still grieving. The two of them had operated a small community theater and now that responsibility had fallen to her, but nonetheless, she would give our project every consideration.

A week later we got the news. Miss Stapleton, having read the script, had decided that Jessica Fletcher was not for her. She graciously apologized and wished us well. When Dick hung up the phone, the silence hung over us like the fog in San Francisco Bay. Our charming little project, our neat script, our potential series, all cut down in a heartbeat. We were dead in the water or as they say in television, in "turnaround" which is a polite way of saying, "Take a hike."

Ah, but we had failed to consider Harvey Shepherd who let us know in no uncertain terms he was a hundred percent committed. I love this project, he told us. We're going to make this. Go find somebody else.

Momentarily ecstatic, we then looked at each other. Great. Get who? We hadn't a clue and we weren't about to toss just anybody into the part to film a pilot which surely would fail. We had failed nine years earlier with Ellery Queen because our leading man, the engine that was supposed to drive the show, didn't measure up. To be fair, it wasn't Jim Hutton's fault. He did exactly what was asked of him. He played likeable, laid back, absent-minded, often disengaged, to a tee. The problem was he was directed to play Ellery without a lot of drive and absent this drive, the show lacked the energy to succeed. The lesson learned: your leading man or leading lady is more than half the battle. If the audience doesn't buy him/her, you haven't a prayer.

And then, like *deus ex machina*, possible salvation suddenly loomed before us. Angela Lansbury, one of those actresses we had never bothered to consider because she certainly wasn't going to get involved in television, suddenly let it be known that for the right project, she WOULD consider a television series. Immediately a meeting was set up for the next day at 2:00 in Robert Harris's office where Dick, Bill, and I would meet this theatrical legend and if that God in his Machine wasn't pulling our collective legs, we might bring Jessica back from the trash heap. (We were trying to ignore the fact that concurrently she was also considering a half hour sit com from TV legend Norman Lear to co-star Charles Durning. If we'd really thought about that, we might have cried.)

Angela was already seated when we arrived. She rose, shook our hands. When she shook mine, she turned on the warmest, most delightful smile I had ever seen. (Outside of my wife, of course.) Dick went through his spiel, we all exchanged pleasantries, laughed a lot. I kept thinking, this feels a lot like lunch with Jean Stapleton but with one exception. I was totally, irreversibly captivated by this woman. Could she play Jessica? No, she WAS Jessica. To hell with The Manchurian Candidate. We'd found our lady. We could only hope that she had found us.

We got the news a few days later. Reportedly, Angela had read the script, liked it a lot and said "I can do something with this." We had our Jessica and while the lawyers in business affairs worked out the details, I called Angela at her New York apartment to reintroduce myself, to thank her and to give her a rough idea of the shooting schedule.

She answered the phone.

"Hello."

"Miss Lansbury?" I ventured.

"Yes."

"Miss Lansbury, this is Peter Fischer, " I said.

"Oh, yes, " she said with a smile in her voice. "It's so nice to hear from you."

"Miss Lansbury, " I started again before she cut me off.

"Oh, for God's sakes, please call me Angie" she said with a twinkle.

For the next seven years I was done for.

How did I get to this point in my life? As I look back it was a combination of a modest amount of talent, a great deal of luck and in a few instances, being in the right place at the right time. In so many ways my career has been a fairy story, an improbability that, if concocted by a screenwriter for a movie, would be tossed in the trash after the first couple of pages. In my case, truth really is stranger than fiction.

> 2. How old was Angela Lansbury when she played 34-year-old Laurence Harvey's mother in "The Manchurian Candidate"?

Well, It Just Doesn't Happen That Way

IT'S 1970. I am 35 years old and as previously disclosed, I have decided to get serious about my writing. I will know soon enough if I have what it takes to succeed or if I have been deluding myself all these years. I have a wife, three kids, and a mortgage and I live in a modest tract house in Smithtown, New York, a small town on Long Island about sixty miles east of New York. My wife Lu teaches English and I own and operate a small monthly publication called 'Sports Car News'. It's not making me rich but with Lu's salary we're getting by reasonably well. The little magazine is grooved and operates on cruise control leaving me a couple of weeks a month to seriously explore my writing ambition. I've had it all my life but an early marriage and three children put a crimp in my ability to get serious. Or maybe that's not really the case. Maybe family obligations have been my excuse not to test myself, to be able to say, Gee, I could have been the next Rod Serling if only I hadn't gotten married so young. But now that feeble alibi no longer applies. Now I DO have the time. So what now, big shot? Do you want to write or do you just want to talk about it?

My first real stab at writing a movie took me a month. It was about 120 pages. I forget what it was about. I knew nothing about formatting a script, pagination, all the little things that professionals learn in Screen Writing 101. I had a story and some characters and I thought it was interesting so I sent it off to Hollywood.

Let me be more precise. I sent it off to my younger brother, Geoffrey, for his criticism and advice and, if he thought it was any good, his help in getting it to someone who might know someone who might be acquainted with somebody who could put it in the hands of a person who could do something with it. At the time, Geoff, a year and a half my junior, was an established casting director at Universal Studios.

Within days I got back a long three page letter with lots of notes, criticisms and suggestions. He also sent along two shooting scripts so I could get the formatting right in case I wanted to do a rewrite or to try something new. In that regard he was encouraging. The script I had written was not good enough to be shown around but he truly believed I had a knack for script writing and encouraged me to try again. He did, however, caution me about getting my hopes up. The idea of someone in the boondocks sitting down and writing a shootable script and then getting it made, well, it just doesn't happen that way.

Buoyed by the hope he'd given me, I determined to try again. A new project. Something special, I hoped. Not a rehash of the usual things I'd seen on television but a story line that was fresh and different. A week later, it came to me.

My eye was caught by a newspaper article about a new law passed in China. Because of overpopulation, married couples would be restricted to having one child, no more. No surprise. Peoplewise, China was a mess. But even in America a lot of people were concerned with ZPG (Zero

"The Last Child" got me into the business against all odds. Van Heflin (l.) in his last role shared the screen with Michael Cole and Janet Margolin.

Population Growth). Suppose it wasn't Beijing that passed that law but the U.S. Congress. Suppose that some time in the future the population problem had become so unmanageable that older people were being cast aside and allowed to die (or even forced to die) to make way for younger generations. Reach 65 and medical treatment was not available, only pills to deal with the pain. The more I thought about the concept the more excited I became. The first thing I needed to decide was how to incorporate all this into an interesting movie. Simple. We make it a chase picture with socio-logical overtones. Our likable young couple has a baby. It lives 15 days and then dies. Too bad. That was your one child, says the government. You're not entitled to another one. In defiance she becomes pregnant again. They hope they can get away with it but they get caught and rather than endure a forced abortion, they make a run for it. Destination: Canada, where they will find safe haven. Hot on their trail, a Javert-like enforcer from the De-partment of Population Control. Along the way they are aided by an elderly ex-Senator who is secretly receiving medical help from his family doctor. It seemed to have all the elements. I sat down at the typewriter. From the start it seemed to write itself. Three weeks later it was finished. (I was always a fast writer. Still am.)

I titled it "We Know What We're Doing", not particularly zingy but an ironic description of government mentality. I shipped it off to Geoff and with great trepidation, waited for a reaction. It wasn't long in coming. He loved it. He couldn't say enough about it. It was everything it should be in terms of story telling, characters and dialogue. He knew some people, he said. He would see what he could do.

There was a lot of back and forth, letters, phone calls but here's the upshot after the smoke had cleared. Geoff had managed to get it to an independent television producer named Bill Allyn who had taken it to Barry Diller, then the driving force behind ABC's newly instituted Movies of the Week. Barry liked it well enough to send it to Aaron Spelling with the suggestion that he might want to film it. Aaron readily agreed. I was suddenly a bonafide television writer and I had a $5, 000 first payment to prove it. (I would eventually get two more checks just like it, In those days big money for a shoestring magazine publisher.)

In December of '70 I was summoned to Hollywood (expenses paid) to do some rewriting on the script prior to shooting. I got on a plane at JFK in 40 degree wind swept weather and landed in L.A. to be greeted by a balmy zephyr-like breeze and temperatures in the mid 80's. It was at that moment that I questioned why I had been spending most of my life living on a snow-tormented, traffic-congested place like Long Island.

The rewriting took almost no time at all. I formed a good relationship with Bill Allyn, spent a great deal of my week on the coast with my brother and went home, determined that one way or another I would be back. Geoff put it succinctly. If you want to be a part of the business, you have to live here. He didn't have to tell me twice.

(Note: another confidence builder courtesy of Bill Allyn who told me that Spelling, upon receiving the script, sent it over to television icon Rod Serling, asking him to rewrite it. This sort of thing happens all the time in television and film when producers can't bring themselves to trust their own judgement. Some producers have had three or four different writers working on the same project simultaneously. And God knows, Spelling probably thought he had good reason to worry about a nobody from Long Island who had written this thing at his kitchen table. Cut to the next day. Serling returns the script to Spelling with a note. "This script doesn't need rewriting". When Bill told me this, I damn near cried. One of my two heroes—Paddy Chayevsky being the other—had endorsed my work. Unbelievable.)

On October 7, 1971, the movie made it to the small screen. Retitled temporarily to "The Day They Took The Babies Away", it finally aired as "The Last Child" on the ABC network. Teen idol Michael Cole and Janet Margolin played the youngsters on the run, Van Heflin (in his last performance ever) played the aging Senator, and Ed Asner appeared as the bulldog cop hot on the trail of the fugitives. Directed by a sly old codger named John Llewellyn Moxey, the ratings were phenomenal (number two in the Neilsens for that week), the reviews mixed though mostly favorable. The picture was honored at the upcoming Emmy Awards with a nomination for Best Made-for-TV Movie. It was up against the pilot for The Waltons as well as "Brian's Song" with James Caan and "Duel", the Steven Spielberg film with Dennis Weaver. We lost.

3. Van Heflin won the Best Supporting Actor Award in 1942 for what picture?

a) Tennessee Johnson
b) Johnny Eager
c) Green Dolphin Street
d) Shane

A Whole Lot of Nothing Going On

OF COURSE, my brother Geoff was right. If I wanted something more than a flash in the pan success, if I really wanted a career in television, I couldn't remain in Smithtown. So Lu quit her job, I sold my magazine and we sold our house. My friends were sure I had lost my mind. Had I been one of them I might have agreed but Lu and I were totally committed. If I didn't pursue this lifelong dream, if I didn't take the gamble, I would always wonder what might have been. To me, it was a no-brainer. My friends nodded solemnly. No brains seemed to be the operative phrase.

Leaving the three kids behind with Lu's folks, we packed up the little Datsun station wagon with all the carryables we wanted to keep and huffed and puffed our way cross-country. A week after we arrived we were settled into a rented house and sent for the kids and the dog. All together now in a new state with new adventures lying ahead of us, we were on top of the world. Well, at least I was. The kids were homesick for their Smithtown pals and Lu couldn't find the right curtains for the windows. But me, I was raring to go. Nothing could stop me now.

I went from euphoria to depression in a short few weeks. Instead of sitting atop the mountain, the mountain was sitting on me. You would think with a major credit like mine (albeit just one, I grant you) that someone might be interested in giving me a job. No, nothing was really happening. I spent some time at my typewriter fiddling with some ideas for a Movie of the Week. I sketched out and then discarded a couple of notions for series. Often my boys and I would wander down to the local park and they'd shag fly balls or we'd toss around a football. I ended up managing or helping to coach park league teams that my sons were on. Most days it was mornings at the typewriter, a chicken salad sandwich for lunch while I followed the adventures of Erica Kane on "All My Children". As I recall she was unhappily married and contemplating divorce to a guy anyone could plainly see was a nogoodnik. Poor Erica, the more I watched, the worse things got for her. As for me. I was becoming an addict. All in all things were mostly dreary.

There were a couple of bright spots. I met Steven Bochco. Not only met him but played poker with him most Thursday nights in an game brother Geoff was involved in and got me a seat. A really fun bunch of people, many of whom were in the business. Like Vic Tayback (Mel, owner of the diner in "Alice") and Mike Constantine (the loony father with the windex in "My Big Fat Greek Wedding") and Chris Stone who had already been a regular on a couple of series. The gossip and the banter around the table kept me tangentially connected to the business at a time when I felt I was becoming more and more isolated. Of course I always had Geoff and beyond that, Steve and I hit it off right away. He was then a contract writer for Universal and the current story editor of "Columbo". This being one of my favorite shows, I had written a spec script and I gave it to him to read. He liked it but not well enough to buy it though he did pass it along to the incoming Columbo producer, Dean Hargrove. (More on this script later.)

Through Geoff I got an interview to write a 30 minute medical pilot being produced by James Hirsch. I showed up precisely on time wearing my spiffiest sports jacket, white shirt and tie, and spit shined loafers. Jim took one look at me and gave me a piece of advice I never forgot. Never, ever, go to a meeting wearing a jacket and tie. It is a clear signal that you need the work and you must never, ever, let them know that you NEED the job. Jim gave me the assignment. I wrote a pretty good script, the pilot was filmed but the series was never picked up. I went back to twiddling my thumbs and noodling with ideas for MOW's or TV series. The phone stayed mainly silent. I had one lunch meeting with Bill Allyn and Mike Connors ("Mannix") about another script I had written. Nothing came of it.

It was during this dry period that I learned several valuable lessons. The main one was this, passed on to me by a very experienced old pro whose name I cannot remember He said that the way business was conducted in Hollywood it was a miracle that anything ever got made. The number one time filler for writers and producers was doing lunch. You don't eat lunch. You don't meet for lunch. You DO lunch. At this lunch which you are "doing", someone is trying to sell the other person on the most valuable property to come down the road since "Gone With the Wind". Invariably this meeting will not result in anything tangible except for the fact that it has chewed up two hours in an otherwise uneventful day. This is all to the good, particularly if the participants are in "development". This is a euphemism for "unemployed". Sometimes one of the lunch "doers" is employed and is actually in a position to enter into a deal. 99% of the time, this will not happen. This is because studio executives can never be held responsible for the deals they don't make but they most certainly can be fired for the turkey of a deal they DO make. Thus, the time honored tradition of "doing lunch" does not result in actual business being transacted but sets the stage for another lunch months or years down the road where no business can again be not transacted.

Six months had passed and by now I was running out of money. The fee for the movie plus what I had made selling my house and the little magazine was mostly gone and I was, as gamblers like to say, down to the cloth. Within the next few weeks I was going to have to knuckle down and find another line of work or skedaddle back to Long Island, battered, bruised and beaten. The neighbors threw us a farewell party when departure was imminent. Meant as a gesture of love, it only brought me face to face with reality. I had failed. Period.

And then heavenly powers once again interceded. My agent called to say that he had set up a meeting for me with Nina Laemmle, the story editor for the highest rated show on television, "Marcus Welby". Since Welby was a Universal show and brother Geoff had strong ties to its executive producer David Victor, I think Geoff had more than a little to do with getting me this meeting. He never let on and I didn't press him on it.

Nina turned out to be a lovely lady who loved writers. At the moment she was in script trouble. She had seen "The Last Child" and liked it. Someone had told her (my brother?) that I wrote good and I wrote fast. She had a germ of an idea for an episode and would I be interested in working on it. Sure thing, says I. I went home, got to the typewriter and the next day messengered over a fully fleshed out story. She was suspicious until she read it but then gave me a go ahead to write the script. Thanks to the Writer's Guild, this now meant that there was going to be money in my pocket no matter how it turned out. Long Island Revisited would have to wait. Did I mention she told me they had a time problem? Not to rush me but if she could see a first draft within 8-10 days she would be very grateful.

Back to the typewriter. Two days later the script was finished. I sent it over. Now I am sure at this point she was wondering what she had gotten herself into. But no, she liked what I had done. It was a Monday afternoon. She called. Could I possibly come in tomorrow at 2:00 to go over the script? Could I? I would have come in at two in the morning if that's what she wanted.

At two o'clock I was in her office, sipping on some excellent coffee, as we went through the script page by page, changing a line here and there, sharpening tag lines, dumping some superfluous dialogue. Inside of an hour we'd finished up. "Good", she said. I said, "Do I go right into second draft now?" I asked. She smiled. "Peter, that WAS the second draft, " she said.

A week later, with Nina's blessing, I drove to a neighborhood in Van Nuys where the Welby company was shooting my episode. I had never actually seen a script shot and for a star struck neophyte from the other end of the world, this is pretty powerful stuff. I was carrying my pristine white script which says "Written by Peter S. Fischer" on the cover page. I knew I was in the right place long before I got to the actual address. The street was crowded with trucks and other vehicles, mostly unmarked. This is what Bob O'Neill, my future producer, loved to call the "Third Army". Props, wardrobe, makeup trailers, lighting equipment, backup cameras, tons of stuff which may not be used but which had better be available immediately if something goes wrong. As I walked by one of the trucks which seemed relatively empty, I noticed five men in tee shirts sitting around a makeshift table, downing cold beers and playing poker. I will later learn that these are the teamsters, the truck drivers who get the equipment to and from the location sites. I learn that, while at the actual site, their contract obligates them to play cards, eat and drink, read comic books or girlie magazines, or take refreshing naps. I may have been misinformed about that but they seemed awfully good at all of the above.

At the actual shooting site, I was momentarily stopped by one of the crew but I quickly put his mind at ease. I am the writer, I told him, pointing to my name on the script. Strangely, he didn't seem overly impressed. I also noticed that he, too, is carrying a script but his is comprised of pink and blue pages. I wondered why I didn't have one of those. Inside the house I ran into the assistant director. He, too, didn't seem awed by my status as the writer. He told me the company is in the back yard setting up. That's where I would find the director, Marc Daniels. Marc was a lovely man. He seemed genuinely pleased to meet me. He liked the script and said it will make a fine show. He explained that the pink and blue pages are updates to include script changes. So far these have nothing to do with my dialogue; it's all about accommodating the script to the actual locations. He introduced me to James Brolin. I manage to mumble something incoherent. Brolin smiled, shook my hand and we shared some pleasantries, then he wandered off to chat with one of the actors about the upcoming scene.

I noticed way off to one side under a canopy, a table laden with fresh fruit, donuts, chips, M&Ms, soda, coffee and other goodies. It was here that I got my first inkling that the writer was not the most important cog in the production wheel. I approached the table which was being "manned" by a formidable looking woman of a certain size who was eyeing me with suspicion even before I reached for a Diet Coke. 'Scuse me, ' she says, 'you with the crew?' I say, 'No. I'm the writer'. Her eyes narrow thoughtfully as if I were Wimpy there to steal one of her hamburgers.

She scanned the front of the script I was holding up, hesitated for the longest time, then sighed, 'Yeah, I guess it'll be all right'. In fact, as I stood around watching them film, soda in hand, I realized that I was about as welcome on the set as a banana slug in a fruit salad. It was a few days later when I first heard the joke that would stay with me for the rest of my career. Did you hear the one about the dumb blonde who wanted to get ahead in

Hollywood so she slept with the writer? That pretty much summed it up but I wasn't going to get depressed about it. I was a writer whether anybody liked it or not.

From that point on, things only got better for my fledgling career. The episode was aired with Lief Ericson as Welby's long time friend and mentor who secretly suffered from atherosclerosis but wouldn't face up to the fact that he could no longer perform surgery.

Meanwhile David Victor had another show on the air, "Owen Marshall, Counselor at Law" starring Arthur Hill and Lee Majors and produced by Jon Epstein. On David's recommendation, Jon had me in to talk about a script and I walked out with an assignment. Even before I had finished the first draft, Nina had brought me in for a second Welby and that was followed by a second Owen Marshall and then by a third Welby. Suddenly I had more work than I knew what to do with and I was loving every minute of it. What was going on here? A year and a half earlier I had been selling ad space to Aston-Martin dealers and now I was walking onto sound stages and being introduced to the likes of Robert Young and Arthur Hill. I considered myself then, and I still do, as one of the luckiest people on the face of the earth.

4. In 1963 Arthur Hill won the Tony for Best Dramatic Actor playing opposite Uta Hagen in what famous Edward Albee play?

Good Griff! (Not Really)

LORNE GREENE was one of the good guys. One of those you liked working with even if things weren't going as well you hoped. Network television past and present is littered with egomaniacal "stars" who, having tasted success in a series, believe the flattery of the press and the sycophants around them. Although actors, they also believe they have boundless talents as writers, producers and directors. In some cases they are right. In most cases, they are dreadfully wrong. The trouble is, a successful star is almost untouchable when it come to criticism. Like the vamp in Damn Yankees whatever the hambone wants, the hambone gets. Later I'll tell you about some of these beloved icons.

But Lorne, as I said, was a good guy. He just had the misfortune to get involved with a train wreck entitled "Griff".

David Victor, the aforementioned executive producer of "Marcus Welby, M.D." and "Owen Marshall, Counselor at Law" scored a triple in 1973 when he got another series on the air. "Griff" was about a retired police detective who comes out of retirement to work as a private eye. The impetus, I believe, was his crusade to solve the murder of his son, a case the police force had mainly given up on. Lorne was cast as Wade "Griff" Griffin. Ben Murphy was his sidekick associate, Mike Murdoch.

(In those days, everybody had a sidekick. Bob Young had Jim Brolin, Arthur Hill had Lee Majors, Telly Savalas had Kevin Dobson, Karl Malden had Michael Douglas. Refresh my memory. Whatever happened to that Michael Douglas guy?)

From the start there were problems. A big one was "Barnaby Jones" with Buddy Ebsen which had an almost identical premise. This was not a case of two brilliant minds coming up with the same overpowering idea. The critics and columnists sort of tittered. How did something like this happen?

How indeed. Had they never watched television? It happened all the time.

Assigned to the project in his first gig as a producer was my friend and soon to be TV superstar Steve Bochco. To keep the budget down he told the execs he would function as his own story editor but as weeks passed and the burden of producing duties weighed heavier and heavier, everyone knew that wasn't going to work out.

I don't know whether Steve thought of it on his own or whether David Victor put a bug in his ear, but I was asked to come on staff as a story editor. I had a vague idea what a story editor did (Nina Laemmle was a good role model) and I thought I could pick up the ins and outs of the job as I went along. It was a wonderful opportunity. A steady paycheck, a chance to write more scripts, a possible avenue to more opportunities at Universal. I jumped at it.

So here we were. Me. Steve who would go on to bigger and better things, Phil DeGuerre (writer, director and producer who would eventually ramrod his own shows), a proven star in Lorne Greene and, oh yes, an associate producer named Robert Francis O'Neill who, in a few years, would become a huge part of my professional life.

I'm not exactly sure why "Griff" didn't work, but it didn't. Maybe it was lack of cast charisma. Maybe it was Steve being stretched too thin on his maiden voyage. Maybe it was my lack of experience as a story editor. (Can you say dull scripts?) It wasn't that the show was awful, it was just pedestrian and considering the talent involved, it shouldn't have been. I remember we had Nick Nolte in one of his first TV guest star roles and Ricardo Montalban as a Mad Bomber but nothing worked. Ratings were dismal.

The ship was leaking and we had no idea how to caulk the holes. On one particular Friday afternoon, we realized we needed a script to start shooting the following Tuesday and the cupboard was bare. Steve and I sat down and in a couple of hours, we outlined the "mad bomber" script. Over the weekend Steve was going to write the first half, I'd write the second half and God willing, we'd have a shootable script on Monday morning. Came Monday morning, the script was finished. I had finished it. Trouble was, Steve hadn't started it. He'd gotten tied up in production problems on a current show or post production on a show about to air. No Act 1. No Act

2. I got back to the typewriter and tried to put it all together.

About Steve. In addition to being a first tier producer and showrunner, he is also an excellent writer. He really knows how to create memorable characters and he is able to construct a scene that can make you roar with laughter or weep torrents of tears and sometimes both at the same time. But Steve, in those days, had a flaw and he was the first to admit it. He couldn't write a third act, i.e. tie it all together and wrap it up in a neat package. Several years later, after leaving Universal for MTM Productions, Steve asked me to screen his new pilot, "Hill Street Blues". I was flattered but I didn't have to flatter Steve in return. Anyone who ever watched the series knows how good it was. My only carp: I was disappointed that the characters played by Mike Warren and Charlie Haid were blown to bits in a gunfight right at the end. Well, apparently so were the test audiences because when the pilot was aired most of the bloody excesses of the battle were cut and a voice-over informed us that the two policemen were in serious condition but would recover from their wounds. Good thing because both Mike and Charlie became integral parts of the ensemble.

I couldn't wait to make the show part of my regular viewing routine and after three weeks I finally caught on to what Steve was up to. One episode led to another, start a storyline, overlap it for a couple of weeks and keep a lot of balls in the air at the same time. In other words, week after week would go by and Steve never had to concoct a third act. He had found his formula and he repeated it with great success in both "L.A. Law" and "NYPD Blue".

But enough about Steve Bochco, superstar, and back to the disaster that had us in a death grip.

One afternoon Lorne came to the office unannounced to discuss some problems he had with the current script. First off, the star never came to you, you went to the star. Secondly, I was in a meeting with a writer and instead of terminating immediately, I made Lorne wait fifteen minutes before I saw him. He was terribly gracious, soft spoken, never said a word. And here was this dolt of a story editor, a gauche dunderhead who didn't know a damned thing about protocol.

One of the few good things to come out of the experience was a brainstorming session in the office of Frank Price, then head of Universal Television. Steve let me tag along and I was just going to observe and keep my mouth shut. What, Frank asked, could we do to pump some life into the show because as things stood, cancellation was only a couple of episodes away. Everybody kicked it around. Nobody really had any answers. I thought of an angle, not very original, but at least it might give us a better handle on things, something to change the show's dynamics. Unbidden I piped up. Everyone turned and looked at me. I think it was the first time they realized I was in the room. I said, why not have our stars play good cop/bad cop? That is, Ben would pretend to be the tough menacing kneecap buster while kindly and gentle Lorne would cajole like an understanding Dutch uncle. As I said, not particularly original, but the room perked up and Frank Price seemed to notice me for the first time since we'd walked in the room. Later as we were leaving, Steve said to me, "You did yourself a lot of good in there". He was smiling. He meant it.

Well, it may have done me a lot of good but it did nothing for the show and in a few weeks we were officially cancelled. Since my contract was for the show alone and not an overall Universal contract, I was let go with nice words ringing in my ears. (I worked with Steve over the next couple of years writing three scripts for "MacMillan and Wife" for him as well as one for "Delvecchio" before he left for MTM Productions.) Out of steady work, I went home, got ready to start free-lancing again and waited for another shoe to drop.

It didn't take long.

> **5. Lorne Greene, who started his career as a news broadcaster, was born in what city?**
>
> a) St. Paul, Minnesota
> b) Albany, New York
> c) Ottawa, Canada
> d) Pierre, South Dakota

Don't Let the Scruffy Raincoat Fool You

ABOUT THAT 'SPEC' SCRIPT that I had written for Columbo and which I had given to Steve Bochco in hopes of getting an assignment. Steve had liked it but not well enough to buy it but he had promised to pass it along to Dean Hargrove who was taking over the show in its second year, even as Steve was leaving it. Hopefully I had waited to hear something from either Dean or his co-producer Roland Kibbee or the new story editor, Jackson Gillis. Months passed. I heard nothing. I assumed no one had read the script and if they had, they hadn't cared much for it. Too bad.

And then, unexpectedly, when "Columbo" was deep into its second season, I got a call from the studio. Would I take a meeting with Hargrove and Kibbee? Would I? Where? When? As before, two o'clock in the morning would be fine with me. Dean and Roland turned out to be a couple of likable, talented, albeit somewhat overworked gentlemen who couldn't have been more gracious to me. Yes, they had read that spec script and yes, it was okay, but they would really prefer that I come up with something new.

I promised to give it my best shot and over the next few days wrestled with some ideas until I came up with one I thought might work. When I presented it to Dean and Roland they agreed and sent me off to write the story outline and eventually the script. The episode was entitled "Publish or Perish" and starred the flamboyant Jack Cassidy as the killer and in a marvelous piece of casting, Mickey Spillane as a Mickey Spillane-like author.

Needless to say, I was happy. What I didn't know was that Peter Falk, the dynamo that drove the show, was even happier than I was. One of his biggest complaints was the quality of the scripts he was getting with particular emphasis on the cleverness of the "gotcha" clues that capped every story. Good characters, good settings, good dialogue, all of it went for naught if Peter didn't like the cluework, not only at the end, but throughout the script. Apparently I had passed muster and he didn't mind telling people about it.

A few weeks before the show aired, I had gotten a phone call from Peter complimenting me on the script and asking if I could drop by his office for a chat. I was flabbergasted. I was finally going to meet "Columbo" and I couldn't wait. And as it turned out, I actually did meet Columbo because in so many ways, Peter was much like his character. It wasn't only his speech cadence, it was the twinkle, the sense of humor, the lack of sartorial elegance, the quick mind and the down to earth intelligence that would show itself only if you dug for it. Unlike some of his contemporary TV stars he was one of the good guys though there were those in Universal's executive suite who would violently disagree. It was my experience, then and in the years to come, that Peter was a hard-working dedicated co-worker with his fellow actors, directors, writers and sometimes even his producers. He did not, however, have much patience with the "suits" (executives) that populated the executive offices. In fact I think he got a real satisfaction out of making them squirm because to Peter, the true test of the show was its quality and not budgets or shooting schedules. He also had little patience with people whom he felt didn't know their job.

During the first year on the air, the producers of "Columbo" were its creators, Dick Levinson and Bill Link. The show was part of a Sunday night "wheel" which meant it alternated with other mystery programs and at least six of these 90 minute movies were needed with almost no prep time to get on the air. Dick Levinson later told me that at times it was a battle of wills between Peter and he and Bill. They finally stopped sending Peter story outlines. He got the shooting script only at the last minute. Because Peter had a habit of wanting to check on what the film editor was up to, they arranged for Peter to shoot at distant locations, far from the studio. If by chance he was let go early, the editors were called immediately and told to lock their doors and go home.

Finally seven episodes were filmed and aired and it was a highly successful season, better than anyone could have expected. And on the heels of that success, Levinson and Link quit. Peter was perplexed. Trouble? What trouble? Did I give you guys trouble? I was just testing you. I trust you now. Let's do it again. Dick and Bill were in no mood to do it again.

Which brings me to my meeting with Peter who very adamantly was hoping that I would join the Columbo family because I obviously knew how to write a Columbo script. I was elated and deflated simultaneously. Elated and flattered by his confidence in me, deflated because I was still on staff with 'Griff'. It was almost certainly going to be axed but a contract was a contract and Steve Bochco was a good friend so regretfully I had to decline. Peter was gracious. He understood. If I could find the time, would I be interested in writing another script? I said I would and we left it at that.

Almost immediately after 'Griff' was cancelled I got the call from Dean and Roland and the next day I was in their office discussing an idea for a new Columbo. They had an undeveloped premise they'd been noodling with and it was a good one. The two key elements were: (a) the killer was going to be Columbo's superior, the Deputy Police Commissioner and (b) there were to be two killings and the Commissioner's friend and neighbor would be complicit in both of them. In TV shorthand, it was 'Strangers on a Train', the Hitchcock classic. You kill my wife, I kill yours. Basically that was all they had but it seemed like more than enough to me and I couldn't wait to get at it. But wait! There was a caveat. This was to be the last episode of the year and Peter was on an unmovable timetable. He was scheduled to start a movie and that start date was inviolate. They needed the script fast. Very fast. I wasn't bothered by that. Fast was the way I worked but I sometimes wondered if the people who hired me did so because of the speed with which I could turn out pages and not necessarily the quality of what was on them.

In any case, I attacked the story and script and very shortly they had something they were happy with. It was titled "A Friend in Deed" and Richard Kiley was cast as the Deputy Police Commissioner. Need I say, Richard was delightfully malevolent. The show ended with a whizbang of a clue and of all the Columbos I have written, this is one of my favorites. Peter thought it "delicious", his pet word for something that is really terrific.

When he pulled out that word, you had succeeded admirably.

It was right around this time that I got a call from my agent, Sylvia Hirsch, saying that Frank Price, president of Universal Television, wanted to meet with me. She suspected they wanted to make an overall Universal deal with me. Really? You mean no more free-lancing? A steady paycheck every week? Whatever it was about, this meeting could only be good.

Frank turned out to be cordial, gracious and complimentary. The studio respected my talent, he said, and was sure I would be a wonderful addition to the Universal family of writers and producers. All sorts of opportunities would flow my way and so on and so forth. A former writer himself, he couldn't have been nicer and as we wrapped up the meeting, his face fell just a little when I told him I was very flattered and I would think about it. Here again, my naivete and inexperience showed themselves. Anyone in his right mind would have jumped at this offer but I wasn't quite sure what the ramifications were and how it would affect my freedom to put my own ideas to paper. How long would I be tied up? There were semi-annual options. Was it their option or mine or was it mutual? A lot of questions popped to mind. I also wanted to talk it over with my wife Lucille. This was potentially a very big step in my career and she deserved a vote.

Sylvia called. She had heard the meeting went well. I agreed. She was sure an offer would be forthcoming. She would be in touch immediately.

Now here's where my memory fails me. It could have been Steve Bochco or my brother or maybe even Dick Levinson, but I was told in no uncertain terms by someone who would know that Peter Falk had been up in the executive offices, pounding on desks, and threatening to quit "Columbo" for good if the studio didn't sign me up to work on his show. I'm sure this is an exaggeration, but with Peter's flair for theatricality, I can't guarantee it.

The next day, I got the call from Sylvia. She was gushing with the most marvelous news. Universal had made me an absolutely fantastic offer. A seven year contract with options, a starting salary of $1300 a week with 5% annual increases and some other boilerplate that I hardly listened to. I knew by now that there was nothing fantastic about a seven year deal wherein every six months, the studio has the right to fire you.

When she was finished talking, I asked her if she knew what had been going on between Peter and Universal's executive corps and when she said she didn't, I told her as it had been told to me. There was a long silence on the other end of the line. Really? she queried. Really, I said.

She and I realized that I had the whiphand in this scenario but I had no intention of exercising it. I was the new kid in town with only limited experience and being an insider at Universal opened up a lot of possibilities for the future. Although I'm pretty sure Sylvia wasn't happy about it, we countered Universal's offer. Five years, not seven. Annual options, not semi-annual. The money was okay but we wanted decent raises during each year of the contract. Oh, yes. One other thing. Scripts extra. That meant that any script I wrote would have to be paid for outside of the contract and not applied against my weekly salary. (At the time the going rate for a 90 minute Columbo script was about $12, 000, a fee I was not about to give away). They agreed and I went to work at Universal where I stayed, happily, for another 18 years.

Yes, I was happy but I suspect Peter Falk was even happier. At the end of Year One, Levinson and Link (both writers) had quit the show. At the end of Year Three, Hargrove and Kibbee (both writers) were functioning as Executive Producers. As the studio got ready to prepare for Year Four, a new line producer was brought on board. Everett Chambers was a good producer but he was not a writer. Jackson Gillis had departed the premises. The only knuckles and knees writer on staff was the Story Editor. That was me.

I felt very lonely and to tell you the truth....

STOP! STOP EVERYTHING!

> **6. In what film did Peter Falk make his motion picture debut in a major role for which he was nominated for an Oscar?**
>
> **What famous female singer also made her film debut in the same picture?**

Writers of the World, Unite!

A FUNNY THING HAPPENED on my way to becoming head writer (only writer) on "Columbo" that season. The Writers Guild of America, that hotbed of social reformation posing as a union, decided for the twentieth time in twenty years to go on strike. This is something they decide but they rarely follow through. However in 1973 something strange was in the air. There was a hint, maybe more than a hint, that this time they might actually go through with it.

I had joined the Guild within months of arriving in Los Angeles. To qualify you needed a certain number of points according to the work assignments you had received. In my case, one MOW was more than enough and to tell you the truth, I was a little proud of being a member of an organization that boasted many of my writing heroes. Not that I had any brief for or against unionization, I just didn't know much about it. Most of what I had learned about organized labor came from "On The Waterfront" and since I didn't see anyone around who even vaguely resembled Johnny Friendly, I didn't feel I was in much danger of being ill used by the collective bargaining process. I probably should have looked closer. Instead of keeping a weather eye out for Johnny Friendly, I should have been concentrating on the likes of Clifford Odets.

At the first pre-strike meeting of the membership where the Board of Directors outlined their game plan, I noticed a certain similarity in dress and demeanor amongst a substantial number of board members. Sixtyish, long haired, "casually" dressed often wearing sandals, usually unemployed or unemployable, revered among themselves as the warrior class of the Guild who were not about to brook any slight, real or imagined, from the networks or the studios. I mentally subtracted thirty-five years from their perceived ages. That would have put them in their mid-twenties in the 1930's, an era not noted for its devotion to capitalism. A quick scan of the attendees uncovered dozens more just like them and they were not shy when it came to grabbing the microphone to voice their opinions. At that very early juncture I began to harbor the notion that this strike was a foregone conclusion, no matter how the membership at large felt about it.

One of the things a union does early on is ask for a "strike authorization" vote. They are quick to tell you that this is not a vote to strike, merely a vote of confidence to give them something to fight with when they meet with management. Don't you believe it. Once they have their authorization, the deal is sealed. And so it was. The old Bolsheviks in the Guild were literally orgasmic at the opportunity to carry their signs and chant epithets at the gates of every major studio in town. Up the workers! Down the fatcats! We shall overcome!

As strikes go, it was a pretty ludicrous affair, at least in the beginning. The Board, in its infinite stupidity, had chosen to strike just after one season had ended and long before scripts would be needed for the following season. In short we were striking at a time when there wasn't much work to be had no matter what. Their reasoning was, they were disrupting the programming process by denying management the ability to authorize pilot scripts. Without pilots and programming for the Fall, the networks and studios would be topsy turvy. They would HAVE TO cave and quickly. Of course they didn't.

As far as the strike itself was concerned, Johnny Friendly would not have approved of anything they did. First, we had no support from the Directors Guild or the Screen Actors Guild. Had they weighed in on our side, the strike would have ended within a week. Moreover we got no help from the craft unions, the stagehands, the teamsters, or just about anyone else engaged in movie making. We were hanging out on a flimsy branch on an unstable tree all by ourselves. Clout? We had none.

How about that picketing? We did not cover every entrance to every studio 24 hours a day. And why should we when no one was honoring our strike. Actors, directors, pizza delivery guys—all passed us by with either a stoic straight ahead stare or worse, a thumbs up 'go get em' grin while they and their agents met with management to discuss their next big movie. Members were divided into teams and teams into shifts. One day I would be outside MGM from 9:00 until 1:00 with maybe a half dozen of my peers. Two days later I would be at Universal from 1:00 until 5:00, usually at the main gate. There were several other ways to enter the lot. None of them were picketed, allowing dishonest writers in Groucho disguises to come and go freely, meeting with producers or delivering contraband scripts to the boys in the Tower. As for us picketers, we passed the time playing trivia games, lying about our resumes or our sexual conquests, or even pitching pennies to relieve the boredom.

Naturally we kept a sharp eye out for any Guild members who would be so audacious as to try to run the picket line in plain view. Never happened as far as I knew but we also were doing little to prevent the breakfast get-togethers between producers and writers at some obscure diner in the northwest corner of the Valley. We were all threatened with dire consequences should we not observe the strike. We would be pariahs. We would never work again. Myriad plagues would descend upon our families. (Of course, when the strike was finally settled, all of this would be forgotten and the miscreants—which included a couple of Board members—would get on with their lives.)

Now several months have gone by and I am itching to get back to work and for the first time, it looks as if the game plan might be having some effect. There is talk from management that there may not be a "next season". The network schedules will be filled with reruns of classic old TV, or cheap game shows, or variety hours which can be slapped together at the last minute. We are supposed to be terrified and some of us are but the strike holds. The networks announce that the following season will be delayed by three weeks. Orders will be shortened from 22 episodes to 18. The strike holds. In between my tours of duty on the picket line, I am home eating lunch and catching up with "All My Children". Erica is getting a divorce. She is sleeping with her best friend's husband. Why am I not surprised by all this?

By May 30th things had come to a head. The motion picture pipeline is drying up. Unproductive overhead is killing the studios. Time for Lew Wasserman to step in. Lew is the Godfather of the management team. Aloof until now, it is now his duty to take over and broker a deal. Within three weeks, the strike is settled. There will be peace until at least 1977.

I've had a little fun pooh-poohing this strike and in truth, at times we all felt like we were in the middle of a Mel Brooks movie. But the truth is, as badly as it was handled, this strike, unlike others to come, was absolutely necessary. In the 50's in New York a writer could earn $5000 for a live TV hour script. Somehow, in the move to film and twenty years later, that figure had shrunk to $4500. Management had no fear of writers. Those silly powerless fools would take what was offered and like it. But when the strike ended that number was up to $7500 with provisions that would take it even higher. By the mid-1990's, the going rate for a one hour episodic script had swelled to over $22, 000. This year (2013) it is close to $40, 000. That never would have been possible had it not been for the 1973 strike, the only really "good" strike in WGA history.

Let's hear it for the lefties.

> **7. Peter Falk attended high school in the shadow of what famous prison?**

The Prisoner in the Black Tower

AS I WAS SAYING before we were so rudely interrupted....

In 1974 the Universal Studios facility on Lankershim Boulevard still retained much of the "small lot" charm that had characterized it since the days of its founding six decades earlier by movie pioneer Carl Laemmle. To be sure, the Black Tower, which rose fourteen stories and dominated the main entrance was brand new, but the rest of the studio retained a certain slow-paced quaintness. In the shadow of the Tower were about a dozen individual bungalows each housing a production unit for shows like Dragnet, Adam-12, Night Gallery, The Virginian, Name of the Game, Banacek, and on and on and on. In those days Universal was thought of (mostly by competitors) as a factory for one hour dramas. Very snide and not very accurate but there was no question the lot was busy. (So much so that within a year it would have to start sending production to other lots around the city. The Lankershim site wasn't big enough to handle all the business.)

Besides the bungalows, there were the two story buildings scattered here and there. Alfred Hitchcock had his own office complex and one day in the future Steven Spielberg's Amblin Productions would be sprawling in the farthest reaches of the back lot. There were over forty sound stages, some tiny, some mammoth. Number 28 was known as the Phantom stage because it still housed the original Paris opera house set used in the Lon Chaney version of "The Phantom of the Opera" as well as the Claude Rains sequel. It has also been used for countless "theater" scenes in a wide variety of films. Beyond the sound stages was the backlot, a collection of exteriors with false fronts that doubled for everything from a busy New York street to a quaint French village or a sleepy Mexican town. The most famous of these was probably the Transylvanian town with its moody alleyways, dark castles, spooky streets, all of which had been used in the 30's and 40's heydays of Universal's monster epics like "Frankenstein" and "Dracula" and "The Wolf Man".

Now you would think, since I had just joined the "Columbo" unit that I would be assigned to one of those quaint little bungalows, sitting primly on neatly winding paths, only a stone's throw from the parking lot and the cafeteria. Well, you would be wrong about that. For reasons known only to God and Frank Price, I was assigned an office on the fifth floor of the Black Tower. To this day I am not sure why. Maybe it was to keep a sharp eye on this new addition to the family and make sure he kept himself tethered to his typewriter, diligently churning out pages instead of hobnobbing with fellow writers as fellow writers are wont to do when unobserved by the executive watchdogs. Instead of mingling with the likes of Steve Bochco and Steve Cannell and maybe even Levinson and Link, I found myself surrounded by lawyers and accountants and others who toiled relentlessly in Business Affairs. Not that they weren't nice people (they were) but I could never get my head around an imbalanced balance sheet any more than they gave a damn about the blonde dog hair found on the murder victim's wrist watch.

Since I was there mostly to write and not to socialize, I accepted my isolation stoically, mostly pleased with my large, airy and brightly lit office with the panoramic view of the Lakeside Country Club on the other side of the Los Angeles River. (The river itself was not much to look at it. It was at least fifty yards wide, constructed of cement and its only purpose was to allow for the runoff of excess water when flood conditions prevailed in the valley. Since this hadn't happened since Clark Gable worked as a one-line walk-on in a Norma Shearer film that may or may not have been a talkie, the "river" was used mostly for car chases and motorcycle stunt work.)

So here I was in the Tower office they had given me. And then they gave me something else. A secretary. I didn't get to interview anyone or to pick someone from a police lineup. No, she just appeared. Let's just call her Cassandra. She was a pleasant looking fortyish old pro in the Universal hierarchy who had been around a long time. Probably too long. Her overall demeanor was dour. If I came into the office at nine, full of enthusiasm for the day ahead, within an hour or two she had me reduced to a glum shadow of my real self. Whatever I liked about my job, she'd give me a dozen reasons why I shouldn't. No, it really wasn't a great place to work and she'd spend the next twenty minutes telling me why. If I mentioned that I liked Joe, the lawyer, down the hall, she'd give me a fistful of reasons why that was a mistake. And oh, yes, to top it all off, she didn't care much for typing which to my mind was the number one reason I needed a secretary in the first place. I probably should have fired her after Day One but I didn't. First of all I didn't know how and I wasn't all that sure I could. Up until then I'd always been a potential fire-ee, not a fire-er. Or maybe it was just plain old fashioned cowardice. In any case, before I got the chance to leap out of my office window in complete frustration, she went on vacation.

The next thing I knew a bundle of sunshine appeared at Cassandra's desk and she was going to be with me for the next two weeks. Sandy Quinn was also an old pro in the studio system but instead of resenting it, she thrived in it. Barely 30 she'd started when she was still in her teens and had worked for or been friends with many, many important studio executives. She was on a first name basis with Lew Wasserman, the CEO of MCA, and Sid Sheinberg, the President of Television Production and right behind Mr. Wasserman in the pecking order. And as for those buried bodies that

Yours truly with Sandy Quinn, loyal assistant for over twenty years. Lucky me.

every corporation has but doesn't like to talk about, she knew the location of every one of them. Did I mention that she smiled a lot? And laughed. And, yes, she liked to type and she was good at it. VERY good. And here's the best part. She got to like me as much as I liked her. It took a couple of phone calls and a little cajoling but very quickly, Sandy's temp assignment became permanent. It stayed permanent for the next eighteen years. Cassandra went on to other assignments.

Freed from the pall of misery that had been hanging over me, I was now free to attack my job with wild abandon. To reiterate what a story editor does. Basically, he or she meets with free lance writers and listens to story ideas. If he hears a good one he can either commit to giving the writer an assignment or he can recommend the story to the producer who then makes the yes/no decision. The story editor is also charged with a great deal of rewriting in case the freelancer isn't up to series standards or cannot write the main character properly. (We got a lot of that.) And finally, the story editor may also write his own scripts. In Season Four, which would be my only full time season on staff, I wrote three of the six episodes, did major (uncredited) rewrites on two others.

When I took over there was nothing usable left over from the previous season. There were, however, a batch of story "notions", complete with so-called usable clues that had been bought from Larry Cohen, a well known TV and screen writer, who specialized in low budget, high concept B movies. I sifted through the material and frankly, there wasn't much there. With one exception. I forget what Larry's story premise was (unusable) but he did have a doozy of a clue. As Peter Falk would have said, "Delicious." The gimmick was this. If you put on a pair of sneakers, the loops and the knot fall a certain way. If a pair of sneakers are put on by someone else (like a dead body, for example), the loops and the knot are reversed. I tried it. It was true. Levinson tried it. He agreed. Everett Chambers tried it. No question about it.

So I went off and wrote "An Exercise in Fatality". Bernie Kowalski directed and Robert Conrad starred as the Jack La Lanne inspired killer and overall it was a pretty satisfying show. We also had a minimum number of "trailer calls" which I got used to after a while. A trailer call came about when Peter was sitting in his trailer, script in hand, and unsure whether the scene they were about to shoot was (a) dramatic enough or (b) understandable or (c) needed fleshing out with additional dialogue. (As to the latter, I don't ever remember being called to the trailer to eliminate dialogue. Not ever.) Peter had a knack, totally well-intentioned, of turning a line like:

"Excuse me, ma'am, my name is Lt. Columbo and I hate to bother you but I need to ask you about those three dwarfs that were seen running from your garage last night" into something akin to an unabridged "War and Peace". Peter was constantly worried that a terse scene would be short on information (though they seldom were). He belonged to the school of "Tell 'em what you're going to tell 'em, then tell 'em, then tell 'em what you told 'em." This does a great deal for lucidity but slows the story telling to a snail's pace and when it involves a "trailer call" it costs a lot of money in down time.

At times the set would be shut down for hours while Peter worried a scene to death. We would make suggestions. He would nod. "Yeah, you're right. That's a very good thought. I like that. It's just that—" He'd mumble something and look back at the script, shaking his head, then go back into deep thought. Once in a while, he'd suddenly stand up and announce, "I'm going home." Then with script under his arm he would hop down from his trailer and take the offending scene home with him. I would look at the director, the director would look at the Assistant Director who would call one of the producers, then throw up his hands in defeat. Shut down the set. Send everyone home. Back tomorrow. Same scene, same set up. And more often than not, Peter would show up with the equivalent of a one-act play to replace the scene he couldn't get a handle on. And it would be filmed. Over and over. When it got to Take 12, the scene didn't get any better but Peter was unhappy. It wasn't right. Not yet. Keep in mind. None of this was malicious. It was Peter being a perfectionist. And all the while, the bean counters in the Tower were losing their collective minds.

The situation, untenable as far as the studio was concerned, led to a bizarre agreement between Universal and NBC. Having been pushed to the limit by huge budget overruns, the studio finally had had enough. They notified NBC that they would no longer supply episodes of "Columbo" to the Sunday Night Mystery wheel. NBC was aghast. McMillan and McCloud were doing okay but "Columbo" was the real jewel in the mix. Without "Columbo" they didn't have much so NBC made an unheard of deal with Universal. NBC would pay for ALL production costs for the "Columbo" episodes and they would tack on 10% (it might have been 15%) to give the studio a profit. Now think about that for a minute. A 10% add-on. Say an episode cost a million dollars in production costs. Universal had no risk. NBC was responsible for every dime. But beyond that NBC would be handing over $100, 000 in no-risk profit to the studio for the convenience of having Universal continue to produce. Now instead of fretting over every dollar Peter was costing them, the Tower executives barely fell short of goading him to spend as much as he liked. $2, 000, 000 a show. Go to it. That's $200, 000 in our pockets. Knowing how much Peter liked to stick it to the suits, I wondered how he felt about this new arrangement. I never did ask him.

One of the canards circulating the industry around this time was the notion that Peter, for all his success, resented Columbo and felt trapped by the character and that perhaps he was even being stereotyped into a narrow dramatic range. Sure, he looked forward to doing movies and plays but he never lost affection for the ill-kempt detective with the scruffy wardrobe. It was Peter who had found that wreck of a raincoat somewhere in the depths of the wardrobe department. It was Peter who spent hours in the back lot at Transportation looking over every vehicle in stock until he stumbled upon that beat up Peugeot convertible. And I believe it was Peter who rescued "Dog" from an animal shelter and made him the second best known canine on the Universal lot. (Lassie was number one.) And most important of all, it was Peter who season after season protected the character from going off the rails and becoming someone he wasn't.

You might think, given what I've said about Peter rewriting and fiddling with the scripts I had given him, that writing for 'Columbo' might have been a thankless chore. You would be wrong. Even when he had misgivings his hesitancy was couched politely and when you had gotten it right, his praise was lavish. I remember writing a scene between Peter and Dick Van Dyke in the episode entitled 'Negative Reaction'. Van Dyke was a world renowned photographer who had murdered his wife using a phony kidnapping scheme to muddy the waters. It wasn't working. Columbo was already onto him. But at the end of this scene, Columbo, in one of his ploys to lull his quarry into complacency, asks Van Dyke if he might have a photo of a cocker spaniel around somewhere that he could tack to his living room

wall because his Dog was very lonesome, the cocker from next door having moved away, and maybe the photograph would make things easier on
the little guy. I wrote this in a fit of fantasy never thinking for one moment
that Peter would actually play a scene this outrageous but was I wrong.
He loved it, played it with relish and it was left in the final cut untouched.
Delicious, he told me. And that's why I loved writing 'Columbo', for those
kind of moments, .

In my long career writing for various stars and their roles, Peter and the
lieutenant were at the top of my fun list. No question about it. Not being
an actor I did not "act" my dialogue when writing except for Peter. I would
be sitting at my desk at home on a Saturday afternoon, banging away on a
script and now and then one of my kids would peer in and yell to my wife,
"Mom, he's at it again!" Click, click, click...." I just have one small problem,
sir".....Click, click, click..... "Just one more thing, sir".....Click, click, click......"
My wife makes the most delicious ziti. Have you ever had ziti, sir. It is really terrific".... As I typed I was playing Columbo, right down to the tilt
of the head, the scratching of the hair, the chewing on the cigar (which I
smoked). If pressed I can still do a pretty fair impersonation. But only if
pressed very hard.

Those were wonderful days and I remember them with great fondness
as I do Peter himself despite the tinkering and the trailer calls. I was prepared to stay with the show until either Peter or I died of old age.

That is, until Levinson and Link made me an offer I could not refuse.

> **8. In 1969 Peter Falk was nominated for his
> first EMMY as a guest star on a series entitled
> "The Law and Mr. Jones." What veteran character
> actor was the star of the show?**
>
> a) Walter Brennan
> b) Walter Pigeon
> c) James Whitmore
> d) Thomas Mitchell

The Boys from Philadelphia

AROUND THE UNIVERSAL LOT, when someone asked you what the boys were up to, they could be referring only to two people: Richard Levinson and William Link. The "boys" were the stars of the Universal television arm, a team of talented writers who had started working together in junior high school in Philadelphia some twenty years earlier and were still at it. Together they had written and produced such groundbreaking and award-winning television dramas as "My Sweet Charlie" (about race relations), "That Certain Summer" (dealing with the issue of adult homosexual relationships), and "The Execution of Private Slovik" (based on the true story of the only American soldier to be executed in wartime for the crime of desertion.) These three alone would have made them the stars on any lot in Hollywood but they had other credits of which they were also proud including a little stage play they had written and actually had been able to get produced. It was called "Prescription: Murder" and it had to do with a wealthy psychiatrist who kills his wife and in his hubris, is certain that no one will ever learn the truth. Enter an unkempt homicide detective in a beat up suit, a raggedy little notebook, always without a pencil and acting just like a traffic cop marking time until he can collect his pension. But the dogged Lt. Columbo is no fool, he is a charming and disarming clone of Petrovich in "Crime and Punishment". Underestimate him at your own risk. (In San Francisco and subsequently on tour he was played by Oscar-winner Thomas Mitchell, an unprepossessing bear of a man which is how he was described in the play.)

The boys convinced Universal and NBC that the play would make an excellent Movie of the Week and got the go ahead. Unluckily many of actors they were considering were either unavailable or not interested. Eventually they got to Peter Falk (seventh choice) and though he was nothing like the shuffling older character they originally had in mind (Bing Crosby was atop the list), Peter took the role and when it aired it finished in the top ten in ratings for the week. Obviously a hit in the making and the critics couldn't have agreed more. The only person who might not have been overjoyed was Gene Barry who played the arrogant killer. It's rumored he bemoaned the fact that he didn't accept "the other part" though I seriously doubt it was offered to him. True? Who knows? In Hollywood, the land of dreams and fairy tales, truth and fiction are in the eye of the beholder.

Everything looked like a "Go" but when Peter was approached about doing a series, he said no. He wanted no part of the weekly TV grind. Two years later, the notion of a series was revived but this time "Columbo" would be a 90-minute movie rotating with two other shows. There would be no 22 episode schedule. Six or seven "Columbo" movies each season. No more. This time Peter agreed. A second pilot entitled "Ransom for a Dead Man" was shot from a script by Dean Hargrove and boasted a icy killer played by Lee Grant. Again, excellent ratings and this time around, Columbo and Peter Falk were on their way to becoming household names.

It is now early 1975. Season Four is over. I have spent a couple of years getting to know Dick and Bill through Columbo where they functioned as consultants, reading scripts and giving notes. They took a shine to me and God knows, I was flattered by the attention. But beyond that, I genuinely liked them both and we would often have lunch together in the Universal commissary, playing trivia games which we were all good at or discussing the gossip of the day like three old biddies. More often than not, as the new guy in town, I was the butt of Dick's jokes. He considered the San Fernando Valley where I made my home as "terra incognita" and anyone who lived there an unsophisticated rube of embarrassing proportions. I took it in good humor. If Dick Levinson could waste valuable time ribbing me, I had to have something going for me.(Note: a perfect example of Dick's wicked sense of humor. Everyone knew that Peter Falk had a glass eye, stemming from a childhood illness. At the "wrap party" for the first season, Dick and Bill gifted him with a half-bottle of Murine. Peter laughed harder than anyone.)

45

In 1971 the boys had been involved in a two hour pilot for a new version of Ellery Queen which had been tried twice before with unspectacular results. Aired as a Movie of Week, "Don't Look Behind You" starring Peter Lawford as Ellery and Harry Morgan as his father, Inspector Richard Queen, was less than a rousing success. The boys had written the screenplay but in the production process it had been tinkered with and eventually butchered so badly, in self defense they took their names off it. Credit was given to "Ted Leighton", their pseudonym.

Cut to 1975 and suddenly NBC is very interested in a weekly Ellery Queen series and they want Dick and Bill to produce it. They agreed to have a swing at it, wrote and produced "Too Many Suspects" with Jim Hutton as Ellery and David Wayne as Inspector Queen. NBC loved it and ordered 13 episodes.

Which brings me to the offer I could not refuse. The boys asked me if I would join them as a producer on the series. They would executive produce, and an ex-agent named Michael Rhodes would be the line producer (overseeing the nuts and bolts of episode preparation and riding herd on the director and crew on a daily basis.) I would be the "writing producer", working with the story editor to develop scripts as well as writing a few myself. Was I flattered? Hell, yes. Was I scared to death. Yes, indeed. What the devil did I know about producing? Beyond that, what did I know about Ellery Queen and the "armchair detective" formula? It was one thing to write "Columbo" which I loved but as much as I enjoyed reading Agatha Christie and Dorothy Sayers and others, I had never tried to construct a closed murder mystery.

So I made a deal with the boys. I took home a book of Ellery Queen short stories. Let me pick one out. I'll try to write a one hour episode based on one I like. I chose one of the EQ classics, "The Mad Tea Party", and even as I was hastily sketching out a framework, I could tell this was going to be a lot of fun. I gave the boys the finished script a week later and they were delighted. So was I.

But before I could agree to join the new show, there was someone I had to talk to. Peter Falk had gone way out on a limb for me a year earlier and I owed him a great deal. I couldn't and wouldn't walk away from "Columbo" if he felt he needed me. Peter and I had a long talk and he was gracious and generous. He knew this was a big step up for me and he wasn't going to stand in my way. He asked just one thing. Would I remain in touch with "Columbo" on a semi-official basis, keeping my name in the credits as Executive Story Consultant, and jump in if needed should the show get in real trouble. I agreed, of course, but I told him I didn't think there was a lot to worry about. There was already talk of William Driskill joining the staff for the next season (he did and we shared screen credit) and beyond that, I was leaving behind a great deal of material that was exceptionally good in its early stages.

Peter was satisfied that I wasn't leaving him high and dry and he wished me good luck. I promised to be there if he needed me and off I went to conquer new worlds in the wonderful world of television.

9. In what movie did Angela Lansbury play Elizabeth Taylor's older sister?

Cult Successes Don't Pay the Bills

WITH MY ESCALATION to the grand and exalted title of "Producer", I was about the escape the Black Tower. The studio had erected a new building directly across from the commissary. The Producers Building was three stories high, state of the art and eventually would house dozens of writers and producers, either attached to on-going projects or in development. The Ellery Queen unit was one of the first to move in. Each suite contained three separate offices. Fronting these offices were three desks for the use of the secretaries (or in my case, my beautiful executive assistant.)

Mike Rhodes insisted on having the somewhat larger middle office. Whether that was a power play or not, I have no idea. I took the office nearer the door to the hallway. It was also the only office with a private, separate entrance to the bathroom. No fool me. The third office was occupied by our story editor, veteran writer Robert Van Scoyk who had been around, it was rumored, since the day Marconi invented the wireless. (I exaggerate.) Like me, Bob had worked briefly as a pageboy at NBC in New York and when WWII came to an end he started selling radio scripts all over town. Within a couple of years he graduated to live television and eventually wound up in Hollywood when TV weaned itself from live production and started using film. He was prolific and known to have a flair for mysteries. He also boasted a pixie-ish sense of humor which would serve him well in the days and weeks to come.

As the season progressed, I also made the acquaintance of a new although not-so-young writer who was going to play a major part in my professional life down the road. Robert Swanson came in one day for a meet with a well worked out idea for a script which he entitled "The Adventure of Colonel Niven's Memoirs". Until then he had only two credits, a Baretta and a Kojak. We liked Bob so much we hired him for two more episodes. Bob would move on to other assignments as well as staff positions on other series but when I needed him most ten years later, he was there. He was then, and is now, a close and dear friend.

In the meantime, Dick and Bill were handed a suite across the hall making it very convenient for Dick to drop in uninvited to steal cups of Sandy's coffee which he did on a regular basis. His own secretary had told Dick from the start, 'You want coffee? Make it yourself'.

From the beginning I was determined about one thing. We would have enough scripts on hand to face any crisis. There was on the lot those days a producer who was always in desperate trouble with nothing to shoot. I kept wondering how he had gotten himself into this fix. It wasn't until some time later that I realized his situation was not only self-induced but deliberately so. Frankly, he wasn't much of a producer or a writer (though he claimed to be), but he had this need to operate out of crisis. If his staff had 'let him down' yet one more time, he was always ready to jump in and save the day, even if it meant around the clock filming, no time for proper post-production, and budget overages designed to cause an outbreak of white hair among the beancounters. Somehow he always managed to get the product on the air and the studio and the network were so grateful, they hardly noticed that the quality was almost always pretty cheesy.

So scripts were a priority and when Mike and I early on had a getting-to-know you lunch date with David Wayne, I assured him we would have eight shooting scripts available before the first day of production. (I lied. We had ten.) David was a delightful man who loved to present himself as a curmudgeon, but who had a wonderful sense of humor and dozens and dozens of stories about the "business" and the people in it. One of the things I regretted most about Ellery's early demise was losing David although I would find opportunities to work with him several times on future projects.

I never did get to know Jim Hutton very well. Don't know why. He was a very nice man but I got the feeling he was something of a loner and given the choice, I gave people their space. He was also a bit of an eccentric. At one point, he started living in his bungalow situated on the lot. Slept there. Ate there. It was strange. From Monday to Friday, he was the perfect professional, always on the set ready to go, letter perfect on his lines, but I was told by crew members that weekends were a different story. Often alone in his bungalow, he took to drinking a little too much. On this much most of those close to the set agree, he was not a happy man. (Note: In retrospect I wonder if perhaps Jim wasn't self-medicating, considering the tragic way he died of pancreatic cancer only a short time after the show was cancelled. It came on June 2, 1979. He was only 45 years old.)

One of my fondest memories (and most ironic) involved, not Jim, but his son Timothy. Tim had come west during summer vacation from high

Ellery (Jim Hutton) wasn't all that pleased when comic book mogul Tom Bosley turned him into a two-fisted crime fighter.

school in Tennessee where he lived with his mother to spend some time with his Dad. For several weeks he hung around the set, lapping it all up, and one day he cornered me at the coffee machine. He wanted to become an actor, he said. Did I have any advice or suggestions? Well, I had one big one but I didn't voice it. *Forget it, kid. The business will break your heart. For every success like your Dad, there are hundreds if not thousands of talented youngsters who will never get a break. What will break will be their hearts.* But I didn't say this. I gave him the second best advice I could muster. Finish school. Study hard. Take acting lessons. Try to get in with a stock group. Apply to one of the first class schools like the American Academy or Neighborhood Playhouse or the Pasadena Playhouse. And then pray to God you get lucky because luck plays a huge role in the difference between fame and anonymity. I'm not sure how much of this advice Tim took. Probably not a lot. But I do know that five years later he was onstage accepting the Oscar as Best Supporting Actor for his role in "Ordinary People". Ah, Fischer, what a great judge of talent you are.

One of the plusses involved in producing EQ was making the acquaintance of Leonard Hill. Len was the network birddog, assigned by NBC to liaise with the producers and give critical advice when called for and generally protect the network's interests on a week to week basis. Let me put it this way. If EQ is a big hit, Len Hill is going to have a sack of brownie points slung over his shoulder. If we fail, his peers will start giving him funny looks. If it's bad enough, he may go into development.(Remember "development" in TV-speak is synonymous with "unemployed".) Every hour show on television has a guy or gal like Len attached. Most try to toss their weight around by giving script notes but as you might guess, these notes are coming from someone who has no clue as to how to write a script. The less destructive of these people will suggest that your hero not wear a suit and tie in a certain scene but something more informal like slacks and sweater. These notes we easily accommodate. (They also take great pride in spotting incorrect grammar and misspellings.) The network policeman you have to be afraid of is the one who questions character motivations, scene transitions, and expository dialogue, just to name three areas where he can

Loveable Betty White, the killer of the country's favorite high school teacher, Eve Arden? Impossible, you say, but that's the way it was.

create havoc. You ignore him at your peril and you take him seriously at even greater peril. Like getting infested with chiggers on a hunting trip, he comes with the territory.

Shortly after we got our commitment to proceed we heard from Len Hill who wanted to get together with me and the boys. A kind of a getting to know you meeting. We invited him to lunch at the Universal commissary. He arrived, fresh faced, curly headed, old enough to pass for a high school senior. Dick was prepared to put him in his place but he never got the chance. Even before we had ordered food, Len announced that he had total faith in the three of us. He knew our work, knew there was no advice he could give us that would make any sense so we had a free ride. He asked only one thing. Don't make him look bad. May I say we loved him from that moment on. Len didn't stay with NBC long. Soon he was running his own company supplying Movie of the Weeks to the three networks. A few years later in one of my slow spells, Len got enamored of one of my original scripts called "Busted Straight" about a gambler and a keno runner in Vegas. He tried everything. We even took a meeting with Ted Danson (pre-Cheers) who wanted to do it but we never could get it off the ground. The rumor is that Len finally cashed in and bought himself a South Sea island where he is living in idyllic splendor far from the hurly burly. As I say, it's only a rumor but I wouldn't bet against it.

In June we started filming EQ. Not at the Universal lot because the sound stages were all in use. No, we were relegated to working from a sound stage at General Services Studios on Las Palmas Boulevard in Hollywood. This season, Universal had 27 different television shows shooting simultaneously. It was so busy that the studio had contracted for nine sound stages at GSS and while they didn't immediately need them all, they wanted to make sure they were there if they were needed. Because of the distance involved, "dropping in" on the set was a major hassle and I avoided it whenever I could.

We had a lot of fun that year turning out what we thought were pretty good shows, ever mindful that the viewing public didn't agree. At least not in large numbers. We garnered a lot of good reviews but realists will tell you these are good for wrapping fish. We invented a couple of characters that the original authors, Dannay and Lee, never thought of. John Hillerman portrayed world weary radio detective Simon Brimmer with just the right touch of ennui. Ken Swofford appeared in five episodes as bombastic Winchell-like newshound, Frank Flanagan. Both always had the murder figured out. Both were always wrong.

All 22 of the episodes we aired were entitled "The Adventure of....." and every episode featured an all-star cast of one-time big name movie stars or television personalities. Our opening show starred Joan Collins, Farley Granger, Barbara Rush, Ray Walston and even bandleader Guy Lombardo. The next week our second episode boasted Ida Lupino, Susan Strasberg, Don Ameche, Anne Francis, Jack Kelly from 'Maverick', and 'Peter Gunn" himself, Craig Stevens. These people cost money but we were happy to pay it. Why? Two reasons. First, familiar faces help keep the suspects separated in the viewer's mind. If three of your suspects are the accountant, the lawyer and the banker, most people won't remember which is which. But if Van Johnson is trying to blackmail Troy Donahue into killing Veronica Lake, that they can follow. The second reason is even more important. A mystery show that is trying to get by on the cheap will hire a half dozen non-entities to play the suspects along with "Special Guest Star Ricardo Montalban". Guess who is playing the killer. Years later we would use this same approach on "Murder She Wrote" for the very same reason. I know that a lot of the old-time actors, especially from the MGM days liked to credit Angela for getting them work but it just wasn't the case. It started with Ellery, although Angela admits to having a wonderful time on the set with old friends from the Metro days like Kathryn Grayson and Betty Garrett and Gloria De-Haven and June Allyson to name just four.

Despite anemic ratings, we were hoping for a second season. Sadly it eluded us. In fact it had been a close call whether we would even be renewed past the original 13 to complete the season. We did and in a move to help ratings we were moved to Sunday night. At the same time ABC signed up Sonny and Cher and threw them up against us. They thrived. Despite our glamorous casts of one-time stars, we didn't. At the time we were quick to blame Sonny and Cher for our poor ratings but if we were honest, the fault, dear reader, was not in the stars but in ourselves. In the years since it went off the air, Ellery Queen has become something of a cult favorite. Devoted fans from every part of the country have been harassing Universal for 35 years to put the series out on VHS or DVD and in 2010 it finally happened. Such devotion requires a lot of perseverance and a great memory but I am happy it happened. It helps take away the sting of that second season we never got. Cult favorite? Absolutely, but cult favorites don't pay the rent. Let's just say that our best efforts resulted in a noble ratings and financial failure. But why? I have my theories.

A major problem was our mystery solutions. Though I loved Dick dearly I always thought he was fashioning the show, perhaps subconsciously, for the critics and other murder mystery aficionados and not for the viewing public. In some episodes the solution was so obscure and contrived that it almost defied explanation. This is not the way to hang onto a mass television audience and in the future, when I had control of "Murder, She Wrote", I vowed that I would not repeat that mistake. I didn't and while I was sometimes accused of making the murders and the solutions a little too easy, I would point to the ratings which had us in the top 5 shows week after week after week. Ellery should have been so lucky.

And the second major problem was Jim Hutton. Not Jim, the actor, because God knows he was a charming and accomplished performer. But it was what we asked him to do that, in my opinion, kept the show from garnering a wider audience. Jim played low key, easy going, laconic, intellectual, almost but not quite bored. He was not outgoing, dynamic, or a go-getter with a mission. The killings were a pastime. His reaction was not visceral. It almost seemed at times that he didn't much care. Now this is basically what we put on paper but Jim did not transcend it and I think if he had tried, he would have made us all very nervous. It was those Frank Flanagan episodes that really showed the difference. Flanagan was driving the show and Jim was being driven. One critic said, unfairly I believe, that if Ellery doesn't care what's going on, why should we?

As I said, those are my theories. I'm probably wrong, but in any event this single season of Ellery Queen will always remain as one of the happiest experiences of my professional life. Dick Levinson became a semi-permanent fixture in my office, dropping in at least once a day, even when there was no coffee to filch. We got to know each other pretty well in those days and formed a bond that never severed. Looking back I realize how much he meant to me, not only professionally, but personally. There are few people I can say that about.

An actor I know, a very pleasant and talented young man whom I worked with a lot, once told me that there was no such thing as luck in building a career. He had succeeded on talent alone. I stared at him. I had no answer for that.

My career had been pushed along at various stages by plenty of luck. Help from brother Geoff, support from Bill Allyn and Barry Diller and Aaron Spelling, a boost up from Steve Bochco, the unqualified backing of

Peter Falk, and the endorsement of Levinson and Link who said, in effect, that I belonged. Sure, you have to be able to deliver when you get that big chance but my big chance was a one in a million fluke and everything that followed was because I was in the right place at the right time. Luck? Hell, I've been loaded with it all my life.

> **10. David Wayne won Tony Awards for playing a leprechaun and an Okinawan in what two big Broadway hits?**

Murder, She Wrote had nothing on Ellery Queen when it came to guest casts. From left to right: Dina Merrill, George Furth, Pat Harrington, Jim Hutton, Ken Swofford, Kip Niven, Paul Stewart and David Wayne.

And Then There Was Robert Culp

ELLERY QUEEN was history. I came to the office each morning for my coffee and danish. The phone didn't ring much. My typewriter, a bulky Triumph, which I had been pounding on for years sat collecting dust. I kicked around a few ideas for a movie of the week. One thing I did NOT do was start dreaming up ideas for a prime time series. I was new to the business but I had already caught on to one thing. If a Tower executive (or more ideally, a network executive) comes up with a series idea, it is practically greased all the way to a pilot episode. If a writer dreams it up, the chances of success plummet dramatically. Some writers succeed despite this, even though it takes barrels of subtle manipulation, schmoozing, wining and dining and other forms of civilized groveling which hopefully ends up with the network executive convinced that your idea was actually HIS idea. So rather than go through all the necessary machinations, I didn't bother. However I did let everyone know I was ready to pitch in whenever they needed my talents. They listened and for a few months it kept me busy.

For starters, Steve Cannell had created a series called "Toma" with Tony Musante and it wasn't really going anywhere and Musante made it clear he wasn't all that wild about doing a series. So Steve, with the blessing of ABC, came up with a "new" version of "Toma" which was called "Baretta". It starred a very talented, colorful performer. That would be a parrot. It also starred Robert Blake. It was a mid-season pickup and they were desperate for scripts. I met with Robert Harris, one of the producers, and got an assignment. (Fischer writes fast. Need a script yesterday? Grab him.)

I was home that night around six, cooking up some spaghetti when the phone rang. On the other end of the line was Blake. He was excited. Couldn't wait to work with me. Had some ideas about the series. Wanted to do this, didn't want to do that. Lucille finished up dinner. She and the kids ate. I didn't. Blake went on for an hour before I was finally able to hang up with a monster headache. But that phone call did one terrific thing for me. After that hour I had Blake's cadence and delivery down pat and when I wrote the script, everything he said he said as Baretta was pure Robert Blake. It was called "The Five and a Half Pound Junkie" and it turned out okay. Not really great. It was the second episode on the air and Baretta had not yet found its style. I was lucky I had nothing to do with producing that series. At the time Blake was an accomplished self-promoter who perceived all sorts of shortcomings in those he worked with but none in himself. He was soon regarded as the most difficult star to work with on the Universal lot.

Jack Laird, who produced "Kojak", also rang me up. He, too, needed a good script fast and I whipped something up, based on my first job as an insurance investigator. The plot revolved around arson and murder ("Close Cover Before Killing") and Telly Savalas, like Blake, was easy to write for if you had the ear. This show, too, was watchable but again, nothing special. However I was busy and earning my paycheck.

And then I heard from my buddy, Steve Bochco, who was Executive Story Consultant on "MacMillan and Wife". He wasn't desperate but he could always use a good script and was I interested? For Steve? Absolutely. I had already written one "MacMillan" in the days just before Ellery. We sat down together and jointly talked through a rough skeleton of a story that would involve the upcoming marriage of Mac's sister (the first the audience had ever heard of her) and the obligatory visit from Mac's mother. (Who knew about her either?) Called "Love, Honor and Swindle" it was to become one of my favorite scripts.

Back in my office, I was again twiddling my fingers, staring out my sliding glass doors at the patio beyond where bevies of attractive secretaries loved to congregate and share studio gossip over lunch. Unbeknownst to me, across the hall, Levinson and Link were hatching a plot.

I believe it went something like this.

Dick: This is a great idea for a movie of the week.

Bill: I agree.

Dick: Do you want to write it?

Bill: No. Do you?

Dick: No.

They stare at each other for a few moments. It comes to them simultaneously.

Dick: How about what-his-name across the hall?

Bill: Why not? You think he'd do it?

Dick: Are you kidding? He's sitting over there counting the tiles in the ceiling.

Which is how I got involved in a project called "The End of the Line" (later renamed "A Cry for Help" when it aired on ABC.)

The narrative line was simple. I mean Dick and Jane simple. An acerbic call-in radio host gets a phone call from a young woman who puts him down for being nasty, sarcastic and mean spirited. If the world is like him, she wants no further part of it. She's going to commit suicide. Harry, the radio jock, scoffs and hangs up on her but pretty soon people are calling in, ripping him to pieces for his insensitivity. Quickly, Harry does an about face and starts to enlist the help of his listeners to keep a lookout for the girl and to stop her before she succeeds in doing away with herself. At the end, they get to her just in time. Harry is so relieved and grateful he cries. There is, in fact, a lot of humanity in this man.

Now that was the thread. All I had to do was get from A to Z in two hours, keeping up the suspense. And that, of course, was the tricky part. No one knew her name or what she looked like. She could have been 17, she could have been 30. Was she local or had she called in from a town dozens of miles away?

Calls started coming in. I think she was in my diner. Poor kid had no money so I gave her breakfast. I think she was headed toward the freeway. I think I saw her near a phone booth down by the 7/11. What was she wearing? A raincoat, I think, and a red wool cap. Next call. There was this young woman in my church. She just sat there for a long time and then left. And on and on it went as the circle seemed to get closer and closer and then she would slip away.

Produced by Dick and Bill and directed by Darryl Duke, it was a project we were all proud of and is remembered, even after all these years, by many,

many viewers. However, the real key to its success was Robert Culp, who played Harry. I had never seen him better. Neither had anyone else. He was outrageous as the snide host at the start of the movie and then as you watched he very subtly segued from I-don't-give-a-damn to a man who, against his will, was forced to show his inner self, who became more and more frightened for the well-being of a young woman he didn't even know. If he ever hit a false note, I didn't see it. We had all seen Culp in his first series "Trackdown" and later in "I Spy" with Bill Cosby and he floated through both shows, a likable and genial leading man with not much to do. He could also be a mannered actor, using signature gestures and the like which he often fell back on, especially when dealing with weak material. None of that was visible here and why he didn't win an Emmy for his performance is beyond me.

Elaine Heilveil co-starred as the young lady in distress and she, too, was excellent as was Ken Swofford in a smaller part as the radio station manager. Ken and I had worked together on Ellery Queen and over the years we have become the best of friends. His wife Barbee and my wife, Lucille, have become even better friends. When Ken saw the picture for the first time in a screening for cast and crew, he was bowled over. We were all thinking Emmy. Then when he saw it on the air, it was still excellent but it had lost a bit of the magic. It was Ken's theory that the constant interruption of the commercials kept breaking the thread of suspense that in theory should have been building and building and building. I think he was right.

Robert and I would work together one more time in an episode of "Murder, She Wrote." I wish we'd done it more often. Sadly he passed away March 24, 2010, of injuries sustained in a fall. Those who knew him and worked with him miss him a lot. To me, he was special.

---

11. In the "Murder, She Wrote" episode entitled 'Murder by Appointment Only', Robert Culp played:

a) The victim

b) The killer

c) The cop

d) A private detective

There Are No Palm Trees in Hawaii

WITH THE EXCEPTION of "The Last Child" where my connection was as an absentee writer and not much else, my career had taken a comfortable and perhaps predictable course. One hour scripts for existing shows, then story editor on a new untested show, then longer scripts for "Columbo" followed by graduation to Executive Story Consultant. After that a producing assignment on Ellery Queen where I was, in reality, a producer in name only. Next up, a classy Movie of the Week, still a non-producing producer and my most curious thought was—*what next?* It popped up almost immediately.

Universal had just made a deal with NBC for a prestige show called Best Sellers, which was to be an umbrella for the airing of three mini-series based on well-known books. They were "Captain and the Kings", a sprawling rags to riches tale of a young Irish immigrant who comes to America in the 1800's and rises to a position of great wealth; "Seventh Avenue", a sprawling rags to riches story of an ambitious young man who rises to the top in the dark and competitive NYC garment business; and finally, "Once an Eagle", which was also sprawling but whose main focus was the military career of a dedicated officer named Sam Damon who rises from private to General over a twenty-six year span, his professional conflict with an egotistical rival modeled after Douglas MacArthur, and the good and bad times of family life, during and between wars.

As I understand it, the boys were offered "Once an Eagle", but turned it down. I think Dick and Bill were much more interested in developing original material than adapting someone else's novel, no matter how good. Then, in a fit of what I can only call temporary insanity, the studio offered it to me. I am trying to get my bearings. Five years earlier I was writing a spec script at my kitchen table on Long Island; now they're entrusting me with a $10 million project to air over nine hours. This television, she is a funny business, no?

I said yes tentatively, took home the book, read it in two days, came back and said, 'Where do I sign up?' I'd also touched base with Dick and Bill to make sure I wasn't stepping on any toes. They wished me well.

If I had had any worries about the Tower tossing me into the pool to sink or swim, I needn't have worried. Here again I was to be one of those non-producing producers. William Sackheim, a prolific movie and television producer, was brought in to oversee everything including notes and suggestions on script. Joe Kramer, a TV veteran of many decades experience, would be the line producer. I would not have to check wardrobe, oversee set construction or interview extras any time soon.

While I was writing the opening two-hour episode, we were simultaneously casting the four leads. With director E. W. Swackhammer (known to everyone as Swack) sitting in, we all pretty much agreed that Sam Elliott was ideal for our stalwart hero, Sam Damon. He had just come off a low budget picture called "Lifeguard" and he had all the qualities, chief of which was a quiet strength and a masculine screen presence. Casting the other leads was not quite so easy. The part of Courtney Massengale, the arrogant and ambitious West Pointer who served as Sam's main rival throughout the series, proved difficult to nail down. He needed to be almost as strong and resolute as Sam but with those subtle flaws that marked him as a man not to be trusted. On the advice of Monique James, a powerful executive in the casting department, we interviewed a contract player, Cliff Potts, who was mostly known for action parts and primarily cowboys. To our surprise whatever we thought Courtney needed to be, Cliff had it in abundance and he and Sam fed off each other well in their scenes together.

For the part of Tommy Caldwell, who was to become Sam's wife, we signed up a very pretty, very outgoing young actress named Darleen Carr and in the part of Emily, who enters into a loveless marriage with Courtney, we cast the lovely and talented Amy Irving.

The fifth major part was taken by Glenn Ford, who played Tommy's father, George Caldwell, a career Army officer who served as a mentor to

Sam during the grim and unfulfilling peacetime years between 1918 and 1941 as well as his quick rise in rank as a battlefield officer in the Pacific in WWII. Glenn had always been a favorite of mine since the "Gilda" days and being the film buff that I was I was awed to be working with him.

We had also scored a coup, we thought, by casting Don Meredith, the ex-football player, as Sam's lifelong friend, Ben Krisler. Sam loved the idea. We all did. But 'twas not to be Two days before we were to start shooting, I got a call at home from Dandy Don backing out of his contract. This is unacceptable behavior at the highest level but maybe Dandy Don, being relatively new to acting, didn't know any better. His agent should have. Luckily for us we knew an actor who was perfect for the part and available. Robert Hogan might not have been the "name" that Meredith was but he was certainly a better actor and we came out way ahead.

We also had a disagreement about casting the part of Jack Devlin who Sam befriends in boot camp and who becomes almost a surrogate brother. The studio wanted Gary Grimes, the young actor who had starred in "Summer of '42". Gary was a good choice but I thought we would do better with a fresh newcomer named John Ritter. I put up a good fight but after hearing 'Who the hell is John Ritter?' one time too many, I gave up. Grimes got the part and to be honest, he gave an excellent performance.

For those of you who have never read Anton Myrer's "Once an Eagle" I highly recommend it. It is one of the two or three works of fiction that are *de riguere* reading at West Point. It is big in scope, it covers a canvas that includes three continents over a thirty year period and oddly enough, while it is pro military, it is anti-war. Both Sam Damon and George Caldwell believed that a strong military serves as a deterrent against aggression. Most responsible military officers in every era would agree. It was only our unpreparedness and perceived weakness that led the Japanese to attack Pearl Harbor. (Note: Like "Ellery Queen", "Once an Eagle" has been a cult favorite for over thirty years and like Ellery, the drumbeat of loyal viewers finally reached the tin ears of the folks at Universal. In the autumn of 2010 the studio released the full length mini-series on DVD. For this we can all thank Tom Hebert, an ex-GI whose middle name is apparently "perseverance" or is it "obstinacy". Tom has been beating the drum for years to get OAE released by Universal and it finally came to pass. He has a website you can reach by typing in once-an-eagle.com and you can read all about it. I heartily endorse it if you are a OAE fan.)

Because the story was so big (the novel runs between 500-600 pages depending on the edition), it presented a huge challenge in getting the complexities of the action and the many relationships onto the screen. I know I got the first two hours right. After that, I'm not so sure. I was certainly new to screenwriting and most particularly to the adaptation of something as rich and literate as Myrer's book. Bill Sackheim believed that the screenwriter owed no allegiance to the novelist, that in condensing action and

Sam Elliott as Sam Damon personified bravery during a World War I raid on a German position. By the final episode of "Once an Eagle," he was a General fighting the Japanese in WWII.

deleting scenes, you ended up with a better screen product, although not something purists would approve of. In writing the script, I tried to walk a fine line and often came up with something that pleased no one, especially myself. (Note: As I said I got the first two hours right. I knew it when I read the final shooting script, I knew it when I saw what Swack, the director, had brought to the screen, and I knew it several days after the first part aired and I got a letter from Mr. Myrer, lauding what we had done. It was, he said, the best adaptation to the screen of any of his works and he was thrilled by it. We subsequently aired the final seven hours but this time, considering all the licenses I'd had to take, I did not hear from Mr. Myrer. I was not surprised.)

I won't bore you with a blow by blow of what was done, but the chief problem was that, to my mind, the story had a natural ending during WWII when Courtney double crosses Sam, causes the death of thousands of his men including his best friend. They confront each other. My gut was to end it there because we were in a perfect spot to tie up the relationships and have a satisfying ending that wouldn't violate what Myrer had written to that point. The fact was, the book went far beyond WWII, into Korea and ultimately into what Myrer had called the Khotiane Mission, a thinly disguised version of the Viet Nam conflict. Sorry, but nobody in those days wanted anything to do with Viet Nam, thinly disguised or not. Secondly, a great deal of what happened in the book after WWII centered on military operations, world politics and I had no idea how to handle it dramatically. So we ended the nine hours in an airplane hangar on a South Pacific island where Courtney was about to fly back to Washington a hero and Sam was going to expose him for the arrogant son of a bitch that he was. There were other changes along the way, but that was the big one.

Sam Elliott was a good man to work with, always professional and always pleasant and always walking around with an empty coke bottle in his hand into which he spit mass quantities of tobacco juice. Sam liked his chaw. Considering all the westerns he eventually wound up doing, one would think he'd been born and bred on a Wyoming ranch. In truth he was born to a middle class family in Sacramento and had a pretty normal non-cowboy upbringing. The rest of the cast was just as professional, especially Glenn Ford, from whom you

Glenn Ford as Major Caldwell pins a battlefield commission on Sam Damon (Sam Elliott) in the opening episode of "Once an Eagle."

would expect no less. He was the movie star in the crowd, the "daddy" of the group. Glenn is no longer with us, but one of my fondest memories of this man was the day we were prepping a very important scene he was to play with Sam.

Sam, as Sam Damon, had had enough of war. The armistice had been signed. He just wanted to go back to the family farm in Nebraska. Glenn, as Colonel Caldwell, has recognized in Sam a natural born leader of men. Caldwell, who had given Sam a battlefield commission for bravery, wants him to consider the military as a career. I had cobbled together some dialogue from the novel, condensed a little, added a little here and there and what we ended up with was quite a long speech which eventually persuaded Sam to stay in the service. Glenn was game but he wanted to make sure he had his cue cards. He was certain he would never be able to memorize what we had given him. I looked at him and said, Glenn, I don't care if you don't get one word right. I want you to read this over and over and I know you will grasp the intent. And then when the camera rolls, I want you to just start talking to Sam, letting him know how you feel. The words are secondary. The meaning is everything.

With great trepidation, he did what we asked and he was marvelous. Everything he knew about performing revealed itself, the low key delivery, the sometimes halting way he usually delivered dialogue. The words weren't perfect but who cared. It remains one of the best scenes in the series.

Most of the show was shot at the studio. Dick Michaels alternated with Swack as director and kept things under control. We went on location to the Napa Valley to shoot a lengthy WWI battle scene in which Sam and the squad capture a French farmhouse held by the Germans. The final two hours required major scenes on a South Pacific island and we weren't about to duplicate that anywhere in the Los Angeles area. So we packed up and headed for Hawaii. Little did we know that the scenery we were looking for, the lush beaches, the heavy green jungle vegetation and most particularly, the palm trees, were not all going to be readily available. That's because there were no indigenous palm trees in the state of Hawaii. (Who knew?) Our intrepid location scouts did find one stretch of beach where a real estate developer, in hopes of sprucing up and selling some beachfront property, actually imported some palm trees from islands in the South Pacific but they weren't going to be enough. Not by a tenth which is why most of the trees we shot and eventually blew up were made of rubber.

We were there on Oahu for a week and they had found me a penthouse suite at the top of the Turtle Bay resort. My wife Lu was with me. Had she not been, I would not have been welcome when I returned home. And that would have been the very least of the misery I might have endured. So on Saturday morning, our last scheduled day before flying home, I was dozing comfortably at around 7:00 a.m. when the phone rang. It was Joe Kramer. Major trouble. Not trouble. A disaster.

We had spent two days dressing the set at the beach with the rubber palm trees for the aftermath of a bloody battle. Wrecked jeeps were littered here and there, the sand and the trees had been painted with black. Smudge pots and other fires were ready to be lit. It had been designed to look like hell on earth. And then early that morning, a very large wave had washed up on shore and destroyed all the work that had gone before.

Yes, this truly was a disaster. This scene could not be cut from the picture. Sam Damon, limping on a jerry rigged crutch, staggers through the carnage, his face a visage of fury, his heart breaking for the dead and dying around him. And then he finds his best friend (Robert Hogan) lying face down in the sand. Overwhelmed he collapses. No, this was a scene that could not be cut. And then everybody jumped in. The business people extended hotel rooms until late in the evening. Joe Kramer got the art director and the set dresser out to the site with their crew and working feverishly, they had it all put back together by one o'clock. Even as the light was fading, we were still shooting but we got it all. Relieved and weary, late that night we were all on a plane heading back to the mainland, film in hand.

As the assistant director likes to yell when the last shot of the last scheduled scene is shot, "That's a wrap!"

And it was.

> ## 12. A 26-year-old Sam Elliott appeared as Doug Robert, a regular on what well known hit TV show in 1971?

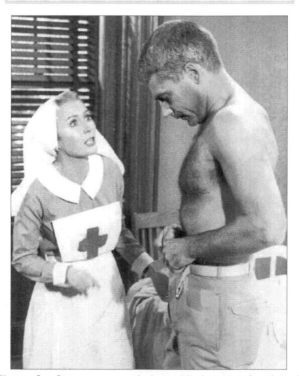

Sam Elliot, as Sam Damon, gets out of a hospital bed to go confront his arch rival in the final hour of "Once an Eagle." Juliet Mills thinks it's a bad idea.

From One Horse Opera to Another

BEFORE I CAN catch my breath the boys are after me again. This time they have a terrific idea for a western series. Did no one tell these so-called geniuses that westerns were passe? Out. Boiled, broiled and overcooked. At one time a few years back there were some 28 westerns on the air in one season. They all reworked variations on the same old plots that had been around since the days of Ken Maynard and Hoot Gibson and the audience palled on them almost immediately. In today's climate "western" is a four-letter word.

Dick put my mind at ease. "It really isn't a western," he said, "it's a detective series."

Oh, well, in that case....

I wrote it and we produced it. It was set in Arizona Territory and featured horses, lizards, rattlesnakes and cacti. A blind man could see it was a western. It was also pedestrian. Clu Gulager, in a deviation from type, played a sly, witty and totally charming rascal of an insurance investigator named Charlie Cobb whose finest talent lay in kiting his expense account. Clu was terrific but despite his best efforts we were an inconsequential piece of fluff which went nowhere except to syndication heaven.

Let us get on to bigger and better things, I thought to myself.

In my newest contract it stated that I had the right, if it in no way interfered with my Universal obligations, to accept work from the outside. Excluded from this provision were series pilots and episodes for competing studio's television series. But if someone wanted me for a movie idea (or a TV Movie of the Week), I was free to pursue it. That meant my agent would have to hustle a little on my behalf. Now Sylvia Hirsch, as lovely a lady as she was, had done little or no hustling for me so when Rowland

Perkins asked me to lunch during the Ellery Queen season, I accepted. He invited me to join this brand new agency (Creative Artists Agency) which he had just formed the year before with three former colleagues from the William Morris office. Because I was getting no outside nibbles and CAA was on the way to becoming the biggest, most powerful agency in town, I accepted. When my contract with the Morris office expired I made the switch. (For several weeks I entered the parking garage at night with great caution, worried that Sylvia might be hiding in the shadows with a sawed off shotgun—or something even more dangerous, a lawyer—but I needn't have worried. Sylvia was a lady through and through and probably out of guilt, I think I hired more of her clients than I really should have.)

So here I was at CAA and as is always the case, Rowland, as a very important founder-executive, fobbed me off onto one of his minions, a young man named Mark Rossen which I didn't really mind because Mark was a nice guy and very sharp. He was not, however, sharp enough to find me something to work on (although, in the future he would.) So while I waited for the studio to find me something to fill my days, I goofed off.

Not for long.

Charlie Engel, one of the Tower suits I liked best, dropped by the office. NBC was at it again. More mini-series. This time it would be in family hour (eight p.m.) and two of the books to be dramatized were "Little Women" and "Black Beauty". Each would air for five consecutive nights, Monday through Friday. "Little Women" was spoken for but would I be interested in writing and producing "Black Beauty"? This time around there would be no Executive Producer looking over my shoulder. The Executive Producer would be me. It would be my project alone, to succeed or fail as the case might be. What an opportunity. I hastily agreed on the spot. Much too hastily, I might add.

On the way home that evening, I stopped by a bookstore, picked up a copy of Anna Sewell's novel (her ONLY novel) and after supper I settled down in the den and opened to the first page.

Chapter One....."The first place that I can well remember was a large pleasant meadow with a pond of clear water in it......"

I stopped reading. My God, the horse talks. I skimmed quickly through the pages. He was still talking. Not only that but he was having conversations with other horses. I was aghast. Was I really going to write a script with a voice over provided by a black stallion. I was able to tolerate "Mr. Ed" only because it was a mindless comedy, but this was too much. I was reminded of "Sunset Boulevard", Billy Wilder's masterpiece. The movie opens with William Holden floating in a pool and he starts a narration about how he ended up in this compromising position. Originally Wilder had Holden in the morgue and dispensing the same exposition by talking to the other corpses who, in turn, were talking back to him. At the first screening, the audience laughed so loud at this ludicrous scene that Wilder knew major surgery was needed. Like Wilder, I could hear titters rising from television homes all over America.

I could have called Charlie and said, no thanks. But I didn't because I thought to myself, *give it a few days.* There is a basic story here, the travails of a horse from birth through a life that goes further and further downhill until he is only days away from being shipped to the slaughterhouse. Miss Sewell, who was an invalid during the last part of her life but who had a deep and abiding love of horses, wrote the novel as a protest against the prevailing cruel practices toward horses that existed at the time. Throughout the pages Black Beauty described the various people who owned and controlled him, kind as well as cruel. There was plenty of material if I could just find the right voice for the narrative thread. And I would have to do it on my own as my two crutches, Dick and Bill, were deeply immersed in writing a disaster of a feature film entitled "Rollercoaster". Disaster is not a pejorative here, it was designed to be a disaster like "Earthquake" and "The Towering Inferno". The genre was all the rage in those days.

I read the book taking careful notes. Then I did it all over again and I knew immediately that I was going to have to take liberties almost everywhere. Yes, it was a well-loved book and with good reason. Young girls in particular have been enamored of it for a hundred years but reduced to essentials it was mostly a polemic and only rarely dramatic. Nonetheless I thought I could walk a fine line by including all the major characters and key scenes but adding my own thread to hang it all together.

For example the first three chapters are mainly Beauty frolicking in the meadow in wonderment about the world around him. I didn't know how anyone could script that. In Chapter Four Beauty is sold to Squire Gordon where he is to have several pleasant years. Thus starts the horse's life journey from master to master.

I scrubbed the first three chapters and set the action in Maryland in the 1880's. The first scene is the birth of Beauty to a brood mare named Duchess.(Not in the book but alluded to).As Edward Bulwar-Lytton penned so ingloriously a couple of centuries ago, "It was a dark and stormy night." Duchess is in pain. It is a breech birth. The vet is summoned. Beauty is delivered. Duchess survives. Tom Grey breeds horses and sells them for a living. His son Luke, who is in his early teens helps out. Boy and horse become inseparable. Luke "breaks' the horse gently like a horse whisperer. Tragically Tom Gray suffers a terrible stroke. The family will have to move to Philadelphia where Luke can get a proper education. They have no money except what they can get for the farm and the horses. Luke knows his duty is to his family but before he turns Beauty over to the Gordons he rides him out to a high hill and swears to return to find Beauty, however long it takes.

The character of Luke, who is to become a lawyer, is woven through the five hours as he tries to juggle his job at a New York law firm with his on-going search for his horse. We used third-party narrations to deal with plot segues. These were voiced by David Wayne who appeared in the final hour as Luke's employer at the law firm and who, regretting the so-called practical life choices he had made, encourages Luke to go back to Maryland, to the life he loved and to follow his dream.

Other than those changes, everything in the five hours was straight from the book: near-death at the swollen river; the fire at the wayside inn where Beauty and his stablemate, Ginger, barely escape death; the midnight ride where a drunken Reuben Smith nearly maims him; the roadside accident where Beauty comes upon Ginger, lying in the roadway, dying; the young man who buys Beauty to go courting but boards him with a scheming, uncaring stablemaster who cheats him and abuses the horse; the tender years with gentle hansom cab driver Jerry Barker and his family; and finally the terrible treatment at the hands of Nicholas Skinner and his fleet of hired drivers who consistently beat the life out of their horses until they were worthless. I embellished, of course. I had to, but what Miss Sewell had in mind, I was very true to.

All five hours were shot on location in and around Lexington, Kentucky, and while we were there, cast and crew were treated like welcome guests. For a line producer, I had hired Ben Bishop, a man who had never before produced. Ben had been the Unit Manager on Ellery Queen and he was the quintessential hard-nosed grouch with the heart of gold. He could yell obscenities with the best of them, often turning beet red in the process. On the set, if things were falling behind, he would stand very close to the director and start jingling the coins in his pocket. The director always got the message. What most people didn't know about Ben was that he was not a cut-and-dried bean counter. One day we were falling way behind and we were concerned that the slow pace of work would put us over into an extra (very expensive) day. Ben saw that I was worried so he pulled me off to the side and in his gruff way said, in effect, 'We want to make this for the money, but we also want to make it good. There's no sense on staying on budget if you're going to turn out garbage. ' And that is why I had asked Ben to be my producer. What Ben didn't know about making film didn't exist and I knew he would never sacrifice the good of the show to budget constraints.

On the other hand Ben felt it wasn't his privilege to spend Universal's money willy-nilly and if there was a budget to adhere to, we should do our best to respect it. Our resolve in this area was tested on the first day of shooting. The general rule of thumb for episodic television in those days was 8-10 pages of script a day. If you had a 56 page script you could do an hour episode in seven days. That was about average. With a mini-series you got a little more leeway but the kind of care given to a feature film was out. That's why when people see a movie for television on television, it's because that is exactly what it is. Bare bones set ups, quick and easy lighting, restricted camera moves, all that and less. On Day One I was in the office noshing on a sandwich when Ben came in. I could tell from his face it was trouble. What's the problem, I ask. The DP, Ben says. He's out at the farm painting pictures. I groan. How much in the can? An eighth of a page, he says. The Director of Photography, let's just call him Toby, is an excellent cameraman and we had been led to believe he also shot fast. We had been misled. He has to go, Ben said. Agreed, I agreed. Ben said he and Jack (the unit manager) would handle it that evening after the day's work had wrapped. I shake my head. The buck stops with me. I'll do it. Meanwhile, see who's available. That evening, the four of us sit down. I tell Toby he does fine work and will do so in the future but we can't afford him. We are one day into shooting and already one day behind schedule. At this rate we'll be still shooting by Thanksgiving. Toby is miffed. "Well, if THAT'S the kind of picture you want...", he says snidely. I say, No, that's the kind of picture we

The horse talks. Who knew? Ike Eisenmann as young Luke and Black Beauty.

can afford. I'd heard DPs could be prima donnas. This only proved it. We put in a call to Johnny Jones who had filmed "Once an Eagle" for me (and won an Emmy nomination in the process). He was on the next plane to Lexington. The next day we look at the dailies including the eighth of a page that Toby took four hours to shoot. It is gorgeous. It is perfect. It belongs in a feature film. If only you could shoot something like that in one hour instead of four. But you can't and that is the reality of the business.

There were many weekend parties as locals vied for our attention. The Governor came to visit one of the locations and made me a Kentucky Colonel, why I will never know. A few of our stars were invited to posh dinner parties. Most behaved themselves. One, a notorious ladies man with fabled equipment to match, fell asleep in the middle of the roast lamb, the victim of too much bourbon. Location romances sprung up everywhere, a phenomenon with which I was heretofore unfamiliar. I suppose it's a part of every profession when out of town trips are called for but it seems to me it's mainly peculiar to the film business. Lonely people, mostly bored, seeking escape, maybe pining for home, quickie attachments just as quickly detached when the picture wraps. Everybody knows who's with who and nobody really cares. Another facet of the business I find fascinating.

Meantime a personal highlight for me was an escorted visit to Claiborne Farms where I got to meet Secretariat. This was some piece of horseflesh and it was easy to see how he had become a horse racing legend. The head groom let me in on a little secret about the big fella. After winning the Triple Crown he was immediately brought back to Kentucky and put into stud. His fees were substantial and the waiting list for his services was lengthy. Well, I am told, that often when you try to stud a very young horse, they don't quite know what is expected of them and for a couple of weeks, no matter what strategem they used, they couldn't get Secretariat to perform. He would even balk at being led to the mating stable all set up with the requisite equipment. Then one day it happened, almost by accident, and from that day forward, everything changed. When Secretariat was led from his stall to perform his duty of the day, he started snorting and tugging at the lead and fought to gallop all the way to the "brothel shed". (I believe this is the origin of the word 'stud' as applied to the young horndogs of America.)

Meanwhile our company of players is coming and going in shifts to perform what were, in most cases, cameo roles. We had an all-star cast of movie and TV stars including Van Johnson, Martin Milner, Eileen Brennan, Diane Ladd, David Wayne, Diana Muldaur, Cameron Mitchell. Edward Albert, Glynnis O'Connor, Farley Granger, Jack Elam, Mel Ferrer, Forrest Tucker, Peter Breck, and Clu Gulager among others.

Our leading man was black, hairy, and ran on four legs. His name value as an actor was zero. So, despite the glittering cameos, there were two substantial roles that needed careful filling, not only because we needed strong believable performances but also some exploitable name value as well. The part I was most concerned about was John Manly, the horse's groom in the first two hours of the series. The part cried out for a stalwart leading man with a sense of humor and who, hopefully, was a recognized star. We had found exactly the right actor in William Devane who had shot into prominence based on his performance as John F. Kennedy in the TV

Bill Devane on the set of "Black Beauty" with Eileen Brennam.
We got rock solid performances from both of them.

miniseries, "Missiles of October". Bill was willing to do it, thanks in large measure to pressure from his daughter who loved the book. Trouble was Bill's "quotes" (his usual fees) were beyond what we could spend on the part. I went straight to Frank Price, told him why Bill was vital to the project and without hesitation, Frank okayed the extra money. Ex-writers look out for their own. We also needed an actor of stature for the part of Jerry Barker, the kindly cab driver, who takes Beauty into his home and treats him with love and kindness. We decide to go right against type and offer the part to Warren Oates who thrived on playing weasly villains and whose biggest role to date was John Dillinger. Warren, tired of playing psychos and perverts, signs on and thrives in the part. We couldn't have done better.

So, in shifts, we are all gathered in Kentucky. Because we were all together on location, for the first time I actually got to spend a little time with the cast members. I remember sitting under a tree with Bill Devane and kicking around the idea of doing a p.i. series. He would have been a perfect Philip Marlowe or Sam Spade. He was about to start principal photography on a film called "Rolling Thunder" and I'm sure he was hoping to embark on a movie career. That never quite happened but a couple of years later he was starring in the series "From Here to Eternity" playing the Burt Lancaster part.(Proving that Hollywood is indeed a very small town, my brother Geoff, having graduated from casting, got one of his first writer-producer credits in that series.) A couple of years after that Bill appeared for several seasons as the star of "Knots Landing".

I also got to know Warren Oates who was a shy and softspoken man who, as I said, was mainly typecast as villains but who we cast as the warm-hearted family man Jerry Barker who showed Beauty nothing but kindness. In a key scene where Jerry is confronted by three drunken louts, I learned an important lesson. We had "snowed in" a section of Paris, Kentucky, for this New Year's Eve scene. I was standing across the street. Warren and three local actors were playing the scene alongside the cab as our fake snow fell from the skies. I became worried. I could hear the three locals just fine but not Warren. It was as if he wasn't there. The next day, watching dailies I was treated to the scene of the three locals "acting" for us and Warren,

Mulling our next move on the set of "Black Beauty." From left to right: Al Yank, our horse wrangler; Ben Bishop, producer; me; and Dan Haller, our director.

keeping his voice modulated, being very real and natural as Jerry Barker. Another lesson learned. You don't have to shout at an overhead boom mike. Warren died five years later at the age of 49. Too young. Much too young.

People came from miles around to either work as extras ($10 for the day plus a box lunch) or to gawk at the stars. Lawyers, accountants, bankers, it made no difference. They all wanted to dress up and become a part of movie magic. They were quiet, polite, and never once cost us time. In one scene, however, they posed a problem. We had signed one-time teen heart throb Van Johnson as an uncaring cab driver. We were shooting in the Paris town square which we were doubling for 1890 Baltimore. The actors were sitting off to the side on their folding chairs and Van was quietly being "mobbed" by starstruck ladies of an earlier generation. Mel Ferrer and Warren Oates relaxing nearby were virtually ignored. We had quite a crowd that day and that was creating a major problem. In the scene we were about to shoot Beauty is pulling an overloaded cab and it is too much for him. He staggers in his traces and falls to the ground. Now there are several ways to humanely put a horse down but they don't really LOOK humane. Al Yank, our horse wrangler, was worried that the spectators would be outraged and we could ruin much of the good will we had amassed. But it had to be done. It was key to everything that would follow.

It was Ben Bishop who came up with the solution. Al Yank and his crew gently lowered the horse to the ground, still in his harness. The cameras started to roll. The trainer gave Beauty the cue and the horse struggled to his feet. The crowd applauded. What they didn't realize was that when we put the picture together, we would run this clip backwards so instead of seeing the horse arise, you would see him fall to the ground. God bless Ben. Always there with the answer.

Lucille was on hand for the final days of shooting and we made a vacation of it. In the cast was Christopher Stone playing the swain of Beauty's fourth owner. Chris was also a personal friend and he and Lu palled around a lot while I was trying to help Ben make order out of chaos. Maybe it was just to show off for my wife but Chris decided he was going to take Beauty for a ride. What he didn't know was that there were actually THREE Beautys on the set. The "actor", the stand-in and occasional double, and the third, a one-trick pony whose only talent was to collapse in a heap when you tugged on his left rein. Unfortunately Chris mounted the wrong horse and if Al Yank hadn't been standing nearby, our good friend might have ended up with a broken leg—or worse.

After the final shot of the final scene of the picture, we all gathered for the traditional wrap party at a local restaurant, imbibing and noshing, dancing and singing (mostly off key choruses of "California, Here We Come"). We were tired and mostly homesick but it had been a helluva seven weeks.

Back at the office, post-production loomed and with one major exception, there was nothing out of the ordinary to write about. That one exception was John Addison.

John passed away a few years ago but to my mind, he was one of the most talented and prolific motion picture composers that had ever plied their trade both here and abroad. His credits include "Tom Jones" (he won the Oscar). "A Bridge Too Far" (he won the British 'Oscar'), "A Taste of Honey", "Sleuth" (Oscar nomination), "The Entertainer, "The Loneliness of the Long Distance Runner", "A Fine Madness", "Torn Curtain", "The Seven and a Half Percent Solution" and many more classic films. His score for "Black Beauty", particularly the stirring main title theme —Beauty's theme—which recurs throughout, is a masterpiece. A kind and gentle man without bombast or ego, he would work with me again, creating the theme music for two pilots and subsequent series. For one of these he would win the Emmy.

13. Published in England in 1877, to date "Black Beauty" has sold how many copies world wide?

a) 15,000,000

b) 25,000,000

c) 50,000,000

d) 75,000,000

Me and beautiful wife Lu goofing off in Mendocino while others do the heavy lifting. Executive producers answer to no one.

Funny, He Doesn't Look Irish

ALTHOUGH I HAVEN'T GOTTEN into discussing the movie business, you have probably figured out that there is a world of difference between feature films and TV films and series. In the movie business the producer is a hustler, con man, conniver, and a smooth talking snake oil salesman. He has to find a property (hopefully, cheap), hire a writer to put it to paper (also, cheap), grovel before studio executives looking for money and/or a distribution deal, abase himself at the feet of a powerful agent who represents an even more powerful mega-star (not cheap), round up a supporting cast (how cheap can we hire these nonentities?) and worst of all, hire a director who will, without question, make his life a living hell for the next six to eight months. He will age a decade trying to find locations that the director will hate, he will take phone calls from the studio suits shrieking that the dailies suck and why doesn't he rein in that profligate director (as if anybody could). He may or may not have a quickie romance with the third extra from the left while his wife tours Beverly Hills in a pickup truck with enough room to clean out Cartier's. In the movies, directors can get producers fired. It does not work the other way around.

In television a producer's life is considerably simpler. He has a studio behind him with all their various departments ready and willing to pitch in. He need not raise money. He can hire a director and if he doesn't like what that former stuntman-dialogue coach (or whatever he once was)) is doing with the picture he can fire him and bring in the next non-entity. (Note: To all my director friends who are truly talented gentlemen, I exaggerate for dramatic effect).

That is one main difference. Here's another. In the movie business the Executive Producer is the guy whose wife put up half the production money, or the guy who knew the book author well enough to introduce him to the producer over spaghetti at Musso and Franks. He knows nothing about filmmaking. He wants money and he wants screen credit and sometimes he wants the film's star to attend his oldest boy's bar mitzvah, but that is the extent of it.

In the television business the Executive Producer is God. He is the guru to whom all bow down. All power is held in his hands unless, of course, he is a spineless jellyfish and a chronic appeaser in which case the series star will crush him like a tiny Prius that made the mistake of getting caught between two tractor trailers. In my opinion being a Executive Producer on a television series (particularly a successful one) is the best job in Hollywood. Television production goes on and on like a tiny Pac-Man chewing up anything that gets in its way. It is a treadmill that once started won't stop until the final episode of the year is in the can. Hot or cold, rainy or clear the crew and the line producer and the director are on the set or out on location at 6:00 in the morning. At six in the evening they may still be there. Hell, they may be there until midnight. The actors are weary from sitting around doing nothing except for those brief moments when they actually get to perform for the camera.

The Executive Producer, on the other hand, is the one who sleeps until 8:00, eats a leisurely breakfast, wanders into work around 10:00, answers a few phone calls, schmoozes with fellow producers or agents or actors, maybe sets up a lunch date. If there's a crisis on the set, he orders the line producer to handle it. Around 5:30 he thinks about heading home to see the wife and kids. Only rarely is this blissful existence interrupted by something negative like, for example, being hauled up to the Tower to take the heat for the lousy scripts, the uncooperative star and the parade of directors who couldn't direct traffic on a one-way street. Clever Executive Producers use these moments to fire the story editor, kick the line producer in the butt and hire a whole new slate of directors who will prove no better than the ones they've been using. No one chastises the star. Everyone talks about it. No one does it. If you are doing a cop show called "Eight Brave Men in Blue", you don't have a star, you have an ensemble. Each of the eight actors knows he is destined for a fatal bullet in the next episode if he causes even a modicum of trouble. If, however, your series is entitled "The One and Only Fearless Captain Braveheart" you have a problem because the guy playing Braveheart knows you can't muscle him. I mean, how could you do the show without him?

So, now you have some idea of how it works. This will help you to understand my excitement when I tell you I was offered the chance to create my own series and oversee production as the Executive Producer.

At one time Dick Lindheim was a Tower suit. A very nice man, he had a sharp intellect, especially for Neilsen numbers and how to get them. He could analyze a project, make a decent projection about how it would fare depending on time slot and competition. He was right most of the time and he loved to schmooze with Dick and Bill and me, sometimes at lunch, sometimes just sitting around the office. We got to know each other well and he was persuaded that I had some idea of what I was doing. He also liked a series idea I had mentioned to him in passing although I never pressed it. (Mostly I was busy with other things.) Then Lindheim left Universal for NBC and before long he was put in charge of prime time dramatic programming.

You may remember that many pages back I observed that the chances of getting a pilot commitment and perhaps even a series vastly improved when the network people came up with the idea. Sure enough, Lindheim came up with the idea of developing that series idea we had chatted about. Before they had even handed him the key to executive washroom, Lindheim was on the phone with me. Let's do it, says he. Why not, says I.

Although Lindheim and the others at NBC might have thought the project would have a better chance of success with Levinson and Link involved, there was no chance of that. The boys, disappointed that Ellery had not gone beyond one season and irked that Clu Gulager and Charlie Cobb hadn't even gotten a short-order shot (6 episodes as a mid-season replacement), they had soured on series television and were deep into their movie-of-the-week phase. And quite a productive phase it was. Now writing again, over the next several years they turned out a bevy of high class television films such as "Crisis at Central High", "The Story Teller", "Murder by Natural Causes", "Guilty Conscience", "Rehearsal for Murder" and several others. They also found time to wend their way to Broadway where they had written a charming musical comedy called "Merlin" which starred Doug Henning. No, they were definitely out of the series business and Dick Lindheim decided, on the basis that I hadn't completely screwed up "Black Beauty", that I could handle it on my own. Besides, whose idea was it, anyway? (Note: It was my theory that every network programming guru had a little list in a desk drawer that was headed: "Guys You Can Hire Without Fear of Immediately Losing Your Job". I believed my name was on it—at least for the time being—along with a couple of dozen other "show-runners". (Synonym: Executive Producer).

My short three page outline which Dick had seen was entitled "Shannon". Shannon was a young lawyer who was not really a lawyer; that is, he never actually set foot in a courtroom. He was more like a detective, but with the trappings and protections afforded an attorney. He was also casual. It's doubtful he owned a tie. His idea of dressing up was a windbreaker and jeans. He was eccentric in his thinking and in his methods. He was not only outside the box most of the time, he was rarely in it. He worked for one of the West Coast's most famous courtroom lawyers (Melvin Belli?) and their relationship was mostly warm and involved mutual respect. Oh, and there was one other thing that I believed set Shannon apart from other lawyers on television. This was 1978. Television morality was still vintage 1956. Shannon lived in an duplex. A few feet away was the doorway to the other half of the building. Living there was the bright and beautiful secretary from the law office (divorced) and her 8 year old daughter. Shannon would come and go on a regular basis to "visit". It was as close as I would be able to get to having them live together without causing apoplexy among the network censors. Dick Lindheim had liked "Shannon" in abbreviated form; he liked it even better as I fleshed it out and before I could light up a victory cigar NBC was committed to filming the pilot.

And then came major problem number one. Who would play Shannon? As the writer and creator of the character I had some very definite ideas of who Shannon was and none of the available people whose work I knew was anywhere close to what I had in mind. So with line producer James MacAdams on board with director James Frawley, we started reading unknowns and hardly-knowns. And reading. And reading. The network was getting nervous. If we didn't come up with our star soon, they would have to "postpone". This is a euphemism. The actual definition is "dead in the water". Jesus might have raised Lazarus from the dead but he would have had no such success with a network project that had been postponed. (Another euphemism is "put into turnaround". Wonder why these sharp film school alums couldn't just use that time-honored phrase, "shit canned"?)

We had three candidates that were possibilities but you never could really tell if they were right until you screen tested them. Frank Price was out of town so Charlie Engel gave us the go-ahead and two days later we committed our three possibles to film. An editor slapped the tests together. We viewed the film and I quickly made up my mind. But by now Frank Price was back in town and he was irked that we had gone ahead and tested without letting him meet the candidates in his office. (Meet and greet was pretty much standard operating procedure but as Charlie tried to explain, the network wasn't giving us that luxury.)

We booked a screening room, gathered together with a still-annoyed Frank Price in our midst and watched the tests for the umpteenth time. The lights went up. There was silence. I was sitting behind and to the right of Frank. He turned and looked at me. I'm not sure where it was a statement or a question but he said, "The second one." I nodded my agreement. Frank nodded, then got up and left. And that was how Vincent Baggetta, a swarthy Italian with Mediterranean good looks got to play an Irishman named Shannon.

I had liked Vince before the test and even better afterward. His best role to this point (for me, anyway) had been playing a recurring priest on "Mary Hartman, Mary Hartman", a late night comedy spoof that a great many people adored. He had screen presence, no doubt of that. He wasn't tall, maybe five-seven, but he carried himself like a linebacker with a cocky swagger that never quite got to arrogance. And he had energy to spare.

An Irishman named Shannon becomes lawyer-detective Eddie Capra when bantamweight Vince Baggetta lands the part. Frank Capra is so flattered we've borrowed his name that he threatens to sue.

Whatever scenes he'd be in might have problems, but juice wouldn't be one of them. Frank Price was with us all the way and he sent Vince's screen test over to NBC with a note. This is our Shannon, he said. NBC didn't get to vote.

So now we had a problem. Our hero was going to need a new name because Vince was a far cry from Pat O'Brien or George Murphy. I remember sitting around the living room with Lu and Geoff and his wife Liz and Chris Stone and his then-wife Carol, batting around Italian surnames. We wanted something not too ordinary and certainly nothing with five-syllables. And anything that smacked of the Mob was out. We finally settled on what I thought was the perfect name. *Capra.* It reflected everything good about Italian-Americans and was an homage to one the industries greatest directors. We were quite pleased with ourselves. A short time later when publicity for the show started to appear, Frank Capra threatened to sue. So much for our homage.

We cast the other regulars. Ken Swofford was picked to play the big-time lawyer J.J. Devlin, a young and beautiful Wendy Philips became Lacey Brown, Capra's secretary/inamorata. Seven Ann MacDonald was cast as her daughter. And for the part of Harvey, a somewhat bumbling but bright and eager young intern, we chose an up and coming young actor named Michael Horton. I liked Michael a lot. A few years later I would cast him as Jessica Fletcher's nephew Grady and we would work together for seven fruitful seasons.

The plot of the pilot, titled "Nightmare at Pendragon's Castle", involved an egomaniacal industrialist who had a King Arthur fixation. He gathers his associates around him at his baronial manor one weekend, skulduggery abounds and early on Sunday morning, Pendragon (played with great archness by Robert Vaughn) is found on his front lawn, run through by a sword called Excalibur. The mystery is this. There is a mammoth stone which Pendragon had placed on the lawn. Set in the stone was "Excalibur". Only Pendragon himself could manage to pull the sword from the stone. A demonstration Saturday evening had proved that. George Hamilton had tried. Robert Walker had tried. So who had been able to wrest the sword from the stone and kill its owner?

I'd like to report that filming the pilot was a happy experience. It wasn't. Jim Frawley was dealing with a lot of personal problems and it showed in his work. Some days the work was just fine. Other days it was pedestrian at best. Our leading lady was also having personal problems that affected her concentration and quality of performance. In the end the two hour pilot was pretty good but could have been so much better. John Addison was brought in to score the two hours as well as create the main theme for the pilot should we be picked up and of course, his work was excellent, a haunting melody, Italian in flavor, with plenty of drive.

After the pilot aired as a special (Sunday night, I think) we debuted in our regular spot, ten o'clock on Fridays following 'The Rockford Files". From the beginning and throughout, our ratings were middling. Not so bad that we were cancellation bad, not so good that we were a sure thing for a pick up from 13 episodes to 22. The members of the cast were all hardworking and always prepared. Vince, as the nominal star (we had been titled "The Eddie Capra Mysteries") was no trouble. Even if he'd had a notion to, he knew better than to try to throw his weight around on a show that teetered precariously between success and oblivion. Had we done well, I think he would have stayed the same fun easy going guy. We became good friends. At last count we still were.

Since our fall off in numbers from Rockford was small, NBC started promoting the two shows as the Friday night Mystery Doubleheader. We learned from the jungle drums that James Garner was angry about this, as if we were the raggedy homeless poor relations from the other side of town. But naturally, star power being what it was, Garner got his way. We gave some thought to sending Vince over to the Rockford offices to sneer "Oh, yeah!!!" at them but decided it probably wouldn't do much good.

And then a terrible thing happened. As it turned out, it soon was terrible for everyone within spitting distance of the NBC studios in Burbank. Our stalwart champion, Dick Lindheim, was axed as chief program developer and in his place, top management brought in the ex-CBS wunderkind who had gone on to "save" ABC from total oblivion, Fred Silverman. Silverman was to be the Messiah, casting out the wretched refuse that made up the NBC schedule to distant barren lands and bringing in the saviors who would turn the parched earth upon which the NBC studios rested into greener pastures. The sun shone brightly. Glory was at hand. With Fred Silverman at the helm how could anything go wrong?

How indeed. At CBS and then at ABC, Silverman had not been in total charge. Stronger hands and wiser heads oversaw him. At NBC he was made President and CEO. Now he had no superiors to curb his excesses. To make room for what he was sure were ratings blockbusters, he cancelled all nine new shows that his predecessors had launched in September. That included us. He didn't do it with a scalpel, carefully evaluating each show as to its potential, he did it with a machete in order to make the biggest headlines possible. Here he comes on his white horse, banners flying, leaving the slag and dross of previous programmers in his wake.

Some of the shows that arose full blown from his fevered brain and eventually reached his schedule included: "The Man from Atlantis" (an underwater crime fighter, half-man, half-fish); "B.J. and the Bear" (a ripoff of Smokey and the Bandit); "The Misadventures of Sheriff Lobo" (spun off from B.J. with Claude Akins in the Jackie Gleason part); "Supertrain"(crime fighting and soap opera on a bullet train spanning America, week after week after week); "Hello, Larry" (hailed as one of the worst shows ever put on the air, it virtually ended MacLean Stevenson's career); Mrs. Columbo (a misbegotten piece of excrement from day one without sanction from Falk, Levinson or Link.) Happily, Kate Mulgrew survived it. (See Next Chapter); and the best of all "Manimal" (a crime fighter who was half-man and half-animal the latter being whatever beast the script dictated that particular week).

I wonder how James Garner felt about leading into a thing called "Eischeid", a sort of a cop show starring Joe Don Baker, that got ratings considerably lower than the ones we provided on Capra. Sorry, Jim, don't blame me.

Silverman left NBC three years later in far worse shape than he had found it. Almost none of his development worked. By 1980 NBC was earning $80 million less than when he took over. He so infuriated Lorne Michaels that the "Saturday Night Live" creator and producer quit and didn't come back until Fred was long gone. NBC fired Silverman in 1981.

I felt badly when we were cancelled but it happens. I also had a contract. I also knew that sooner or later I would be moving on to other things but what hurt most was what Silverman had done to the cast. For the sake of a self-aggrandizing headline, he had destroyed our tight knit little family and dashed a lot of hopes. A role on a regular series can often provide lifelong security to an actor or actress. My people, my friends, were robbed of that opportunity.

Someone told me later that Silverman was quoted as saying the cancellation of "The Eddie Capra Mysteries" was a mistake. He may have said it.

I don't know. I wasn't there.

I was there when I had to go to the set and deliver the news to the cast as they filmed what would prove to be the last show. I was there when a pall fell over the sound stage and Vince sat in his folding chair staring at the floor. I was there when Ken Swofford talked in quiet dejected tones with the cameraman. And I was there when Wendy Philips cried quietly in her dressing room, shocked, disbelieving and utterly inconsolable.

A couple of weeks later I threw a party at my home for the cast and a bunch of key crew people. It was my way of trying to blunt the pain while saying, 'Great job, guys, we deserved better'. The mood was mellow if not quite joyful and got even mellower when Michael Horton broke out a dozen T-shirts he had had especially made for the occasion. The inscription on each read "Silverman Sucks". I chastised Mike for having no sense of decorum or class and told him we were all better than that. Some of my criticism might have been lost as I was trying to pull my T-shirt on over my head.

Heaven help you, Fred. More about your career in the next chapter.

> **14. One of Frank Capra's earliest successes was "Lady for a Day". Years later he remade it with Glenn Ford and Bette Davis under what title?**

Right: These six foolish people are "celebrating" the cancellation of "The Eddie Capra Mysteries" by programming genius Fred Silverman. Note the T-shirts. From left to right: Ken Swofford, Wendy Phillips, Vince Baggetta, Seven Ann McDonald, Michael Horton and me.

Anyone for a Really Bad Idea?

IT WASN'T bad enough that Fred Silverman had cancelled my fragile, struggling child before it had a chance to grow into maturity, now he wanted to bastardize one of the most popular shows ever to emerge from a television tube. As noted in the previous chapter, Silverman assumed the reins of NBC, galloping in one day on a fiery white steed, armed to the teeth with brilliant insights into what made good TV programming and what didn't. Given his track record at CBS and ABC, few were courageous enough to speculate that the man, left to his own devices, was in over his head.

As previously noted, his first act in taking control was to cancel all nine shows which his predecessor, Dick Lindheim, had scheduled the previous September. Nine shows (including "The Eddie Capra Mysteries") deep-sixed unceremoniously, even when there was no real need for it. But Silverman's ego was monumental and he wanted to make a few headlines. And he did. No, he didn't have the courtesy to let us know in advance. We read about it in the trade papers.

But in addition to letting those nine one-hour shows fade from the tube, he also got rid of one of the network's jewels. "Columbo" was also dumped. Maybe he didn't like the financial arrangement. No question it was expensive but NBC didn't have a whole lot going for it. But "Columbo"? Media observers just shook their heads. What next? What next, indeed.

Silverman apparently thought he could have his cake and eat it too, because he came up with the bizarre notion of making a series out of Mrs. Columbo. Of all the idiotic ideas Silverman ever sired, this was by far the dumbest, but maybe he figured he could parlay the Columbo name into a successful franchise at a tenth of the cost. Remember, at this time, Silverman was still Merlin, still the man with the unfailing touch. He believed that he need only speak the words and the waters would part. Remember "Field of Dreams"? Someone must have whispered in his ear: "Program it and they will come."

I know Peter Falk was disappointed by his cancellation but also ambivalent. He would have liked to do more of the 90 minute or two hour specials but he also wanted to leave room in his schedule to make feature films. But Mrs. Columbo? Words failed Peter and that was a first. Dick Levinson believed "Columbo" was getting a little worn but still had one or two good years left. His reaction to a Mrs. Columbo series, like Peter Falk's, was right on point. It can't work. The audience will turn away in droves. Meanwhile I had other problems. First of all, it was never clear in the seven years "Columbo" had been aired if, in fact, there really was a Mrs. Columbo. Or was she just a device to disarm his antagonist with his folksy irrelevant stories about his home life.

Nonetheless, Silverman was adamant and he came to the three us, me and the boys, to create and produce it. None of us wanted anything to do with it, but Silverman persisted and it became clear that he was going to proceed, with or without us. Dick, who was very good at playing the game that I never learned, decided that maybe the project was better done by us than some nonentity who would not only fail but sully the Columbo image in the process. And being a pragmatist he thought we might need Silverman at some future date on a more viable project. I still was against it and my animus toward Silverman was palpable, but if Dick and Bill were willing, I'd grudgingly go along. At this point the three of us were pretty much intertwined as a trio when it came to series television.

We immediately decided that the woman would be approximately Peter's age, probably ethnic Italian, warm and outgoing, sharply intelligent without flaunting it. She would be childless giving her room to maneuver. She would have the large extended family Peter was always referring to. (These were all issues we would deal with six years hence when inventing Jessica Fletcher). Ideal casting would have been Maureen Stapleton, Zohra Lampert, or maybe Anne Jackson if we dumped the Italian requirement.

Two big stumbling blocks had to be dealt with. First of all, how does she get herself into the detecting business when so far all we know is she's a stay at home housewife baking cookies in the kitchen? And more importantly, if she's going to be out of the house tracking down killers, where is her husband? Dead? Divorced? That was a major imponderable.

The boys and I worked out a story, I wrote the script and we got the okay from NBC to proceed. We started testing actresses (as I recall the above named ladies wanted nothing to do with this turkey). Silverman started sending suggestions. They were pretty silly. The age range had dropped to 30 or younger which meant that Columbo had obviously married a teenager. Maybe not even that old. Sexpot Carol Wayne was one of Silverman's more outrageous ideas. Finally we all thought that maybe, just maybe, Brenda Vaccaro could pull it off, but at the last moment she wisely declined.

Then one morning we checked our *Daily Variety* and learned that, unbeknownst to us, Silverman had signed Kate Mulgrew to play the part. Who? My thoughts exactly. Kate was, and is, a good actress. Her turn in later years on a Star Trek spin off is proof enough of that. But at that time, she was basically unknown, a road company Kate Hepburn, with the same voice patterns, an aloof presence that passed for sophistication. If Peter Falk had ever run into her on one of his own shows, he would have arrested her immediately for murder. There was nothing warm or ethnic about her. Oh, yes, and just to make the package complete, she was twenty-three years old. Good old Fred. He still thought he had the Midas touch. None of his woebegone programming had yet been aired. He still was the Boy Wonder of TV. What Fred proposed, others disposed.

The boys and I disposed by exiting the project that very day. Dick was livid as were Bill and I. He made sure the Tower understood. You cannot have the network casting your shows. Maybe Silverman could buy and sell others but we three were determined to let him choke on his own hubris.

We were replaced by Richard Allen Simmons who had been a producer on the last season of "Columbo". He rewrote the script to accommodate Miss Mulgrew and started filming. From the start, "Mrs. Columbo" was an unmitigated disaster, a not very believable show with lousy ratings. Despite that, Silverman was not one to admit he had erred. He stayed with it for months, then decided that the series title was at fault and renamed it "Kate Columbo". When the viewing audience saw through this ruse, the numbers dropped even more. Not to be bested by the American viewing public ("I know what's good for you so shut up and watch"), Silverman did a revamp. Kate Mulgrew became Kate Callahan in a new and improved version called "Kate, the Detective". New and improved Kate slid farther into the abyss but Silverman was not yet ready to admit he was wrong. Another renaming of the show. Now it was called "Kate Loves a Mystery". At this point ratings were extremely low and when the show emerged under the new banner, both its remaining viewers opted to switch channels and Silverman gave up. As it writhed in pain, incurable and unfixable, he shot it in the head. At long last, unlike the dreaded hydra, it did not grow another one. For those of you who are curious about such things, all of the foregoing took place within a one year span.

By this time, Fred Silverman had been exposed to America's viewing public as that clueless little man behind the curtain. God works in mysterious ways, his wonders to behold.

---

15. In the "Murder, She Wrote" episode entitled 'The Corpse Flew First Class', Kate Mulgrew appears as:

a) A jewel thief
b) The killer
c) A stewardess
d) An undercover policewoman

You Can't Scare People Like That

THERE ARE A LOT of quotes about Hollywood, almost as many as there are lawyer jokes. These are my two favorites. From William Goldman in his book, "Adventures in the Screen Trade"......"Nobody knows anything." From the highest paid executive to the lowliest mail boy, everybody has an opinion but nobody knows anything. Huge hits succeed on flukes, can't miss projects with huge stars tank the first week out. Everybody will expound a reason but these will be no more than guesses. Nobody knows anything! So when a higher up gives you criticism, listen but do not take it as gospel because as Mr. Goldman has pointed out—you fill it in.

The second quote, and I believe it comes from Fred Allen, a one time king of radio comedy, is the following.... "Imitation is the sincerest form of television".

Following the demise of Eddie Capra and another short, self-imposed period of goofing off, I was approached by Bill Sackheim who was deeply involved in a newly sold series to ABC. It was called "Darkroom" and it was to be a Friday night hour long shriek-fest, imitating if possible the huge success that was being enjoyed in movie theaters by the likes of "Halloween" and "Nightmare on Elm Street" and their subsequent sequels. Would I be interested in writing and producing, Bill asked. I was at loose ends with nothing to do. The studio continued to pay me every week. I owed them my labor. I said, sure. The network had no problem. We needed no pilot. We were already committed for 13. We got to work.

The first thing I did was get in touch with Bob O'Neill who had been the associate producer on "Griff". Bob was a plowhorse in the Universal stable. He had worked on countless shows and even had an Emmy to show for his work on "Columbo". (One more than I had or would ever have.) Bob knew every art director, set dresser, prop master, makeup artist, wardrobe mistress, grip, best boy and cameraman within a hundred miles of L.A. He knew every location that was available and those that weren't. He was the ideal guy to take all the nuts and bolts of producing off my back and let me do what I did best. He was available. We grabbed him, a move I was never to regret.

Then, along with story editor Jeffrey Bloom, I started poring through anthologies looking for shootable horror stories that would perhaps approach the scare factor of the feature films being churned out. Friday night was fast becoming a date night for young people. Our task was to convince them to stay home and shiver with fright for free. They would put us on opposite "Dallas", a favorite of the older folks. We would attract the kids.

We sent the network the first batch of possible story lines. They sent them back the next day. You can't put this stuff on television, they croaked in disbelief. Blood, gore, mutilations, beheadings. No, no, no. Impossible! This reaction was coming, not from the programmers who came up with the series premise, but from the office of Standards and Practice, the censors whose job it was to protect the American public from sex, violence and literacy.

I was confused. I thought that rampant violence and terrifying young viewers was the whole idea. We had been charged with delivering whatever they would be able to find in their local multi-plex, minus the popcorn, of course. Politely I suggested that the censors talk to the programmers. I asked the programmers to work something out with the censors. They put their collective heads together and rendered their verdict. We were to develop suspenseful stories that "hinted" at violence. No onscreen blood and gore. They no longer wanted what they had bought and Bill Sackheim and I wondered what we had gotten ourselves into. A new antiseptic roster of stories was needed immediately. I checked out "Heidi" and "Rebecca of Sunnybrook Farm" and decided they just wouldn't do.

We had a unique format. Each hour would contain at least two stories, sometimes three. They might be 30 or 35 minutes or as short as 8 minutes. They would be hinged together by the series host, James Coburn, a photographer who would be working in his darkroom. On a nearby wall would be an 8x10 glossy. As Coburn introduced the next story line, the camera would zero in on the photograph, then it would dissolve into film and the episode began.

We didn't succeed but along the way we came up with some pretty good storylines and the actors to go with them. "Makeup" concerned an unsuccessful actor (played by Billy Crystal) who buys a battered old makeup case at a flea market. Unknown to him, it had once belonged to a famous horror movie star (think Bela Lugosi). When he applied the makeup from the case he actually became whatever character he was going to portray, often a ghoul.

Oscar winner Helen Hunt played an impressionable young girl with a crush on a handsome young man about town who some secretly thought was a vampire. They were wrong. He was a werewolf.

Ronny Cox appeared as a tortured Viet Nam veteran who had taken part in a My Lai type massacre. Venturing out to his barn in the middle of the night because he has heard screaming and gunfire, he is attacked (utilizing remarkable special effects) by his son's toy soldiers.

TV anchorman Robert Webber was re-created electronically through archival footage and while his electronic twin was delivering the network's version of the news, the real Webber was imprisoned in the network's basement complex along with other personalities who were supposedly still performing on television. (Steve Allen did a wonderful turn as a fellow prisoner.)

David Carradine was a drifter who was drowned by diner owner Pat Buttram's pet which turned out to be a giant squid. As I recall (as in "Fried Green Tomatoes") Carradine was then turned into yummy barbecue.

Roddy MacDowell, conned into buying cases of old rare wine as an investment, drinks a toast to his purchase, learning only when it's too late that the wine came from the cellars of Cesare and Lucretia Borgia. (Note: We thought we had a pretty literate script, slyly laced with black humor, but subtlety was not ABC's long suit. Afraid that no one would know who the Borgias were they insisted that we add the line: "The Borgias? You mean the famous poisoners of renaissance Italy?" Amazing how these people continue to thrive with such contempt for their audience.)

However, it was for "Darkroom" that I wrote one of my favorite all time scripts and it was only 8 minutes long. "Uncle George" (the title of the episode) lived in his own bedroom in a quaint Victorian in a peaceful suburban neighborhood. He was cared for by his niece, June Lockhart, and her husband, Claude Akins. Uncle George, had not worked in years and received a disability check from the railroad each and every month. That check helped pay the family bills. And then George died. Unable to face the future without that check, they buried George in the basement, and Akins drove to skid row in hopes of finding an old wino who would be willing to live with them as "Uncle George". Three squares a day, a warm bed and a decent amount of booze. The incomparable Dub Taylor, already blotto, agrees and Akins brings him home. They get him into bed and hand him a fifth of whiskey. Enjoy yourself, old timer. Drink up. By then this new "Uncle George" is feeling no pain and a good thing, too. Curious as to why he is being treated so well, Akins explains about the disability check. And then he describes the terrible accident in the railroad yards where both of George's legs were severed above the knee. Drunk as he was, Taylor suddenly figured out what was happening, just as Akins pulled a chain saw from out of nowhere and in one quick yank, started it up. Cut. We left the gore to the imagination of the viewer.

The next day I got a phone call from Robert Bloch ("Psycho") raving about that little vignette. Mr. Bloch was an excellent writer of terror and suspense who described himself as a man with the heart of a little child. As a matter of fact, he would be quick to tell you that he kept this heart in a jar on his desk next to his typewriter. I was flattered by Mr. Bloch's endorsement but in the end, all of the nice words couldn't save "Darkroom". In fact I had exited even before the axe fell. My story editor, who had always been a better schmoozer than a writer, convinced the Tower execs that I was the wrong guy to run the show and that he had all the answers. No one asked me to step down but our fate was obvious to anyone with more than one functioning brain cell so I stepped aside to see what my ambitious successor was going to come up with that I couldn't in order to save the project. In two words of one syllable, not much.

Debuting in November 1981, "Darkroom" was cancelled in January of 1982. "Dallas" had clobbered it into extinction.

These days, blood and gore abound on the small screen. "Criminal Minds", "The Brothers Grimm", "Dexter", "The Walking Dead". The list goes on and today's writer-producers have free rein to graphically scare the bejesus out of little kids and teens. Me? I was told by the network to make *coq au vin* without chicken, carrot cake without carrots, and peanut brittle without nuts. Maybe that's because the network didn't have the nuts to accommodate me.

> 16. What early and also eerie television show started off each episode with a voice-over telling you, "There is nothing wrong with your television set. Do not attempt to adjust the picture...?"

Two for the Trash Bin

HISTORY TELLS US that the Age of Enlightenment was preceded by the Dark Ages. I was about to enter my own personal deep, dank pit of frustration. From 1981 to 1984 I was involved in several projects, some satisfying from a personal point of view but none successful. There are a couple I would rather forget but I think I'm obliged to tell it like it was, warts and all.

Believe it or not, the boys are back. Tired of writing and producing all those highly praised, award winning television movies, Dick and Bill are once more willing to take a fling at creating a network series and have come up with a vehicle for Telly Savalas, no longer tied to Kojak which has been cancelled. Telly likes money and he likes to work. He has signed on for the project which is called "Hellinger's Law". He will play a flamboyant lawyer named Nick Hellinger who has a reputation for courtroom theatrics as well as borderline ethics but in the fairyland of prime time television, he always prevails. In the two hour opener the government will come to him and ask him to defend a mob accountant who has been accused of murder. Hellinger is told that the accountant is actually a treasury agent in deep cover and that he is innocent. However he has been cleverly framed. Hellinger is told by the government that in defending him, he cannot reveal the accountant's true identity and that Hellinger will have to suffer the slings of public outrage in silence, even as the press labels him a mob lawyer.

It was a good premise that everyone liked. We avoided the typical mob aspect (Italian) by making the villain a Texan who used his ranch as a cover for his illegal activities. Rod Taylor was signed to play the part. Leo Penn, a veteran television director, also signed on.

The boys and I worked together as we always had. I took the premise and fleshed it out, adding twists and turns. If I got stuck, the three of us worked our way out of it jointly. Once the story was solid and approved, I wrote the script. All throughout this process we had heard precious little from Telly. We wondered if he'd seen the story outline. More importantly, had he read it? (Note: During his Kojak years, Telly liked to jet off to Vegas for the weekend. He would show up on the set on Monday a little worse for wear. Often he would pull the director aside and ask for his opinion of the script, the writer's intent, the subtext etc. This was code for the fact that Telly had not read the script and had no idea what it was about or what scenes they would be shooting. Did anyone care? Not really. He was Telly and if the episode made it to the air on time, no harm done.)

Leo Penn was not only a talented director, he was a genuinely nice man and easy to work with. (He had directed my second script for "Marcus Welby M.D.") At the time we were prepping Hellinger Leo'd had some trouble with the Motor Vehicle Bureau so one of his teenage sons drove him to work every morning and picked him up late every afternoon. Every day the younger Penn would sit patiently in our anteroom waiting for his Dad to wrap up for the day. One afternoon Leo pulled me aside and told me that his boy had designs on becoming an actor and was there any chance he could play the small two line part of a horny kid trying to compromise guest star Melinda Dillon's daughter. He needed the part in order to join the Screen Actors Guild. No problem, I said. Consider it done. Which is how Sean Penn was able to get his SAG card and go on to bigger and better things. Looking back I am very grateful to have been able to give Sean this opportunity. Otherwise, he might have ended up in some other occupation. Like politics. Be grateful, America.

Meanwhile I am getting nervous about the silence coming from Telly Savalas. On this pilot, now that I had been blooded on other series, Dick and Bill will be strictly hands off which meant if there was going to be trouble, it would be all mine to deal with. The hammer fell on a Thursday shortly after lunch.

Telly came to my office, and immediately started in with his criticisms of the script. A couple of his points were valid and were easy fixes. Some involved dialogue and that, too, was not a problem. But I also realized that

Telly really had no idea what the script was all about. He was a superb actor in the right role but his story sense was nil. Also, like many actors, his vision was almost entirely focused on his role, making it difficult to see the project as a whole.

He went on, getting more specific. "I see this scene. It's a Ku Klux Klan rally, white sheets, lit torches. I'm confronting the head man. I'm not afraid. I'm putting my life on the line. The Klan guy backs down." I stare at him in numbed silence. There is nothing in this script that has anything to do with the Ku Klux Klan nor should there be nor could there be without a page one rewrite. But Telly has a vision of this scene. This is an actor talking.

He goes on. "Another thing. This kid you've got working for me. That doesn't really work." We have given him a bright, good looking assistant, right out of a Texas law school to help with the leg work. Morgan Stevens is a potential heartthrob for the teenies. We hoped he might be able to do for Telly what Michael Douglas did for Karl Malden. Telly continued: "What I think might work infinitely better would be a black man. Homosexual. You know, gay." I knew what gay meant. Now I am wondering what the hell I have gotten myself into. Telly leaves, sure that I will accommodate his every wish.

Now Telly was not an evil man. In fact, he could be very charming but he had just come off a hit show where he was the irreplaceable star and he had learned quickly that if you are the irreplaceable title character, your power is nearly unlimited. Possibly his concerns and suggestions were legitimate or possibly he was just letting me know what the ground rules were going to be. Either way he overplayed his hand. In my book, actors do not dictate to writer-producers how to write a script. Suggestions, sure. Queries? Absolutely. But the annals of television are filled with egotistical actors and actresses who believe all power emanates from their presence and that their dictates are to be obeyed no matter how ill thought out or misguided.

As soon as he is gone, I call Levinson and Link. I repeat Telly's dictates verbatim. They are as furious as I am. It's not just the trashing of the script. We could live with that if he had made intelligent suggestions. But these were not suggestions and they were far from intelligent. Beyond that I knew that if I knuckled under on something like this, shooting the pilot would be a nightmare and conditions on the series, if bought, would be unspeakable. I told the boys I was walking away from the show. They said if I was leaving, so were they. That is why, if you ever watch this thing on cable, you will see credits that read "Story by Ted Leighton and Lawrence Vail.......Teleplay by Lawrence Vail". (All writers have pseudonyms registered with the Writers Guild. These were ours.)

As I said, this was Thursday. The cameras were set to roll on Monday. (Thanks, Telly, for giving us all that time to deal with your objections.) I went up to Charlie Engel's office, repeated the Telly dictates and informed Charlie that the boys and I were off the project. Sorry, but if the big fella wanted a Ku Klux Klan rally and a gay legman, he could jolly well write it himself. Charlie understood. So did the other Tower executives. They'd dealt with Telly before.

Shooting was postponed a few days. Jack Laird, a former producer of Kojak was brought in to replace me. I never did see the finished product. I have heard it was a disaster and obviously the series never materialized. No great loss.

The second big bonehead move of my so-called career also involved the boys. You wonder how supposedly intelligent and experienced men, particularly Dick and Bill, kept getting involved with these turkeys. Me, I mostly didn't know any better but even I felt that the ground under this project was pure quicksand.

Showtime, just getting started in the cable business when everything was topsy turvy, wanted to get some good publicity and some genius in their programming department wanted Levinson and Link to write a murder mystery and the audience would be challenged to solve it. Everything would be aired except the denouement. That would be aired after the deadline for entries from viewers. A cash prize of $60, 000 was at stake. Naturally the boys needed their favorite fall guy around in case this one tanked. Little did we know it was tanking even as we considered it. It had one big thing going for it. It was a monumental challenge and I really believe that our egos tripped us up on this one.

Here's the problem. You have to "play fair" which means that all clues are there to see and/or hear. If these clues are too obvious everyone will get the solution. If they are too obscure, the movie may be incomprehensible. I realized early on that I wasn't writing a story, I was constructing a puzzle. There was hardly any room for character development because we needed a lot of characters to mask the identity of the killer (or killers). It was a totally plot driven scenario and therefore, in my mind, totally uninteresting.

The first thing we decided to do was set the movie in a space ship. (Hence, it was titled "Murder in Space"). This was the ultimate in a closed environment mystery. Here's what I mean by that. "Ten Little Indians" is set on an island beset by a raging storm. No one could get onto the island. No one could leave. Someone is murdered. The killer must be someone on the island. That is a closed environment. "Murder on the Orient Express" used the same device to good effect in a snowbound railroad train in the middle of nowhere. "The Mousetrap", the longest running play on London's West End, utilizes a country estate, also snowed in and unapproachable. No sense boring you with the plot which I wouldn't do, even if I could remember it, which I can't. I just remember that it was wildly convoluted with multiple murders and least one murderer being whacked by another murderer. One of the twists was that one of the murderers wasn't even in the space ship. Prior to launch he had programmed one of the astronauts with a post-hypnotic suggestion. The astronaut carried out the killing as a proxy.

The budget was barebones. The spaceship set was ludicrous. Hanging drapes that looked like plastic shower curtains separated the areas of the ship. Remember "Silent Running" and "Alien" and "2001". Those sets looked authentic. "Murder in Space" looked like something that had been staged at a local high school. It was almost as amateurish as my script and that's saying something. Just as Kate Mulgrew was able to survive and thrive after "Mrs. Columbo", this epic was unable to cripple the careers of Wilford Brimley, Martin Balsam and Michael Ironside. When it aired, writing credit was given to my pseudonym. That was a mistake that I now regret. On the rare times when I had used my alternate alias, 'Wesley Ferguson', it was because someone else had screwed with the script and it was no longer my work. "Murder in Space" was all mine. Coward that I was, I disowned my own child. Shame on me.

17. For what motion picture did Telly Savalas win his one and only Oscar nomination?

The Good Die Young….So Do Good Scripts

EVEN THOUGH I was a television writer and television writers in those days were looked down upon by the "big screen" community, I was pretty good friends with a very successful movie producer who maintained offices in the Producers Building at the far end of the corridor. Walter Mirisch is an icon in the motion picture world. Along with his brothers Harold and Marvin he had produced two Best Pictures ("West Side Story" and "In the Heat of the Night") as well as smash hits like "The Magnificent Seven", "Two for the Seesaw", and "Midway" as well as scores of others. In 1978 the Academy of Motion Picture Arts and Sciences presented him with the Irving Thalberg Award. In 1983 he was honored with the Jean Hersholt Award. What he saw in me I will never know but every year he would show up for my patio birthday party staged by my b.e.a. (beautiful executive assistant) Sandy Quinn. Between times we would get together and chat but we never actually worked together. In fact, the idea had never crossed my mind.

Then one day he called, asked if I would stop by for a chat. Sure. I always had time for Walter. Over coffee he asked me if I would be interested in writing a script. A movie script. It was like asking W.C. Fields if he could use a fifth of bourbon. I would, I said, managing not to stammer or drool. What did he have in mind?

Walter had (or could get) the rights to a memoir written by Hadley Richardson who was Ernest Hemingway's first wife. He felt there was a pretty good love story there….Hemingway returning home after the war, probably still carrying a torch for Agnes von Kurowsky, the nurse he had fallen in love with in Italy. (See or read "A Farewell to Arms"). He was working for the Toronto Star Weekly, wanted to become a novelist, and ached to move to Paris where the action was. Hadley had some money of her own and was available (and very much in love with him). It had all the elements. Romance, adventure, a panoramic vista, Hemingway's developing career through the eyes of the woman who loved him. I liked it a lot but with great misgivings. I had written a lot of scripts in the past 12 years but nothing even close to what Walter was looking for. I asked him if he was sure he was approaching the right person for this project. He just smiled amiably. A good writer is a good writer, he said. If I was game, so was he.

I read the memoir twice through taking copious notes. Then I read two more books about Hemingway and the early years from the war through Paris, when he was hobnobbing with people like F. Scott Fitzgerald, James Joyce, and Gertrude Stein. During this period he wrote "The Sun Also Rises" which, although fiction, highlighted the thinly disguised lives of people he had met and socialized with in Europe. That book, his breakthrough novel, changed his life entirely.

My script, entitled "Hemingway's Lady", began at a party in Chicago, attended by Hemingway and given in honor of the hostess's friend visiting from St. Louis, Hadley Richardson. We weave through the first meeting, the courting and then to the proposal and the marriage. Hadley was an attractive woman but few would call her a raving beauty. She was also eight years older than Hemingway. They were married in September of 1921 and moved to Paris two months later.

Those who knew them say that Hadley was not as mature as her years might dictate, that she had a fun-loving spirit that Agnes, who was also eight years Hemingway's senior, did not have. In many other ways the two women were very much alike leading to the theory that Hemingway, still pained by his failed romance with Agnes, had settled for a stand-in. Another theory suggested that, while Hemingway liked Hadley immensely, he was also attracted to the financial security she could ensure him.

The script chronicled the ups and downs of both the marriage and Hemingway's career. As the latter ascended, the former grew less and less important to Hemingway. He started a secret affair with a wealthy heiress named Pauline Pfieffer. When Hadley learned of it, she tried to endure the betrayal silently but eventually that became impossible. She walked out, head held high, taking their 7 year old son Bumby with her. Hemingway was so guilt-ridden that he turned over to her all his rights and royalties to "The Sun Also Rises". (Subsequently, Hemingway would marry Pauline, the second of his four wives. All his marriages ended badly. So did his life. He committed suicide with a shotgun on July 2, 1961, at his lodge in Ketchum, Idaho.)

Having finished the script to my satisfaction, I handed it over to Sandy to type up and went off to find a cup of coffee and a newspaper so I could unwind. About an hour later I walked past her desk and tears are streaming down her cheeks. Oh, my God, I said. That bad? She shook her head with a sob. It's wonderful, she said. At that moment I thought maybe I was onto something.

Walter refrained from crying but he couldn't say enough good things about the script. We went through it, scene by scene, sharpening here, softening there, tightening the dialogue. In the end we were both pretty happy with it. From the start Walter had envisioned Meryl Streep in the role of Hadley. He sent it over. She was gracious. She liked it but not enough to push aside things she was already involved with. How much of that was real or just politeness we'll never know but Walter didn't get his Meryl. Walter tried a couple of lesser lights who nevertheless had box office juice. Same story. I was crushed. Walter told me not to fret it. Some scripts get kicked around for years before someone hits on one and produces it, maybe even winning an Oscar in the bargain. (Tell me, boys and girls, can you say "One Flew Over the Cuckoo's Nest"?)

Because the movie was a period piece, it never lost its potential value and Walter kept plugging away. Sadly, in the end, it was never made. Maybe the script wasn't as good as we thought it was. Maybe the subject matter was too out of touch with the younger audiences that made up the moviegoing public. We'll never know. It just seemed sad to me that good money could be spent on garbage like "Hellinger's Law" and "Murder in Space" while "Hemingway's Lady" lay stored away on a shelf, gathering dust.

During this period I got another golden opportunity. As I mentioned, my contract gave me the right to work on a project outside of Universal, provided it was not in conflict with my studio obligations. Mark Rossen, my agent, knowing I was at loose ends, set up an interview with Irwin Allen, the legendary producer of epic disaster films like "The Towering Inferno" and "The Poseidon Adventure". I looked forward to it. Allen was an irresistible force in movies and television.

Mr. Allen (Call me "Irwin") was an energetic man, full of ideas, constantly busy and totally unfamiliar with the word "No". He had an idea for a great TV MOW, something really special, something to rival the best of his all-star movie extravaganzas. Was I interested? Sure, I smiled, but could he tell me something about it? Absolutely, he said with all the pizazz of a carnival hustler and he launched into a twenty minute blow-by-blow of what he had in mind.

First, we have terrorists. In those days the terrorists were Italian. Secondly we have the train from Milan to Switzerland, which will travel through the thirteen mile long Simplon Tunnel which had been dug under the Alps from one country to the other. Thirdly, we have the American Vice President who, along with his wife (a former beauty queen), will be on board traveling to Zurich to attend a state funeral. Also on board will be other interesting personages with stories that will theoretically intrigue us. (I forget why the Veep and his spouse didn't fly but we had manufactured a good reason.)

Halfway through the tunnel, the train is commandeered by the terrorists. Their ransom demands are simple. They want key comrades released from Italian prisons. If the government refuses, all on the train will die. But wait. Don't they read the newspapers? Don't they know the authorities do not negotiate with terrorists? On the other hand, the Italians are not sure they want to endanger the life of the American Vice President. U.S. Special Forces are flown into Switzerland. A daring rescue will be attempted. Both ends of the tunnel have been sealed off by the terrorists but there is possible access through air vents that stretch a half mile up to the mountains above the tunnel. Look, you don't have to be Einstein to see how this plays out. There's a lot of suspense, action, strained relationships, double crossing, and finally, a major action sequence at the end as the Yanks take on the bad guys and freedom, justice and the American way prevail.

I really enjoyed writing this. It played in my head like a movie as I was putting the words to paper. Jason Robards as the flawed VP who dies in the end saving his wife, played by Shirley MacLaine. Harrison Ford was my ideal for the lantern-jawed Special Forces commander. Al Pacino couldn't miss as the boss terrorist. One of the joys of writing, especially something like this, is that you get to "see" a movie that no one else will ever see, even if it gets put on film. Because I had to keep a lot of balls in the air as I cut back and forth from the tense atmosphere of the train to the desperate preparations of the rescuers, it was a lot like a murder mystery puzzle and the structure was easy to put together.

Irwin liked it very much. Just what he had hoped for, he said. He called it "The Tunnel" and sent it over to the network and awaited reaction. It didn't come right away, which made him nervous. When he did hear, the network wanted him to come in for a meeting on the project. He dragged me along. Why? I have no idea. Maybe for moral support.

The meeting was ugly and one I'll never forget. The network executive who met with us may have been 25. Hard to tell. The fuzzy faced kids the networks kept trotting out got younger and younger as I was getting older and older. He displayed an arrogance unseemly for his obvious lack of experience and credentials. The script was way too expensive, he said. Far beyond anything the network could afford. The cast was much too large. The relationships were too pat, too obvious. The were also too contrived and too convoluted. (Hey, Beaver, which is it?, I wanted to say.) He went on like this at length and I started to notice the beads of sweat starting to form at Irwin's hairline. As the network "pischer" (Yiddish for twerp) raved on, the perspiration on Irwin's forehead became even more pronounced. He was close to begging. I felt awful for him. Here was one of the most prolific producers in Hollywood being treated like dog dung by a nonentity half his age. It was one thing to say no. It was another to humiliate. I made up my mind in that meeting that I would NEVER put myself in that position. If the time should come (and it would) where I would have to grovel to find work, I would gracefully retire.

"The Tunnel" did not get made. Irwin tried but couldn't close a deal. The ABC youngster may have been right about one thing. It would have been expensive. Very expensive, especially if Irwin cast the big names that had become a hallmark of his productions. We'll never know. (One of the bittersweet ironies of this experience was a critique which Irwin received several weeks after our debacle of a meeting. Every project at a network has to go through a reading process and an old friend of Irwin's smuggled out the synopsis as well as the reader's evaluation. In short, it said that this was the best script that they had read in over a year and that the network just HAD TO go ahead with it. Good for the ego but a day late and a dollar short.)

I have to digress here with a wonderful story about Irwin and another writer. Writers love to tell writer stories and this is one of the good ones. Years earlier Irwin had been producing a series called "Voyage to the Bottom of the Sea". It starred Richard Basehart and David Hedison and was based on the movie he had produced in 1961 with Walter Pidgeon. The show lasted four years and was a popular success and Irwin made money with it. But the way it works is this. Irwin is given X dollars to turn out 22 episodes. Anything under that amount is his profit. If he goes over he loses money. One year Irwin is in trouble. He has one more show to film and he is almost out of money. He calls in his favorite writer (can't remember his name) and begs him to save the show. He can only afford to shoot the permanent sets with the permanent cast. That means no guest stars, no extras, no secondary sets, and it has to be something he can shoot in four days. The writer goes away, thinks and thinks and then comes back triumphant. I've got it, he cries. And he does. The ship is being attacked by an amorphous glob of ectoplasm (remember "The Blob") and the crew has got to overcome it in 44 minutes of airtime. Irwin is ecstatic. His writer has saved his show, saved his profit. He will be forever grateful. Skip a year. Irwin is again in trouble. One more show to shoot and he's almost out of money. Desperate, he calls on his old pal, the miracle writer. *Save me*, he implores. *What again?* the writer grumbles but nonetheless he goes home and wouldn't you know, he's back in two days with another solution. This time the ship has been overrun with mysterious spirits who have taken on the human form of the regular cast members so there are two of everybody in the regular cast and no outsiders. It takes another 44 minutes to sort it all out and Irwin's season is saved once again. I think I love this story mostly because it demonstrates the kind of ingenuity writers can come up with if backed to the wall. Directors love to think they are "auteurs" but they are not the ones who have to wrestle with the blank sheet of paper. It starts with the page and without the page there is nothing. Or as one well known writer once said as he handed a particularly obnoxious director a bound sheaf of 120 blank sheets of paper, "Auteur this!"

There is one more project worth mentioning here. Even as he was shopping "Hemingway's Lady" around to the various studios. Walter Mirisch said he hoped I would keep my hand in. If I ever came across a project, a novel or short story, that I thought would make a good motion picture, he wanted a shot at it. I'd write the script on spec, he'd put up the money to option the property, and we'd produce it jointly. That kind of confidence took the sting out of the non-reaction we were getting on Hemingway. Spurred on by Walter's suggestion (the studio still had nothing urgent for me), I began checking out plotlines and reading obscure books that most people had forgotten about which is how I came across "Tagget". Written by Irving A. Greenfield, it was set in WWII but the setting could easily be updated to Viet Nam, a subject that was becoming a little less onerous as film fare.

John Tagget is a disabled veteran. He has a bum arm and limps with a cane. He doesn't really remember how he sustained his injuries but for years he has been getting regular treatment at a Veteran's hospital. He is well-to-do, owns a factory which only hires the handicapped. One day he sees a man on the street. It triggers a memory. From that moment on, he starts to have dreams, nightmares if you will, as more and more he begins to remember things about his tour of duty in Nam. The upshot is this. Tagget was picked for a special mission by two officers (actually CIA black ops types). He was fed misinformation which he believed to be factual and vital. The black ops guys sent him off, double crossing him, making sure he got captured. They knew that under torture Tagget would eventually break and reveal what he knew. The enemy would be forced to believe it, even though the information was bogus because of the terrible torture Tagget had endured. Tagget, for his part, feels shamed by his cowardice, and his injuries do not heal because subconsciously Tagget won't permit them to heal. Although he was supposed to die on the mission, Tagget survives. The black ops officers see to it that he goes to the hospital regularly where a combination of drugs and hypnosis keep his psychosomatic injuries as debilitating as ever.

And it goes on from there. Remembering more and more, Tagget becomes a threat. They try to kill him and fail but in the attack, falling back on deeply ingrained training, Tagget is able to defend himself. His leg no longer aches. His arm, once useless, has regained its strength. And now Tagget, realizing what has been done to him, goes on a mission to root out the two men who betrayed him and kill them. He keeps secret the fact that he is whole again.

Again, Walter concurred. Terrific book, great plot line, wonderful gimmick. We proceeded and when the script was in good shape, Walter sent it off to Sylvester Stallone, the top action box office draw of the time. A week or two passed and Stallone finally responded. Nice script. No thanks. Too busy. Walter tried several other stars and again, either no interest or immovable conflicts. And that normally would have been the end of it.

But no. Skip ahead about a year. Out of the blue, my agent Mark Rossen gets a call from Stallone's people. He is committed to "Rambo II". If I am interested, he would like me to write the script. What? I don't know the guy. Aside from "Tagget", he doesn't know me from a hole in the wall. Aha! Tagget. Obviously Stallone was so taken by the quality of my work that he wants to help me graduate to the prestigious world of feature films. I am flattered beyond words. A chance to work with Rocky himself. Truly an honor. Unfortunately I have to say no. I am in the middle of prepping scripts for the second season of "Murder, She Wrote". Even if I could spare the time (which I couldn't) my contract would prevent me from the assignment. Through Mark I thanked him profusely. I told my family. I told my friends. Even though I am not Catholic I went to confession and told the priest. He asked, 'Why are you telling me this?' I said, 'I'm telling EVERYBODY!' (This is a punchline to an old joke. If you don't know it, ask a friend who does.)

Move ahead another year. "Rambo II" has just opened. Lu and I attend an early show on Friday. As I watch, I am struck by something. This story-line seems very familiar. And then it washes over me like a tsunami. Rambo is sent on a vital mission. He is fed misinformation. The Cong are waiting for him. He is tortured. He has been betrayed by the man who sent him on the mission.. He manages to escape and then, knowing what has happened, has but one thing on his mind. Find the bastard who double-crossed him and slit his throat. (He doesn't but that's immaterial).

So much for the high quality of my scriptwriting. Stallone wanted the gimmick. Now I will say this for the man. Most actors in his position would have just ripped us off and forgotten about it. Stallone was an honest man with a lot of integrity. I liked him as an actor before this incident. Now I also respected him as a man. The truth is, however, that the gimmick wasn't even mine. It was straight from the novel and belonged to Irving A. Greenfield.

We move ahead five more years. It is 1991 and "Tagget" actually gets made. Walter still owns the rights and he makes a deal with HBO for one of their original movies. His son Andrew is the producer. Daniel J. Travanti (who had starred in "Hill Street Blues") played Tagget. Richard Heffron directed. I believe it was shot in Canada for money reasons. Two other writers were brought in to work on the script. They didn't make it any better or any worse, just a little different. The three of us shared writing credit.

Of course, I didn't know any of this was going to be happening. It was still 1984. I'd been writing but not producing. I was getting itchy and out of sorts. Then I got a call from Dick and Bill. *What now?* I thought. What now, indeed. Little did I know I was about to embark on the happiest years of my (professional) life.

---

18. Which of the following films did Irwin Allen NOT produce?

a) When Time Ran Out
b) The Towering Inferno
c) The Poseidon Adventure
d) Earthquake

Time Is Not Our Friend

OKAY. IT'S EARLY 1984. I have just gotten off the phone with Angela Lansbury and with my wife's permission, I have fallen in love with her. I do not share this information with Angela's husband. Being British, he wouldn't understand.

Our pilot commitment from CBS is firmly in place and now we must face reality. In terms of film production the first week in May is not that far away and that is the week when the various networks announce their fall schedules. If your pilot episode isn't finished, you are in trouble. Network management likes to have something they can fall back on. Let me translate."We looked at the pilot and it was great. How did we know it would lose big-time to a mouse cartoon?" A lame excuse but legitimate. Then try this one. "Well, the pilot wasn't finished and we weren't positive how it would come out but my gut feeling told me it was going to be terrific so I went out on a limb and authorized an order for 13 episodes." Executives who habitually exercise option two often find themselves in development. Development is where you get fired and then desperately try to catch on at some other network before the bank sends well dressed goons to the door of your multi-million dollar Beverly Hills mansion to collect several months back mortgage payments and repossess your Ferrari.

We had an edge in that Harvey Shepherd loved us, loved the script, and loved Angela. Still, we wanted to get something on film quick so preproduction went into double time mode. The first thing I had done was grab Bob O'Neill to serve as line producer. "Darkroom" may have tanked but not because of Bob. His work was always solid. I can't say enough about this man. Without him there would have been no "Murder She Wrote," at least not the one you got used to watching, He took all the onerous time-consuming details off my shoulders and handled them with ease, freeing me up to write and help with casting and once in a while with the editing. At an age when other men his age were retired and enjoying their golden years he was a well oiled dynamo, totally efficient and absolutely reliable. I never once had to worry about problems with the set, the locations or the cast. Bob took care of it all. He was a great man to work with and a dear friend to boot.

Anyway, Bob had things humming and we had signed up Corey Allen, currently a polished director and at one time an actor (He went over the cliff in a drag race against James Dean in "Rebel Without a Case"). I'd never worked with him but his credentials were top notch.

Then came casting. That responsibility fell to Ron Stephenson who would work with us not only on the pilot but the first seven years of the series as well. From the start we were going to go the big name guest star route just as we had with Ellery Queen. And for the pilot Universal proved to have deep pockets. In the role of the fast food fish king we signed Brian Keith. For Jessica's publisher Preston Giles, we were able to snag Arthur Hill. Ned Beatty came aboard in the role of the small town sheriff. Anne Francis was Keith's unhappy wife. Bert Convy played a theatrical producer looking for money. And as Jessica's nephew Grady, we called on Michael Horton from the Eddie Capra days.

Angie and I got together at one point to discuss various things about the schedule and timetable and she mentioned that she wanted to get with wardrobe and hair to discuss in detail her costumes and wigs. I looked at her and smiled. No, Angie, we're not going to do that. You won't need any wigs and as for costumes, wardrobe will make you look great, but you have to recognize that you will be basically playing yourself with no theatrical distractions. She looked at me, appalled. 'Play myself?' she said. 'I've never played myself in my life. I'm not sure I know how to do that.' I said, 'Angie, as far as we all are concerned, with a little minor tweaking, you are Jessica Fletcher. And be grateful. We will probably have you on an exhausting schedule. You'll be very glad to be operating out of your own skin." (And eventually, she was). I remember discussing with her the costume party at the suburban estate. Brian Keith was Sherlock Holmes, Arthur Hill came as the Count of Monte Cristo. I forget what Angie's first instinct was but I thought it too "charactery". I said, 'I want you to come down those stairs into the main room dressed as Cinderella's fairy godmother, a vision in white and pale blue and lace. Up to now the audience has seen you as this sensible lady from Maine. Now I want you to knock their socks off'. And she did.

A major problem cropped up immediately. Where do we shoot the scenes that take place in Cabot Cove? We could all fly to Maine and find an ideal location. But that would take time we didn't have. In addition we would run into union problems, probably have to hire another camera-man from the east coast jurisdiction as well as other crew members. Bob O'Neill had a better idea. Mendocino, California. Mendocino is a small village on a bluff overlooking the Pacific Ocean that had been founded by New England whalers over a century ago. It has the look and feel of a small Maine town, no question about it. The location people flew up with Bob and they found a perfect two story frame house to serve as Jessica's home. As soon as the papers were signed, the carpenters got busy on Stage 12 and started constructing the interior sets—her kitchen, the dining room, the living room, and the front door entryway—matching it perfectly with the Mendocino house.

(Note: Mendocino proved to be an ideal place to kick back and relax even in the middle of a shoot. Whenever I was there, Lu was there with me. The ocean vista, the small town quietude, all of it made for a perfect mini-vacation even as I was working. In the future we would squeeze in cruises in every part of the world, motor trips around the British Isles, a train trip through Europe. Very fancy, very broadening. Little old Mendocino was right up there with all of them.)

Other locations were found and locked down. Other stages were re-served for additional interior sets that would be required. Everything moved as quickly as humanly possible. And in the end, it wasn't enough. We would never have the pilot finished on time. And the network needed that pilot, not only for their own edification but also to show to potential advertisers and to the critics and other members of the press who made a yearly junket to L.A. to view and eventually critique each network's upcoming schedule.

What to do. One solution which was often used by late starters would be to film scenes with actors other than those who would actually appear in the film. I dismissed this notion immediately. Much of the charm and attraction of the show would be the use of the well known stars. Substituting unknowns was out of the question. But wait. Suppose we started filming the pilot, out of order, shooting key scenes from the beginning of the film, say the first thirty minutes or so, ending with the body in the Sherlock Holmes cape floating in the pool. I would write some connective material for Angela. The camera would find her in her kitchen, seated at her typewriter. She would look into the camera with a smile. "Hello, my name is Jessica Fletcher and I have just been involved with the most interesting murder mystery you can imagine." (Or words to that effect. I can't remember exactly and this piece of film seems now to be lost forever.) And then we cut to an early scene, maybe with a little Jessica voice over. Then back to the kitchen as she leads into the next piece of film. All the scenes, of course, feature our expensive guest stars and reek of our first class production values.

The needed scenes were shot in the first four days of production. Angie came in on a Saturday to do her scene in the kitchen. The editor grabbed all the film and raced off to his editing room where he put it all together in record time. No time for an original score but we added some appropriate material from the Universal library. Sound effects were added and with a day or two to spare we delivered this 25 minute "teaser" to CBS to show to the press along with their other product for the fall season.

I do not exaggerate when I say we were the hit of the press junket. Most critics couldn't wait to see the finished product. A handful of malcontents were less generous. They kept wondering what was the matter with the picture that they couldn't see the whole thing. What was CBS hiding? I guess some people just have to have something to gripe about.

We finished principal photography only a day or so behind. The first cut we saw was excellent. We needed to trim out some footage to bring it down to the proper length. The second cut was even better. We felt very good about what we had.

Next came post-production. This means prepping the film for sound effects, dialogue sweetening, dubbing if the quality isn't there, and other technical aspects. It also means finding a composer to score the picture and I went straight to John Addison for the third time. We had made a tape of the film which John took home and played so he could get a feel for where music belonged and where it didn't. We also needed a main title theme. We had shot a lot of footage of Angie jogging around Cabot Cove (Mendocino) and these scenes, strung together would play on screen underneath the opening credits. Two days after he got the tape, John called me. Could he come in around one-ish? Could I find him a room with a piano? He had something he wanted to play for me. I found him the room and when I got there, he sat down and played this absolutely fun-filled, happy-go-lucky, toe-tapping melody which he felt personified Jessica Fletcher. I'm such a sucker for John Addison. I said, 'Don't change a note'. He didn't and that melody became the theme music for twelve years of "Murder, She Wrote". (Note: John had many irons in the fire and he was not available to score the hour-long episodes. He recommended a talented young composer named David Bell who did some really fine work for us. David alternated shows with another excellent musician, Richard Markowitz. Year after year their contributions were first rate.)

When we finally had the film finished and polished, we screened it for Harvey Shepherd. He grinned from ear to ear. We had our 13 episode commitment. The only thing that concerned me was the fact that I had, from the beginning, seen it as a Saturday night show. Harvey had chosen to put us on Sunday nights at 8:00 following "60 Minutes". Of late this time slot has been a graveyard for every show thrown into it since the heyday of Ed Sullivan. Harvey just smiled. Don't worry, he said. You'll be fine. He was right. Was he ever.

> **19. Jessica writes her novels under the name J.B. Fletcher. What does the B. stand for?**

Season One : Getting to Know You

ONE OF THE QUESTIONS I am most frequently asked is, what is Angela Lansbury really like? I always give the same answer. When you watch "Murder, She Wrote", the Jessica Fletcher you see on screen and Angela Lansbury, the actress, mother and good friend, share the same admirable traits. Good humor, courtesy, compassion, intelligence and an all around niceness that, alas, many series stars do not have. That doesn't mean Angela is a "nice Nellie", too eager to please, too easy to manipulate. Far from it. She has a sharp mind, she's a quick study, she knows what is right for Angela Lansbury and she knows how to get it. But her methods are gentle, her requests (she never demanded) always reasonable. So when I tell you that she was one of the easiest people I ever had to work with (along with Jerry Orbach) I mean it sincerely. In seven years we never had a cross word, we never raised our voices, and we always found a way to accommodate one another.

Part of that was due to Peter Shaw, Angela's adoring husband of thirty five years, a strikingly handsome man, equally as polite and softspoken as she was. But Peter, at one time an agent with the William Morris office, was also Angela's manager so when the time came to protect her interests, he did so, quietly but firmly. Through the seasons, much of this had to do with Angie's working schedule. The long hours of work on series television are tough enough on youngsters getting their first break; for a 59 year old woman, they are brutal. Almost from the beginning, we started devising ways we could shorten her hours. She asked for and got a 6:00 deadline. At six, she was in her studio supplied limo, on her way to her cozy home in Brentwood where hopefully she could relax and recharge. Because of the huge amounts of dialogue she had to learn day after day, we got her cue cards to help out. Mostly she didn't really read them, but they were there to spark her if she hit a snag. She got to be an expert at it and the cards literally saved her sanity.

Even before the cameras started to roll, Angela asked me if we could find a spot for her son Anthony Shaw on the crew. He would act as a dialogue coach, mostly for Angela, but for other performers as well if they needed help. I was happy to oblige. Anthony was a pleasant young man, a former actor who had licked problems with substance abuse (which both he and Angela had admitted to publicly). Now clean and sober, he was a great help and within a short time, we were able to find other things for Anthony to do.

But much of all this was in the future. Now it is mid-May. We have our commitment. Carla Singer calls from CBS, congratulates me, wishes me all the best, says she is going on a three week vacation and when she returns. she will sit down with me to discuss story lines. I have been smoking a mini-cigar as I did in those days. I almost swallow it. This is mid-May. To be on the air in September, we need to start filming in early July at the latest. And I am supposed to wait until the first week in June before I can start developing stories? Like many development people Ms. Singer has no clue as to what it takes to get a series on the air.

I pick up the phone and call Dick Lindheim. Having been let go by NBC in the wake of the Silverman debacle, Dick is back at Universal and he is the Tower executive assigned to keep an eye on "Murder, She Wrote". (Note: I am often asked where the title for the series came from. It came direct from Harvey Shepherd who borrowed liberally from an old Fred MacMurray film called "Murder, He Said" and a Margaret Rutherford movie, "Murder, She Said".) I told Dick about my conversation with Ms. Singer. I am apoplectic. There is no way I can produce this show- nor do I even want to- if I have to wait three weeks for unwanted input from CBS. In the early days of television the studios and their producers were autonomous, but in later years, the networks were trying to creep into the creative process. I wanted no part of it. I finally quieted down long enough for Dick to politely tell me to shut up. Start developing scripts immediately. He would deal with Carla Singer. So I shut up and started developing.

Bob Van Scoyk, who had been story editor on "Ellery Queen" came on board in the same capacity. He started interviewing free-lance writers immediately and also started work on a script of his own. I put a call in to Bob Swanson who had written three Ellery's. I knew we would need him and by God, we did. Bob Van Scoyk ended up writing two scripts that first season, Bob Swanson wrote three. I wrote seven.

(Note: I'll keep this brief. There is a trick to writing closed murder mysteries and either you have the knack or you don't. In many ways it has nothing to do with how good a writer you are. Most episodic writers were either experienced in cop show/detective hours or medical/lawyer dramas but neither of these required the kind of "puzzle" construction needed for a whodunit. Aside from "Perry Mason" there had never been a long running successful whodunit on national television. We had to find or develop the people who could do it, but in the meantime, Bob, Bob and me were the only writers I could count on.)

One of the other critical matters we had to get settled before we could proceed was the budget. Of particular concern was the casting budget because, as I said, we were going for "name" actors and actresses, not only to help disguise the identity of the killer but for the fun factor of seeing so many favorite performers in one show. Some programs in those days were paying as little as $1250 an episode for a guest star. I intended to pay a minimum of $5000 for a well known star. Often we paid more. (You didn't offer Van Johnson or June Allyson or Jose Ferrer or James Coco $1250. It just wasn't done.) We also set two rules which we never violated except in one instance. All billing would be Guest Stars (alphabetically) and our absolute top was $15, 000. We would not break it for Paul Newman, even if he wanted to do the show which, of course, he didn't. Universal went to CBS for the extra cast money. CBS agreed but they wanted approval and input. I said no thanks. We'll cast the episodes the way we want. Nothing slows up the creative process more than having to wait for "committee approval" on something. I stuck to my guns. CBS caved. We got our money and I am pretty sure, approval rights or not, they got their money's worth with the guest stars we were able to attract.

(Note: We are two weeks into shooting and I get a call from a TV critic or maybe a young lady writing an article for TV Guide. Can't remember which. She says she has heard that we will be using a lot of well-known guest stars on the show. I say, we will. She says, can you give me any names? I say sure, and rattle off Carol Lawrence, Gabe Kaplan, Harry Guardino, Martin Landau, Dick Gautier, Jeff Conaway, and Genie Francis. Wow, she says, and will they be in shows upcoming soon? I tell her they will be in the episode we start shooting the following Monday. I hear silence. All those people are in ONE show? Yep, I say to her. Thank you, CBS, I say to myself.)

Start day is almost upon us. Only one thing remains to be cleared out of the way. My new contract. The business affairs people were never really happy with my first contract which had been updated from time to time. It was that "salary PLUS script payments" that nettled them. One of the bean counters once asked in a meeting if there was any way they could get out of my deal. He was only half-kidding. As the seasons rolled by and I continued to be productive there was apparently less grousing. Now came my new contract which Mark Rossen negotiated for me. I got a big raise, a nice hike in producing fees, and one other thing that few people had in writing but which Universal felt was so improbable that they didn't give it a second thought. As a co-creator of "Murder, She Wrote" I was entitled to a royalty of $5000 for each show produced. Nice money. I was delighted. I was also entitled to share in the profits earned by the series once production and distribution costs had been recouped. In real terms this is like winning a national lottery except that in the lottery you actually have a chance to win. In television, production and distribution charges are never recouped. NEVER. There are no profits. EVER. Confederate money is worth more than a contract that promises you a share of net profits. So Mark, clever young man that he is, asks for and gets an "advance on profits, whether or not there are any". This means that I receive X-dollars each time an episode is filmed as my share of these end of the rainbow profits. There is a caveat. This clause does not kick in until the show has been on the air for two years and picked up for a third season. Now Universal is pleased that the boys and I have sold this nice series but their expectations are low. They figure a pick up to 22 unless we really tank but we won't be strong enough to make it to a second year. If the show does succeed, the contract pays the advances retroactively which means they would immediately have to write me a check for $X times 44 episodes. This would not be pocket change but convinced they have little at stake, they happily agree because Mark has backed off slightly on other demands to get it. I sign. We are all delighted. Somewhere down the road, Universal will be less than delighted. They will begin to remember my first contract which they hated with great fondness. But that's for another day.

D-Day comes and we traipse off to Mendocino to film "Deadly Lady". Tom Bosley has been cast as Sheriff Amos Tupper and will be with us for four years doing five shows a year. We have also cast Claude Akins as a local fisherman and Jessica's friend who looks out for her. (Note: Claude won't be with us long. His agent is making noises like the generous fee we're paying Claude is bus fare. Because he's not a regular we can never be sure he'll be available when we need him and beyond that he could put a gun to our head at any time. Besides, Angela was less than thrilled, not by Claude, but by the character he was playing. She felt it unlikely Jessica would have a close friendship with this sort of roughneck.)

This first Cabot Cove show involves a visiting yacht and starred, among others, Howard Duff and a bevy of very talented not-really-big names on the youngish side. "Deadly Lady" was not the best script I wrote for the series but it holds up pretty well. The Mystery Writers of America liked it well enough to present me with an Edgar for Best TV Mystery of 1985. It still sits in a place of honor on a shelf in my living room. Later I was to write some shows that I felt were far better but by then, "Murder, She Wrote" had found its groove.

Like gypsies, we packed up and moved to Seattle where we filmed our second "location" show. This was the second of my scripts and we had a terrific cast including Peter Graves, Lois Nettleton, Andrew Stevens, Grant Goodeve, Andrew Prine, and Greg Morris. We shoot for six straight very brutal 12 hours days and by this time Angie is out of gas. The night before we are supposed to leave to go back to Los Angeles, I find her sitting in a tall folding chair staring into a makeup mirror. Peter is rubbing her back and shoulders. She looks at me, totally washed out. 'I'm not sure I can keep doing this' she says. I tell her we'll fix it. It'll be at the top of my list of priorities when we get back to the studio. Over the season, we make adjustments, write her out of some scenes if we can. It gets better but it's not great.

Two more shows are put in the can without incident and now, after the pilot and four one-hour episodes have aired, the ratings are holding up. It is at this juncture that I believe the bean counters decide to test the mettle of the Executive Producer. Maybe I'm wrong. I don't think so.

We are a very responsible unit. We function with two producers and a story editor. We have a set on one sound stage which is made up of movable walls, windows and staircases. In a matter of 24 hours we can transform it

Angela and first season buddy, Claude Akins. Claude stepped aside in season two to make room for William Windom as Dr. Seth Hazlitt.

into any kind of set we choose just by moving things around, applying a little paint and dressing it with the proper furniture. This week a library, next week the foyer of a convent, the following week a psychiatrists office. As I recall we are the only show doing this and we are saving the studio tons of money. Our first four shows came in no more than 1-2% over budget, amazing for a new show trying to find its way. Episode 5, "It's a Dog's Life", takes place at a country mansion, boasts an excellent cast which includes Lynn Redgrave, Dean Jones, Dan O'Herlihy and a fox hound. (Spoiler alert: the dog is the killer.) We also have a fox hunt and other splashy production values. We are about 5% over budget with no place to cut. I'm not concerned. We'll make it up on another show down the road. Besides some of the studio's more profligate producers go 10-15% over every episode as a matter of habit.

Bob O'Neill and I meet with the Unit Manager. He's the guy who says go or no-go and without his "go" we don't go. He tells us he's sorry but we can't start until we get the budget squared away. This means we will have to skimp on production values and produce an inferior production so that he can save nickels and dimes, all the time making himself look good to the executives in the tower. I am now in my thirteenth year at the studio but this guy (I think his name was Jack) must assume I just fell off the turnip truck. I shrug and get to my feet. I have no intention of making his life difficult for him. We'll just have to shut down the company for a week or so while we try to find another script, cast it, re-do all the sets, work something out with the owner of the country estate, and pay off the fox hound who has a pay-or-play contract for this episode. I tell Jack I'm on my way to the tower to notify them of the shutdown and O'Neill and I scamper out of his office as he starts to fume and bluster. By the time we get to the Tower suite, Earl Bellamy, Jack's boss, knows we're coming and he immediately tries to mollify us. Of course they're not going to shut us down. I say, Earl, I know that. I'm shutting us down, not you. The last thing I want is to get a reputation for wasting Universal's money. Earl, like me, is no dummy and he knows where I am coming from. It will cost the company approximately $50, 000 a day each day we are idle. If it takes a week to gear up for a new script, the studio will eat a quarter of a million dollars instead of letting us go $40, 000 over our budget which is about $890, 000. Needless to say I allow Earl, who is a really nice guy behind that suit, to persuade me to reconsider and I do. Over the next seven years we have almost no trouble with our budgets and in fact, we are probably the only series shooting that comes even close to making budget each and every show. Credit Bob O'Neill with that.

Meanwhile we continue to merrily roll along. We are in the top 12 each week. By years end we will be in 8th place for the season. Starting with our second season we will be consistently in the top 5, often as high as 2 or 3. We discover only one new writer we feel we can turn to in a pinch, Tom Sawyer. In coming seasons we will find a few more.

Casting each show is a joy. Ron Stephenson is a first rate casting director and pleasant to be around. Each show we meet early on to work out our dream lists of who we would like to see appear in the upcoming episode. I have an encyclopedic memory of old movies and TV shows, in particular the performers. Ron's almost as good and more than that, he knows who is still around and who might be available. He comes with his list, I have mine.

"For the part of the minister, " I say, "what about Mel Ferrer?"

"Shooting overseas."

"Arthur Kennedy?"

"Not interested."

"Anthony Hopkins?"

"You gotta be kidding."

"Zachary Scott."

"Dead."

"Dead?"

"Still dead."

I'd forgotten that I'd brought Scott up two weeks ago. I am chagrined but we've stumbled onto something. Now whenever I mention someone like Jack Carson or Richard Conte, he gives me a patronizing look and says, "Still dead."

All kidding aside, Ron was really amazing, We tried for everybody and a lot of them were flattered but absolutely retired. Like Alice Faye and Dennis Morgan and Peggy Dow. And then suddenly he'd come up with an old favorite of mine, John Ireland, as well as delightful damsels like Dinah Shore and Margaret O'Brien and Terry Moore. Amazing.

By October we are running smoothly. Scripts are ready well in advance. There are few if any panic attacks. By trial and error we are building up a stable of reliable directors that Angela likes. John Llewellyn Moxey (who had directed my first MOW, "The Last Child:"), Vince McEveety, Walter Grauman, all will be with us through many seasons. (Note: We were experimenting with directors, trying to find the right mix of talent and compatibility. I wasn't going to give Angie director approval, but I made a deal with her. If we hired someone she couldn't work with, all she had to do was tell us. That person would not be rehired and I would take the heat for it. Unless, of course, I could shift the blame onto Bob O'Neill. That was always a good option.)

In January the Hollywood Foreign Press Association presents the annual Golden Globes for excellence in motion pictures and television. We are nominated for Best Drama Series. Angela is nominated for Best Actress in a Drama. I have no expectations for the show. We are up against "Cagney and Lacey", "St. Elsewhere", "Dynasty", and "Hill Street Blues". As the new kid on the block we are odds on to finish fifth in a field of five but I am dead bang certain that Angela is going to win. I call my bookie to place a bet. He refuses to take it. Angela is off the board. He, too, is convinced she cannot lose. Lu checks in with the parish priest to have him pray for Angela's success. He smiles. A regular viewer, he says she cannot lose. God has told him so.

This is my first invitation to an awards show but I am savvy enough to know that if you are ANYBODY, particularly a nominee, you arrive by limo. So in addition to renting a tux I arrange for a shiny stretch Caddy which will also accommodate Bob O'Neill and his wife Marlene who we will pick up on the way to the Beverly Wilshire Hotel. There is a TV set built in in case we want to catch the news or a Jeopardy rerun. I rummage around and find beer, soda, booze and ice. This is the high life, no question about it. We pull into the hotel entrance already choked with other shiny stretch Caddies and a few self-driven Jags, Mercedes and BMWs. (Peasants, I think to myself.) A horde of photographers is assembled by the entrance waiting breathlessly for the stars to arrive. A claque of maybe 50 or 60 howling fans is nearby, screaming appropriately each time a limo door is opened. We pull up. I get out, turn, take Lu's hand and move a few steps toward the door with her on my arm. I make a little hand gesture toward the paparazzi, the sort Sam Giancana would make in a Vegas casino lobby. No pictures, please. We're just here for the party. I could have saved myself the trouble. All lenses were now aimed at the limo behind us where the fifth billed star of a failing sitcom was emerging from the back seat.

The four of us make our way through the milling crowd. The noise level in the lobby is deafening. People are shouting to be heard. Every nominee is being told by friend and stranger alike that they are a shoo-in to win. Four-fifths of these people will be proven wrong by night's end. They are standing five deep at the three bars strategically placed. Impossible to get to. We decide to make for the ballroom and our table where at the very least we will be able to breathe and talk at the same time. On the way I jostle John Forsythe. He smiles. I smile. We pass close by Tyne Daly, Angela's chief competition. I growl under my breath and give her the evil eye. She doesn't seem to notice.

The Golden Globes are self-described as "the party of the year". They do not exaggerate. We are at a table for ten up near the stage. Lu and I, Angela and Peter, Bob and Marlene, a couple of the boys from the Tower. This is a sit-down affair with good wine, good food, and as Louis B. Mayer once said about MGM, more stars than there are in heaven. Lu and I, the hicks from Smithtown, Long Island, are sitting next to a table with Rock Hudson and Elizabeth Taylor, among others. Bruce Willis is wandering around. At one point in the evening he will make a gallant, tongue in cheek pass at my wife by picking up the train of her gown and helping her negotiate the crowds that have clustered in the vestibule. Lu goes to the ladies room and Susan Sarandon asks if she could borrow some makeup. Every major star in every major movie that season is there because the Golden Globes hands out awards for feature films as well as television. I, who have been a movie

Old times. Angela reunited with June Allyson and Van Johnson, old friends from the MGM days.

buff all my life, am in over my head. I don't know which way to look or how long to gawk without giving myself away as a total rube.

The winners are announced. Angela wins. I am delighted but hardly surprised. My bookie, the priest and I all had it right. I down another glass of wine to celebrate. Oblivious to the reading of the nominees, I dig into Lu's dessert which she won't touch because it may contain more than 5 calories. They announce the winner for Best Television Drama Series. I hear "Murder, She Wrote". I am momentarily frozen in place before I realize he is talking about us. I stumble my way to the stage followed by Bob O'Neill who is calm and cool. He has done this before. He has an Emmy. I am almost totally unprepared. The only thing I remember is Lu's admonition: If we win, don't forget to thank your beautiful wife. It's an inside joke born of watching decades of Golden Globe and Oscar broadcasts. Without notes I start mumbling a few things. First, I thank the Foreign Press. Secondly, I say it is a joy and a privilege to work with Angela Lansbury. True. I say she is the engine that makes the show the success that it is. Also true. While I am talking I look down and see Elizabeth Taylor smiling up at me. I am transfixed by those violet eyes. Elizabeth Taylor??? My God, what am I doing here? How long before security appears and hauls me off the stage? I blather some more, making sure to thank my beautiful wife. Bob says a few words. We are escorted off the stage to go chat with the press who have

Nephew and aunt, Grady (Michael Horton) and his surrogate mother, Jessica (a smiling Angela Lansbury) at the first year wrap party.

absolutely nothing to ask us because they have no idea who we are. The producers of the other nominees must have been thinking, like the reporters, 'Who are these guys anyway?' I don't blame them. It is a banner night in a banner season. Even better, a second season of "Murder, She Wrote" is a certainty. We toast each other with expensive champagne. I take my Golden Globe home and put it on the shelf next to my Edgar.

Later that year we are nominated for an Emmy. Angela is also nominated. I dust off my shelf and move my smallish Edgar and Golden Globe to one side to make room for the Emmy which is a much larger piece of hardware. Eight minutes into the broadcast they announce the winner of the Emmy for the Best Score for a TV Movie. John Addison wins for the pilot. I look at Bob O'Neill. I look at my wife. I can feel it. This is our night! John's award was the last time I heard "Murder, She Wrote" mentioned that evening. The show lost. Angie lost. I went home and put my trophies back where they belonged.

The remainder of the season fell into place like a well oiled machine. I believe we had several excellent scripts that emerged because we were learning our formula, avoiding some mistakes we made early on. Moreover, for performers, "Murder, She Wrote" became the place to be and we were able to continue attracting high powered guest stars. Everybody wanted to work with Angie and as I said earlier, Ron Stephenson and I made a gallant try at accommodating all of them.

20. Angela Lansbury's mother was a well known character actress, Moyna McGill. Before his death when Angela was quite young, what was her father's occupation?

a) Barrister
b) Green grocer
c) Politician
d) Music Hall comedian

Abracadabra! We Make a Show Disappear

SEASON ONE is done with and we have been renewed for a second season. As if I had any doubts. Our ratings have been solid but even if they hadn't been I have learned that "Murder, She Wrote" is Mrs. Paley's favorite show. Mrs. Paley is the wife of William S. Paley, the founder and Chairman of the Board of CBS. I have also learned that the TV sets at 1600 Pennsylvania Avenue are always tuned to CBS on Sunday evening at eight. What's more, at Camp David, there is a double-doored piece of furniture which disguises a small screen black and white television. It is hardly ever used except for an occasional news broadcast and, more predictably, every Sunday evening for "Murder She Wrote". Nice to know we have friends in high places.

After spending a couple of weeks on a much needed vacation, I am back at the office. There is no pressure. Knowing that we would be picked up, I had continued developing scripts. Several were already shootable. No need to panic. The truth is, I never really panic, but I do get insecure. I always think we can use a little more help on scripts.

During the first season the producing staff consisted of three people. Executive Producer (Me), Producer (Bob O'Neill) and Story Editor (Bob Van Scoyk). Have you been watching television lately? Have you paid any attention to the credits as they roll by? Probably not, but these days, hour dramas invariably have upwards of six producers, three or four supervising producers, maybe two or three coexecutive producers and two or more executive producers. I ask myself, what in the world can all these people be doing aside from getting in each other's way? A good producer with a good post-production team can dub a rough cut in one day. With multi-producers all offering their own (and differing) suggestions, it might take three days. A writer finds it easy to deal with script notes from one producer. Script notes from a half-dozen producers could lead to a nervous breakdown.

We'd been lean and mean. Now I thought about making us a little less lean. I'd been after Bob Swanson to come on staff for several months, but he'd always hesitated. He lived in Santa Barbara and had no intention of moving. Who could blame him? To take a staff job he would have to commute at least two hours a day each way. In L.A. freeway traffic, this was no fun. Torquemada type torture. Nonetheless, he finally agreed. The money was good and very quickly he started using a cassette recorder to play back the contents of prior meetings and to make story notes. We both realized that MSW looked like a long-running hit in the making and security seemed assured. I also think he enjoyed this show as opposed to a couple of others he'd worked on after Ellery. Now we had two story editors. (The following year we would promote them both to Producer, principally because it enabled them to make more money.)

Angie was at home in Brentwood and she invited Bob O'Neill and I over for lunch to chat about the coming season and to show off her beautiful English garden which was keeping her very busy. Right away I let her know that we were adding a new regular to the cast to replace the long-gone Claude Akins. William Windom had agreed to play Dr. Seth Hazlitt, a somewhat grumpy old codger whose bluff and bluster was mostly facade. He would serve as a confidant and sounding board and also would be easy to fit into the stories. Where there's a dead body, there had better be a doctor to make sure he's dead.

As we were eating and Angie was daintily nipping away at what she always called a salad sandwich, I noticed she looked thinner but before I could comment on it, she confessed she was on a diet. Apparently she was unhappy with the way she had looked in some of the episodes. She was determined to be thinner and wear more fashionable clothes, pointing out that Jessica was now a world famous globetrotting author. This metamorphosis was only natural. I agreed but cautioned her about losing the down home folksiness that made the audience love her. No argument, she said. Then I told her about a couple of scripts that I'd written that would help her stretch her acting muscles. It was no secret that Angie was not really challenged as an actress in the part of Jessica and at times the repetition would get to her. Her eyes lit up when I told her what we had in mind.

What would be the season opener was a two-hour special entitled "Widow, Weep for Me". After Jessica gets a desperate call for help from an old friend who is staying at a Caribbean resort and feels her life is in danger, Jessica is ready to travel there to help. But before she can depart, she learns that the friend has been murdered. Determined to find out what happened, Jessica arrives posing as Marguerite Canfield, a wealthy recluse, imperious in manner, throwing her weight around as she tries to get to the bottom of things. She had a blast in the part as I knew she would. This was also the first episode in which Len Cariou appeared as Michael Haggerty, man of mystery, who may have been an agent for MI5 or just a con man. Len was and is a well known Broadway personality and he starred with Angie in

Angela never did quite trust Michael Haggerty (Len Cariou), British MI5 agent, who was constatntly getting her into some sort of hot water.

135

"Sweeney Todd" for a couple of seasons. Currently he is appearing in the CBS series "Blue Bloods" as Tom Selleck's father.

The second episode to give Angie a chance to exercise her acting chops was "Sing a Song of Murder" in which she played two roles, Jessica and Jessica's English cousin, a musical hall chanteuse named Emma McGill, fun-loving and flamboyant and a theatrical joy. I named her "Emma" after the dancehall girl Angie played in "The Harvey Girls" and "McGill" which was her mother's name. (McGill is also Jessica's maiden name.)

Emma owns and performs in a small out-of-fashion music hall which has slowly been going broke for years. Nonetheless, it is her life and she doesn't want to give it up. The show's dog-eared comic is ex-Shakesperean actor Oliver Trumbull (Patrick McNee) who hangs on because he has always been in love with Emma. Emma, terrified by several attempts on her life, fakes her own death and cousin Jessica is summoned to London from the States with Emma desperately hoping that Jessica can find out who is trying to kill her. There are several scenes where Jessica and Emma talk to one another through the use of camera magic. And early on in the hour, Angela as Emma performs a song at the musical hall in full gay nineties regalia. We chose "Goodbye, Little Yellow Bird" which was the song she had sung years earlier in her second Oscar-nominated role in "The Picture of Dorian Gray". I always cite this episode as one of my favorites and Angie liked Emma so much we brought her back the following year.

The season is a success. Ratings are excellent. The Hollywood Press Association has once again nominated the show for Best Television Drama and Angie as Best Actress. A bizarre thing happens. We win for the second year in a row. Angie loses. This is impossible. This is like negating the laws of gravity. Angie IS "Murder, She Wrote". Trouper that she is, she takes it in stride. She is happy. She is enjoying her work. I am happy. What could go wrong? I am about to tell you.

The boys have had almost nothing to do with the series except to collect their royalties. Dick drops by daily to chat or to tell me I made the solution to last week's show too easy. I got a lot of that. Then one summer day shortly before we are to start airing the second season, Dick comes by with a new topic to discuss. NBC wants to chat. Two years ago the network suits turned down "Blacke's Magic", long before the boys and I took the idea to CBS. But in televisionland, nothing succeeds like success and now that we have this monster ratings hit that is beating their brains out, NBC is reconsidering.

'What do you think?' Dick asks me. 'I'm busy', I tell him. 'But you could handle it'. 'Maybe but I'm not sure I'd want to'. Finally I agree to go with them to take a meeting. It is my feeling that we had a sale even before we sat down for the obligatory coke or coffee. A couple of caveats. They didn't want some 60 year old doddering grump in the lead. The hero Alexander Blacke needed to be youngish, suave, energetic, theatrical. The premise of the show was that an impossible crime has been committed or any variation thereof. Magic and illusion were to be a key ingredient of every story. We agreed. That's what we'd come to sell them. They commissioned a two-hour pilot and I was sent off to write it. (We were in excellent shape with scripts on "Murder, She Wrote". I could take the time.)

I won't bore you with the plot of the pilot. Here's all you need to know. A famous escape artist has himself bound with chains and locks, sealed into an airtight coffin, and the coffin is lowered into the deep end of a swimming pool. When fifteen minutes elapse, his assistant knows something has gone wrong and orders the coffin raised. Inside, the escape artist is found dead. Has he drowned? No. Asphyxiated? No. He's been shot to death.

When we delivered the final film, NBC was extremely pleased. Their prime time schedule was littered with more turkeys than a supermarket poultry case the day before Thanksgiving so we got a commitment for the pilot and 12 more episodes and we would be going on the air in January as a mid-season replacement.

I swallowed hard. Why did they never give you enough time to do it right and while we had been under the gun with "Murder, She Wrote" this was different. I would have two shows to worry about simultaneously. By nature I am hands on. Now I would have to trust others. I wondered how that would work out.

Hal Linden was signed to play Alexander and a couple of nights before the cameras were to roll, we all went to the local Magic Castle for dinner and some mind-boggling entertainment. Hal had just come off a successful run on "Barney Miller" and was looking forward to this new challenge. He was pleasant, good natured and an excellent dinner companion. He also projected everything the part called for. I began to have thoughts of two hit shows on the air at once. My potentially lucrative contract did not apply to "Murder, She Wrote" alone but to ANY show I was involved with. Visions of sugar plums danced in my head.

As Alexander's father, we signed up that one-of-a-kind scene stealer Harry Morgan. Leonard Blacke was a scheming, untrustworthy con man who had never actually done time although he had often come close. In his straw skimmer, bow tie and white linen suit he cut a dapper figure and was a perfect contrast to his more down-to-earth son. Whenever I recall this series, it is always with a great fondness for Harry and what he brought to the screen.

We were getting ready to go. Despite the short lead time, we had a couple of scripts ready to shoot and two or three others on the way. Bob O'Neill was the Supervising Producer (doing double duty with "MSW"). Doug Benton signed on as line producer. Lee Sheldon became our writer-producer.

The day before we were all ready to fly to San Francisco to shoot the opening sequence, a fellow Universal producer caught up with me outside the commissary. 'I hear you're going to be working with Hal Linden', he said. 'I am', I replied. He gave me a strange look and said 'Good luck'. 'What's that supposed to mean ?' I asked. 'Do you know Danny Arnold?' he asked. 'Not personally' I said. (Danny had been Hal's producer on "Barner Miller'). 'Did you know he had a heart attack while doing the show?', my friend asked. 'I hadn't heard that', I said. He looked at me in that odd way again and repeated himself. 'Good luck', he said as he walked away. Whatever he was trying to tell me, I wasn't sure I liked it.

The first three or four weeks, things went well. I now had two sets of dailies to watch, double the number of story outlines and first draft scripts. I was tired and also a little guilty that I wasn't doing more for "Blacke's Magic" on a face-to-face basis. My two producers were getting along like two mutts trying to figure out which was the alpha dog. I was sick or hearing from them. I asked Bob O'Neill to straighten it out and if he couldn't, fire one or both and start over.

Our opener had revolved about a priceless ten ton marble statue that had been shipped from Italy to a NY museum. It was on display inside a thick protective glass case. Laser beams and other security devices protected it from vandalism. They did not, however, protect it from being stolen. Early in the morning, after the grand unveiling the night before, the security guard found the glass case intact and the statue missing.

Later in the season we would dramatize such "impossible mysteries" as a city street that totally disappears, an impossible escape from a room in a two hundred foot high tower. The walls were all stone. The heavy oak door had been bolted from the inside. Another involved a ghost ship that kept appearing and disappearing. In another, Alexander rescues an old flame from Moscow through slight of hand and misdirection. Some of the solutions to these mysteries were a bit over the top but we made sense of them. Sort of.

The reviews for the show were by and large very, very good (TV Guide gave us a rave) but in the land of network television, reviews are meaningless and the only thing that matters to the network is ratings. We'd be up a couple of points, then down a little the following week. We never seemed quite able to get a firm toehold in the time slot.

And then I received "the phone call". I had heard that Hal was not the most beloved actor our crew had ever worked with. Cast members, too, were less than thrilled and our directors really didn't appreciate it when Hal started giving acting lessons to some of our guest stars or even bit players. I'd left it alone because I thought Bob or Doug could handle it, and I knew if it got bad enough, they would come to me. As far as I could tell, Hal wasn't hurting the show. Not yet. And then, as I said, I got "the phone call".

I was at home around 7:30 in my den, polishing a script. Hal was on the other end of the line. He was upset. He hated the upcoming script. Well, okay, Hal, we'll fix it. Come in tomorrow morning. You and I will sit down and work on it. That was not good enough. Whose idea was that story, anyway? It didn't make any sense. The mystery was ludicrous. I repeated my offer to rewrite. No, no, no, that won't do it, he groused. He went on for a while in that vein and then he said the magic words: "If I had time to rewrite this shit, I would". My blood ran cold. He said he wasn't going to do this script. Period. And he hung up. I sat there for the longest time, staring at the phone, staring at the ceiling, staring at my mug of coffee which had been getting colder and colder as I was getting hotter and hotter. I mulled all my options. None were great but one was not open for discussion. Capitulation. I wasn't about to play patsy for Hal Linden any more than I would have for Telly Savalas.

Let me say a word in Hal's defense. Underneath all that boorishness, he had a real problem. In series television, it is the star that is most identified with the success or failure of the show. How do you like Wayne Rogers' new show? Or isn't Kate Jackson's new show the pits? Like it or not, it's the star's face up there on the screen and they are the focus. People like me or Bob O'Neill or our writers, our names fly by in an instant, even if the audience cared (which they don't). So I understood Hal's anxiety, but whatever fears he may have been feeling, that's no excuse for rudeness or bullying and as far as I was concerned, Hal had crossed the line. I would never feel about him the same way again and I was damned if I was going to become another Danny Arnold.

The next day I went to see Robert Harris. I related the conversation. I warned him and the other execs in the room that giving in to Linden would only lead to more of the same. Without firm action the studio would find itself with another Robert Blake or a Telly Savalas on their hands. Or maybe even a Peter Falk. (They gasped in horror. Peter would have loved it). I thought I had a pretty good solution to the problem and I told them what it was. They liked it. They agreed to back me up no matter what.

I went back to my office and rewrote the offensive script. It didn't take long. I introduced Alexander's younger brother, Benjamin Blacke, who was also a magician. In the stage directions I described him as tall dark and handsome and looking a lot like Robert Wagner. Then I deleted the name "Alex" anywhere I found it and substituted "Ben". Finally I wrote a short scene right at the beginning of the script where Alexander, in Paris on some made up excuse, has a phone conversation with Ben who has graciously come to town to fill in for Alex at some charity event. After that, the script remains basically the same with Ben solving the mysterious crime and Alex, off screen, still in Paris savoring escargot. We have not violated Hal's contract. He will appear in the episode and he will receive his regular salary. I send copies of the revised script to Hal, his agent, and the guys in the Tower as well as Levinson and Link. I sit back and wait for the firestorm. It isn't long in coming.

Hal and his agent want a meeting right away to discuss the revised script. At your convenience, I tell them. At two o'clock that afternoon they are in my office along with Bob O'Neill and possibly Dick Lindheim, I really can't remember. Hal is still adamant. He hates the script. Why not just junk it and go on to something else? No, I tell him, at the moment we have nothing else and even if we did, which scripts we shoot and which we don't is the responsibility of the producer and no one else. Hal won't back off. He's determined to find a way out of this morass he has created. I am equally committed to getting on the phone with Robert Wagner if it comes to that. And then we come up with a solution and it's all Hal's idea.

The script involves an inventor friend of Alex and a new toy which a scheming competitor has stolen and begun marketing under another name. The friend, shattered, has a heart attack and almost dies. Alex is determined to set things right and using his skills to create a "sting", exposes the thief and restores order. In this script Leonard, as usual, has a key but subordinate role. Hal suggests, ' Why not make the inventor Leonard's friend, not mine. Leonard will play the lead part, I'll play what you've written for Leonard. The adjustments will be mainly character and dialogue fixes.' I knew Hal was sharp. This only proved it.

I look at Bob. I look at Dick. I look at Hal's agent. 'Done' I say. 'Great idea. You'll have the new script by tomorrow'. We all stood up, shook hands and went our separate ways. It was win-win all the way around. The studio and I had made a point that Hal would not forget. Hal got his way in many respects. No one lost face. It was an ideal solution to a knotty problem. I

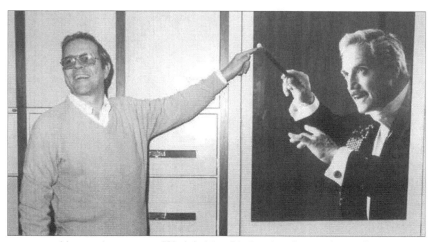

Happier days prepping "Blacke's Magic" before the infamous phone call.

buzz my b.e.a. Sandy Quinn and tell her to take Robert Wagner's number out of the rolodex.

I wondered, however, if the detente would hold. Our ratings continued to flounder. One of the drawbacks to being a mid-season replacement is that you are replacing a show that was trounced by the competition. (Note: We aired on Wednesday evenings at 8:00, replacing the short lived series "Hell Town" with Robert Blake as a priest. The competition that did him in, and us too, was "Dynasty"and "Crazy Like A Fox".) And there was Hal. His performance was unfailingly good but had viewers become so used to seeing him as Barney Miller that they didn't buy him in the part? This happened a lot in those days. Ever hear of "Window on Main Street" or "Kingston: Confidential"? These were the first followup series for Robert Young (after "Father Knows Best") and Raymond Burr (after "Perry Mason") before they went on to "Marcus Welby" and "Ironside". They both tanked big time first time out but came back strong after a decent interval. And what about the scripts? Maybe Hal had a point. Were the mysteries and solutions so over the top as to be unbelievable and the audience just started tuning out?

It could have been any one of the above or all three. After our 12 episode run, we were not renewed. It was too bad in many ways because the reviews for the show had been predominantly favorable. Yet again, reality had its way. No ratings, no renewal. None of us was happy about it, especially Hal who took it philosophically. 'One door closes, another opens' he said as he went on to bigger and better things. It was a good thought. As for me, I had mixed feelings. After that run-in I no longer had any passion for the series. I was secretly happy that I would never have to find out how bad things could get. I was completely soured on the idea of working with Hal at any level. He can be charming when he wants to be but often he is so wrapped up in himself that he forgets that there are others around him who have their own fears and insecurities.

At the time Harry Morgan was still grieving over the loss of his wife of many years and in a ride back to the studio from location, Harry started to reminisce. Hal cut him off by saying he hoped they wouldn't get bogged down in morbidity. It took a lot to anger Harry Morgan who was one of the sweetest men in the world but that was an unkind cut. A year or so later Harry was filming a pilot for a TV version of "You Can't Take it With You" playing Grandpa Vanderhoff who never paid his taxes. A Treasury agent looks him square in the eye and says to him ominously, 'Mr. Vanderhoff, have you ever been in prison?' Harry, rewriting George S. Kaufman, replied, 'No, but I was once stuck in an elevator for two hours with Hal Linden.' If you get to see a rerun sometime on cable, check it out. The line's still in there.

In any event, done was done. I hadn't suffered a heart attack or even a kidney stone, for that matter, and I could get on with my life. I knew I hadn't given "Blacke's Magic" my all but I couldn't have. To me, "Murder She Wrote" came first no matter what. With Season Three looming, I could now kick back and start writing again for my favorite actress.

21. Hal Linden won Broadway's coveted Tony Award as Best Actor in a Musical for what show?

Playing the Game...I Wish I'd Learned

THE THIRD SEASON of "Murder, She Wrote" was about to get underway. The second season had ended on a low note. Both the show and Angela were nominated for Emmys. We both lost. We would be nominated twice more in the seven years I stayed with the show as Executive Producer. We didn't win. Angela went on to be nominated twelve straight times for the twelve years she was on the show. She, too, never won. I consider that a terrible injustice that is more a reflection on the Academy than it is on Angie, but in a way I understand it.

In those days winners were picked by Blue Ribbon panels who would be sequestered in a hotel for a day and forced to watch five one hour shows in a row, broken up by a lunch break. I served on a panel in two different years but after that, I demurred. It was a Godawful way to pick a winner though in truth, I'd be hard pressed even now to think of a better one or a fairer one. Both times I got to vote for Best Dramatic Series. One year all five nominated hours were from "Hill Street Blues" and I had already seen all five at home during the season. Much as I liked the show, this was not the most intriguing day of my life.

As for "Murder, She Wrote" we were in the dramatic category but there really wasn't anything "dramatic" about us. We were an amiable, low key, charming, often amusing non-threatening puzzler, and high strung dramatics would have been totally out of place. Our competition had life and death situations in the operating rooms, breast beating skulduggery in courtrooms, leading ladies trying to beat cancer. Put our pleasant little outing up against the histrionics of "Cagney & Lacey" or "L.A. Law" and we were doomed before they broke out the coffee and danish. And the same was true for Angela. She never appeared in that one special episode which might have prevailed because if she had, it wouldn't have been "Murder, She Wrote". Even when she had control of the final seasons, she couldn't find a way to do it. They just gave Tyne Daly too much scenery to chew and she was very very good at it.

But Season Three loomed and awards or not, we were all looking forward to it with great anticipation. Angie was hale and hearty and looked like a million bucks back in the days when a million bucks was a nice piece of change. The numbers were great, our time slot secure, our script situation was excellent, and oh, yes, my agents had passed on to me a huge check from Universal as my share of the profits to come "whether or not there were any". If Universal was unhappy about all this, they never showed it. We were just making so damned much money for them, they had nothing to complain about. (Note: For years I would receive annual accountings from the business office, reporting the financial condition of the series. They always provided a chuckle. The last one I received was about ten years ago. Although we had been able to make each episode for a figure fairly close to

The desert was the setting for homicide in an episode starring
Piper Laurie and Ed Ames and, of course, the first lady of murder.

its assigned budget, the bottom line indicated the show was tens of millions of dollars in the red. This is called creative accounting.)

It was rumored during my tenure at Universal that the studio kept three sets of books. The first was the one they showed to the artists and other participants with a "net profits" deal. By the time the studio had finished writing off all kinds of questionable costs and cross-collateralizing hits with flops, it was obvious from the balance sheet that Universal Studios was on the brink of bankruptcy and it was only a matter of weeks before the plant would have to be shut down. A good example of something you might find in this fictional fantasy would be the 5% delivery fee charged to the studio for getting the finished film to the network. 5% of the budget might come to $40, 000 which seems a little excessive considering that the delivery was effected by having someone pick up the film and drive it downtown and hand it to a network minion. I may be a little off on the actual numbers but the example applies.

The second set of books was the one they showed to the Internal Revenue Service which is not so easily fooled by obvious financial slight-of-hands. The third set, perhaps hidden away in an underground bunker overseen by armed guards sworn to secrecy, contained the REAL profit and loss figures. Only a handful of people headed by Dr. Jules Stein, chairman of MCA, had access to these figures. If God had wanted a peek he would have had to ask in writing in triplicate and even then it's doubtful they would have complied. As I said, this was only a rumor.

However, the annals of television are filled with stories of artists who refused to believe the fiction that was thrown at them and took their studios to court for an accounting. Two notable examples are Fess Parker ("Daniel Boone") and Harve Bennett ("The Six Million Dollar Man:") both of whom had deals that apparently weren't being honored. The studios dug in right up to the first day of trial and then settled for huge amounts running into the millions. Makes you wonder what's rumor and what isn't.

In any event, none of this applied to me. Each report that I received had an asterisk alongside the debit figures and at the bottom of the report, in small type was the modifier: "Includes $XXX in advances on profits paid to participants". There should have been no "s" on that last word. I was the only one with that deal. Thanks again, Mark Rossen.

Something else was going on as a result of the show's success. Lu and I were being invited to more and more parties. I managed to turn most of them down. Neither of us was a drinker, we didn't puff on or inhale weed, we didn't put foreign substances up our noses and as for me, I was not interested in selling anybody anything and I hated being cornered by hustlers with an agenda. When I was young, in my earlier jobs, I'd been forced by circumstance to attend cocktail parties. I hated them so when I figured out I didn't have to go, I didn't. Two exceptions. Loved to socialize at Dick and Rosanna Levinson's. Great guests, fun people, made new friends like Dick and Ursula Sherman. And Jon Epstein's annual party for all his friends was a genuine don't miss affair. Where else could you sip champagne and listen while Jon at the piano accompanied Vivian Blaine singing "Adelaide's Lament" from "Guys and Dolls"? But beyond that I had no interest. Maybe I should have tried a little harder. It's one of the ways the game is played in the television business. I just never learned to play it very well. Dick Levinson once said to me, and he was very serious about it, "Fischer, " he said, "its a good thing we have talent because if we didn't they'd toss us out on our ears tomorrow."

The season got off to a great start with a two-parter with a circus background starring Jackie Cooper and Courtney Cox. We followed up with a Romeo and Juliet-like story as the kids of two feuding ex-show business partners. If they sounded like Martin and Lewis, it was intentional. Steve Lawrence, a vastly underrated actor, played the singer-straight man and Buddy Hackett played Buddy Hackett. We also had George Clooney as one of the moonstruck lovers. Now why didn't I try to grab George for a series of his own instead of some of the ill-fated disasters I got into later. Well, as Bob Van Scoyk said to me, "Who knew?"

CBS talked us into doing a crossover show with "Magnum P.I." which had been running out of gas for a couple of seasons. Crossover means you start the story on one show and end on the other. It took a little persuasion to convince the Magnum people that we had to go last as Jessica solves murders which means the story is OVER when she reveals the killer. How we could make this work with us going first is beyond me.

Jerry Orbach made his third appearance as Harry McGraw, the seedy private eye with a heart of gold, and as usual, he was terrific and he really showed he could drive a show, Jessica or no Jessica. The germ of an idea begins to form in my feeble brain.

Season Three is working so smoothly I am in danger of taking afternoon naps to pass the time. Scripts are in good order, casting is going better than ever. We have no crises. All around us other Universal shows are experiencing the disaster of the day, some self-inflicted, but more likely, due to studio and network interference because ratings are somewhere south of Cape Horn. When ratings are bad, everybody has the solution. When cancelation finally comes the same experts insist they were not involved in the debacle. Remember Sgt. Schultz in "Hogan's Heroes"? His favorite copout: "I know Nothing!"

But cancellation did not loom in our future and so, without histrionics or fanfare, we kept delivering a top-notch show.

It was late November, I think, when I got a call from Angie. She wanted to talk to me. Did I have time? Of course. For her, always. When she arrived I could tell she was nervous. I could sense it was important but I wondered why she hadn't sent her husband Peter in her stead. She got right to it. Her son Anthony was a big help to her. He fit right in with the crew and staff. He loved his job but Angie felt that his talents weren't being utilized to the greatest extent possible. In short, she hoped that I would see my way clear to give him a chance to direct an episode. I hesitated for a moment. My first rule when it came to "Murder She Wrote" was, above all else, protect the show. I could tell that asking for this had been hard for her but here was a woman who had basically walked away from a career to take her son to Ireland where they hibernated, sticking close to each other as she tried to help him break the terrible addiction that had him in its claws. She had fought for her son then. She was prepared to fight for him now. A dozen thoughts whirled around in my head for a period of seconds and then I agreed.

First of all, I did not want to deny Angela anything. We had made many accommodations to her involving the actual shooting of film (fewer hours, her cue cards, limousine to and from the studio) but she had never made any unacceptable demands on me. Rarely did I have to go to the set to talk over a scene, maybe once in a while, dialogue that didn't work well. We usually fixed it within a matter of minutes. But demands? Never, and even this was a request. I knew Anthony would get the full support of the assistant director and the DP (cameraman) as well as the editor assigned to his episode. As a rule of thumb, I believe that an excellent director, working within the time and budget constraints of episodic television, can turn out a top notch episode out of an excellent script. But it won't be earth shattering or groundbreaking. Conversely, a mediocre or inexperienced director cannot really destroy a script. Anthony was inexperienced but he also had a sharp mind and he'd been around movie sets for years. I didn't doubt that he had absorbed a great deal.

I gave Anthony "The Bottom Line was Murder". It wasn't our best script but it wasn't the worst either. Give him a good cast, Angie there to pitch in and I felt he'd be okay. As expected, it turned out no better or worse than many of our shows. I think Angela realized Anthony was capable of better work and she was determined to do something about it. Over the upcoming hiatus, I'm told she found a coach who worked with Anthony for long hours, teaching him the fundamentals and developing his skills. If so, it paid off. In Season Four we would give Anthony another shot. His work was considerably better. Angie, who always gave 100%, gave 110% when Anthony was directing. He soon became one of our regulars.

Right after the Christmas holidays, the Golden Globes popped up. Again we were nominated for Best Drama. Angie was nominated for Best Actress. This time around we lost and Angie won, making up for the oversight of the previous year. The show was running smoothly, I was having fun writing but in the back of my mind, I was being pestered by a thought that wouldn't let go. Jerry Orbach should have his own show. Harry McGraw deserved to be a series. I was sure CBS would go for it. "Murder, She Wrote" was rock solid. I had clout. I could make it work. I was so caught up in my own hubris that I didn't even have the courtesy to discuss it with the executives in the Tower. Bad mistake. At CBS I pitched the idea to Bud Grant, the head programming guy, and his Number Two, Kim LeMasters. They listened politely. They thought they could see their way clear to a pilot commitment. I said I was really hoping for a guarantee of 13 episodes. Like I said, I had clout. They acquiesced. That was another mistake. I proudly went back to Universal, the commitment in hand. The execs were "pleased". They had to be. They were also pissed. Getting commitments was what they did for a living. I had stepped all over their toes. Doubtless Kim LeMasters wasn't particularly happy that I had muscled them. Soon he would take over for Grant and he had me in his crosshairs. As I said I never did learn to play the game and this time I was eventually going to pay a heavy price for my naiveté.

> ### 22. What do Countess Aurelia, Mame Dennis, Rose Hovack and Mrs. Lovett all have in common?

The Script That Wouldn't Die

I BELIEVE that Jerry Orbach and I came into the world under the same star. Maybe not exactly, but close enough. I was born in Flushing, New York, on August 10, 1935. Jerry was born on October 20, 1935, in the Bronx. I am two months his senior and I never let him forget it. During his childhood his family moved around a lot. So did mine. We both grew up enchanted by radio and movies. In 1952 he went off to Northwestern. I enrolled at Johns Hopkins. He quit after three years to try his luck in New York. I graduated and ended up in New York as a page for NBC at Rockefeller Center. From there our careers diverged.

In 1959 after several years of studying with the best, Jerry was offered the part of El Gallo in "The Fantasticks" off-Broadway. He was also offered a minor role in a Broadway production at 10 times the money. He took El Gallo and it made his career. Two years later he was starring on Broadway in "Carnival". He would go on to star in other hits like "Promises, Promises" and "Chicago" and "42nd Street". He won one Tony award. He was nominated for three others.

A brief fling at film resulted in 'The Gang That Couldn't Shoot Straight" and later "Prince of the City" which got him good notices but didn't help him conquer the movies. Eventually he would make his mark as Baby's father in the highly popular chickflick "Dirty Dancing". For years he would prowl the highways and byways of the world as fingers pointed in his direction. Baby's father! Later that would be supplanted by even more finger pointing. Lenny Briscoe!!

In 1985 he was in New York doing "42nd Street", bored out of his mind. He was looking for something a little different and still dreamed of making some kind of mark in Hollywood. Ron Stephenson got wind of it and offered him the part of Harry McGraw in the MSW episode entitled "Tough Guys Don't Die", one of those silly titles that ranks right up there with "Dead Men Don't Wear Plaid". He accepted immediately and got a two week furlough from Broadway.

We met the first day on the set and whatever it was, we developed a kinship. Jerry did that with hundreds of people. He was undoubtedly the most likable, most easy going actor I had ever met and that includes Peter Falk whom I have always idolized. I have never met anyway who knew Jerry who didn't say the exact same thing. He was one of a kind.

Anyway we are shooting the episode. It is an homage to (i.e. ripoff of) "The Maltese Falcon". Jerry's character, Harry McGraw, is a partner in the private eye firm of Miles & McGraw. His partner is named Archie Miles. Those who know the movie will appreciate the kudo. Sam Spade's partner was named Miles Archer. Archie Miles is busy investigating three separate cases. In the opening scene he is shot by an unknown assailant.

The next day I again visit the set. Jerry grabs me by the arm and pulls me aside. He says, 'Last night I'm in the hotel room watching The Maltese Falcon and suddenly Bogart says...When a man's partner is killed, he's supposed to do something about it...' This is a line from your script. Here it is on page 17, he says, waving the script at me. "I almost fell off the bed", he tells me.

I say, "Jerry, I can't believe that a man who loves movies as much as you do had never seen The Maltese Falcon before."

"Ah", he smiles. "I get it". It turns out, as I will soon discover, that Jerry knows as much about movies and actors as I do and that is saying a lot. But somehow he missed this one.

In the week he was with us, Jerry joined me and the staff at the commissary for lunch and if there was a joke that anyone had ever told anywhere on the planet, Jerry had heard it. Say "peanut butter" and he could come up with a dozen. Say "hooker" and he could reel off a gross. Maybe more. We never tested him.

So we fast forward. We have now done three "Murder, She Wrotes" with Harry McGraw and every one of them has been a great experience so during his third trip west I broach the idea of a series. Would he be interested? I think I can make it happen. He loves the character. He knows a hit show could make him financially secure for life. He jumps at it. I have my CBS meeting and we are off and running. It is early 1987. We have to film a pilot and for that we will need a script.

Here is where I must back up a little.

I call it "the script that wouldn't die" You recall that early in my life in television, I had this "spec" script for "Columbo". Spec means "speculative". It means I wrote it on my own, for my own amusement and the producers had no idea that it (or me, for that matter) existed. This is the script that Steve Bochco passed on to Dean Hargrove which eventually got me the meeting which got me my first honest to God assignment on "Columbo". But the script was never made and I owned it.

Now I have a thing about stories and scripts. If they work, you never throw them away. In writer's parlance it's called "the trunk" where you literally store all those wonderful gems you will some day get around to polishing. So in my spare time, I do a rewrite. If "Columbo" doesn't want it, maybe someone else will. Columbo is transformed into a private eye named Matt Deegan who works on again/off again for a lawyer named Eleanor Maginnis who took over her recently deceased husband's practice. I keep it an open mystery (we know who the killer is). I keep the murder and all the clues and I rewrite for my TWO leads with lots of fun and bantering and the like. Call it "Moonlighting" for a slightly older generation. I like the end product. I show it to a few select people. Most like it a lot. I also show it to a couple of Tower executives. They ask me excitedly if this is an idea from someone at the network. I say, no, it's all mine. They nod with a smile and as their eyes glaze over they say "Very nice", stifling a yawn. It goes back into my trunk.

We cut to 1980. Poor Eddie Capra is a memory. In a year "Darkroom" will become one and meanwhile I am at loose ends. Then Charlie Engel comes to see me. William Conrad, who had starred for five years as "Cannon", has shown some interest in doing another series. Do I have any ideas? I smile. Better. I have a script. I hand him a copy of "Maginnis and Mr. Deegan". He reads it. He likes it. We fly to Hawaii to meet with Mr. Conrad to pitch the idea. I am puzzled. Pitch the idea? The script is already written. Charlie nods. 'Yes, but we don't want him to know that, A script is old goods. An idea is just for him. Trust me, it works better this way."

I take the hint. We meet with Conrad. ("Call me Bill") I resurrect some of my highly suspect acting talents and perform the highlights. Bill likes it. I tell him I have a lot of story notes and I could have a script for him pretty fast. He'd love to read it, says he. We enjoy a wonderful lunch, listen to a lot of great stories as we sit out on the balcony of his suite overlooking the water, drinking mai-tais and chi-chis and letting the world drift by. A wonderful trip and Bill has it made. "Cannon" was very good to him.

Back home, I actually do a rewrite with Bill in mind. Some of the existing stuff just doesn't work. Bill would have been the first to admit he didn't cut a dashing figure on screen. I make adjustments. They seem to work. We send the script and wait. His reaction is quick. He likes the material very much. However he's being wooed by another Universal producer, Glen Larson, whose resume includes shows like "Switch" and "Battlestar Galactica". Charlie was sure I had nothing to worry about. Mine was a much better project. He was wrong. Larson sold Conrad a series idea about an ex-cop who is hired by Hawaii State University to be head of campus security as well as double as the school's football coach. I am pretty sure Charlie is right. My material is probably hands down better but Larson promised he would shoot the show in Hawaii where Bill was living his idyllic existence. We never had a chance. "Battles: The Murder That Wouldn't Die" aired in 1980 as a two hour movie and was never heard from again. "Maginnis and Mr. Deegan" goes back into the trunk.

Now here we are in 1987 and out of the trunk comes the script that would not die. I do a major rewrite, mostly character and fun stuff because Jerry Orbach is not Peter Falk and he is not William Conrad. Harry McGraw's persona flows from the typewriter and he meshes really well with my female character, Ellie Maginnis. I am very excited.

The network reads the pilot script. They like it. A few notes are taken to accommodate. Nothing serious. We are a "go".

A couple of days later I get a call from Kim LeMasters reiterating how much he likes the project. Then he says, "We have to get together and talk about re-casting Harry McGraw". I am momentarily speechless. "But, Kim",

I say, "Jerry Orbach IS Harry McGraw. He's been established for three seasons on "Murder, She Wrote". Kim seems not to care. "Jerry's a good actor but he's not a television star", he says. I disagree. Kim is adamant. So am I. We go back and forth. Finally I mutter something like, I gotta get out of this lousy business. It's killing me. That stops the conversation. Jerry remained Harry McGraw. (Note: I wonder if Kim ever watched "Law and Order" where, for ten years, Jerry served as the mortar that kept that show together. He was THE star and everyone knew it. But did Kim know it?)

I needed an Eleanor Maginnis and one actress jumped to mind. Barbara Babcock. She was a vivacious 41 years old, just the right age. Everything about her shrieked intelligence and class. She'd already won an EMMY for "Hill

High hopes abounded for Barbara Babcock and Jerry Orbach in "The Law and Harry McGraw." Underrated and underviewed, it never had much of a chance.

Street Blues". If the network had trouble with her, they'd have had trouble casting Abraham Lincoln as President of the United States. We quickly signed up our other three regulars: Shea Farrell as Ellie's skirt-chasing nephew, Juli Donald as Harry's niece and sort-of-secretary, known only as E.J., and Peter Haskell as Tyler Chase, the District Attorney. I had no idea Haskell was funny until we used him in an episode of "Murder, She Wrote". He was our version of Leslie Neilsen, Lloyd Bridges and Peter Graves. Typecast stodgy, now vying for laughs. For the Boston police lieutenant, a one shot deal, we sign up Ron Masak. Within a year we will promote Ron to Sheriff of Cabot Cove where he will oversee law and order for eight more seasons.

We head off to Cape Ann and Boston where we will film a great deal of the pilot. We are staying here and there, in small hotels and bed and breakfasts. On a Monday morning we get ready to shoot the "perfect murder", so carefully constructed that it supposedly defies solution, even by that persistent terrier, Columbo, or that beefy bulldog Matt Deegan, or even that gangly, deceptively sharp and outwardly sleazy private eye, Harry McGraw.

The plot? Too cumbersome to go into here but it has all the elements. The perfect murder, blackmail, a doublecross, a frail and frightened young woman framed for murder, a wealthy and powerful father determined to exonerate his daughter and a genuinely hissable villain played with haughty arrogance by William Atherton. (If you loved the Die Hard movies, you'll know who I mean).

Peter Crane does a decent job directing though I'm often unsure if he knows where the jokes are. There are no major snafus, the cast gets along, we stay on schedule and on budget and I even manage to get my sister and two of my nieces on film as extras. We return to Los Angeles, tired but feeling good about ourselves.

We go into post-production, put the pieces together and all in all, we think we have a pretty good two hour opener. CBS is hosting the usual party celebrating the coming season at Chasen's Restaurant for critics, columnists, some advertising people. I almost never go to these things but Jerry and Barbara are attending (it's close to a command performance) so Lu and I tag along. I am ready to accept the congratulations of the intelligencia for a job well done. After an hour or so I am still waiting. Perhaps they don't know who I am. No matter. The food is wonderful, the atmosphere stress-free, and the press is fawning over my stars, especially Barbara whose participation seemed to be validated by her EMMY. Jerry's Tony Award didn't seem to count for as much but maybe that was my imagination although I do believe that a goodly number of people there had no idea what a Tony was.

The stars were also on hand in profusion doing their best to make a positive impression on studio and network executives. As I mentioned Lu and I are not Hollywood party goers and we seldom get a chance to see the beasts up close and personal and believe me in these close quarters it was that and much more. You would think that perhaps being in the spotlight these people would be on their best behavior but oddly enough, it seemed just the opposite. I was flabbergasted by the sight of one of the network's new female stars in a state of chemically induced incoherence while her significant other (also female) tried to wean her away from the festivities. The restrooms seemed to be a favorite gathering place for the younger element while the older folks apparently preferred the open bar. Hair down, warts and all, it was fascinating to watch.

One of those on hand was Paul Sorvino (sober and well-behaved) whose new show "The Oldest Rookie" was billed as his debut appearance into series television. Someone in CBS publicity conveniently forgot about "Bert D'Angelo, Superstar" which had aired a few years earlier. Jerry and I were outside noshing and looking through the picture window at the bacchanal when he elbowed me and pointed to Sorvino who was slowly edging his way toward the piano. "I give him ten minutes" Jerry said, "before he drags out something from Puccini." Sorvino, a very good actor but apparently not quite as good as an operatic singer, never likes to let a good crowd go to waste. Inside of ten minutes, he had humbly agreed to sing a little something for the gathering. Maybe I have a tin ear but he sounded pretty good to me. I asked Jerry when he was planning to sidle up to the ivories and belt out a few of his Broadway hits. He just gave me a dirty look.

We aired on Sunday, September 27th, following "Murder, She Wrote". The reviews were mixed but the ratings were excellent. It was the time slot I coveted. If we had stayed there, Harry would have developed into a successful series. But it was not to be. On Monday morning I received a phone call from Bill Conrad raving about the show. First rate all around and he couldn't say enough about Jerry. Keep in mind that Bill already knew a great deal about the project. It was "Maginnis and Mr. Deegan" in a new form. He confided he wished he were doing it instead of the new series he found himself in. "Jake and The Fat Man" premiered on Tuesday at 9:00. Oddly, our regular time slot was Tuesday at 10:00 right on Bill's heels. The irony of it didn't escape me.

> **22. Talk about your whodunits, Bill Conrad starred in a 1981 TV series about what famous armchair detective created by Rex Stout?**

Angela got a breather from Jessica when she played Cousin Emma, the English music hall queen, seen here with Anthony Newley.

Not So Wild About Harry

SEASON THREE ended successfully and we were deep into prep for our fourth season. We now needed scripts for "Murder, She Wrote" as well as "The Law and Harry McGraw". I was determined that neither show would be given short shrift and that meant an added burden on the writers, myself included. Also, Bob O'Neill who would be Supervising Producer on both shows. We had come up with a couple of freelancers who understood the whodunit concept and could put together very good material. At some time or another, both Philip Gerson and Chris Manheim would join the staff as story editors. In Chris, Angela would finally get the woman writer she'd always been looking for. Both Phil and Chris contributed two scripts each for this fourth season, Bob Van Scoyk two, Bob Swanson one and I wrote three. That left twelve for the freelancers and the Bobs coaxed some pretty good material out of them.

I really believe it might have been our best season in terms of story telling and the stars we were able to attract. Jessica's cousin Emma McGill, the musical hall diva, was back for a second episode which included a bittersweet doomed romance. Anthony Newley supported her as the local constable. As for Jessica she had three lines of dialogue and Emma carried the ball all by herself. She also found time to sing "How'd You Like To Spoon With Me?" which she had performed in the 1946 movie "Till The Clouds Roll By".

Jane Powell was on hand playing a Mother Superior at a convent. Patrick McGoohan stole his episode as a flamboyant lawyer besting poor Juliet Mills in the trial of the century. Eli Wallach joined us as the patriarch of a wine growing family while Cornel Wilde came out of retirement to play an industrial mogul in a modern day 'Macbeth' type plot.

We fortified our reputation as an "international" show when we set our opener in Paris. A cameraman, a couple of assistants and a photo double for Angela and we had Jessica getting out of a cab and walking up to the Eiffel Tower, police cars wailing through the crowded streets of Montmartre with Jessica in the foreground, and Jessica hurrying down the street past the Arch d'Triomphe and going into a fancy dress salon operated by Barbara Rush.

A real highlight was a Cabot Cove episode which introduced the town's gossip mongers who hung out at Loretta's Beauty Parlor. The ladies proved to be so much fun that we used them over and over. Ruth Roman as Loretta, Kathryn Grayson as Ideal Malloy (good hearted but vague), Julie Adams as Eve Simpson (man hungry realtor) and Gloria DeHaven as Phyliss Grant (biggest snoop of them all).

In all honesty, every episodic drama always has a few weak sisters in its season. The general rule of thumb is 40% excellent, 40% good to very good, and 20% which could have been a whole lot better. As I said, looking back on Season Four, I really believe it was our strongest season to date with almost every episode having something special to recommend it.

A good thing, too, because our companion series was having lots of trouble, most of it having to do with ratings. While Sundays at eight proved to be ideal for MSW, Tuesday's at ten was a black hole for Harry and the gang. To begin with, we weren't a ten o'clock show. In those days ten o'clock shows were either high strung adult dramas with plenty of intrigue, sex and angst or hard-hitting crime dramas. We were saddled with both. "Crime Story" on one side of us, and the very popular "thirtysomething" on the other. We were lucky enough to have a few critics find us and say nice things about both the show and Jerry but all of them also noted that America had no idea who or what "The Law and Harry McGraw" was. If a fugitive from the FBI wanted a safe place to hide, the ideal cover would be a guest appearance on our show.

But as we plowed through the first two or three episodes, none of this was readily apparent. Bob O'Neill had put together a crack crew and they were

Murder in California's wine country with Angie and Eli Wallach,
a nice old patriarch who turns out to be the killer.

doing a super job with few problems. Tom Sawyer, who had turned out
some acceptable MSW scripts, was signed up as the writing Producer. As
I recall I ran a lot of the scripts through my typewriter, not because the
scripts were necessarily bad, but I knew "Harry" and I wanted to make
sure his attitudes and dialogue were written properly. Jerry was happy with
the material. At least I never got that call telling me we were handing him
a bunch of crap. Far from it, Jerry felt in many ways his scripts were better
than some of the things we were doing for "Murder, She Wrote". I wouldn't
have gone that far but I didn't argue with him. If he was happy, so was I.
(Note: Even though Jerry had done Harry three times on MSW, I have

already pointed out that an actor in a series named for his character can suddenly become a monster. I talked with several people who knew Jerry well. I said to one, "Jerry's a great guy but I'm waiting for the other shoe to drop". He just laughed. With Jerry Orbach, he said, there is no other shoe. And he was right.)

I discovered early on that Jerry was a trivia nut. So am I. He liked puzzles. So do I. And word games. So do I. I started visiting the set twenty to thirty minutes a day when I knew Jerry was between shots. We would sit off to one side, laughing and challenging one another. Barbara watched us with great curiosity, then with amusement and finally with tolerance. Years later I turned on Jeopardy and there was Jerry vying against 14 other celebrities. I turned to Lu and said "Jerry is going to murder these people, " and he did, going on to be Champion of that season. (What I knew that his competitors didn't was that Jerry had a photographic memory. He could look at a page of dialog for a few seconds and he'd have it cold. It also explained why his brain was loaded with useless information). I never did tell Jerry that I, too, had appeared on Jeopardy long ago in the Art Fleming days. I couldn't handle the lights, the heat, my opponents or the questions. I was trounced by some slick lawyer (redundancy here) who won his fifth straight match at my expense. I felt that this was something Jerry had no need to know.

Since Jerry was out in L.A. alone with wife Elaine back in New York (she wouldn't leave her cats alone), the two of us spent a lot of weekends playing golf which Jerry had just taken up. He had been an ace tennis player but tennis elbow put a stop to that. Jerry was a quick learner. He went from duffer to a bogey golfer in a matter of weeks. You wouldn't know it to look at his screen personna but Jerry had many well hidden athletic skills, notably pool at which game he was a shark. He once played Minnesota Fats in a match on live TV and beat him. He was also an inveterate poker player who had more good nights than bad but when they were bad, they were BAD. He told me that at one point during his Broadway years, he ran afoul of the Gallo brothers, a couple of very serious, very well connected mob guys. It could have been a gambling debt, I'm not sure. In any case Jerry had to get to a better connected member of the "family" to intercede for him and call off the contract that the Gallos had put out on him. During this time with Jerry we established a bond that remained through the years until his untimely death due to prostate cancer. It was Christmas 2002. He was only 67 years old.

But long before all that, we are doing our damndest, all of us, to try to make the show a hit.

A few weeks in we're going to shoot an episode called "State of the Art" about a small time burglar who boosts some paintings from an estate but inadvertently gets mixed up in a murder. The burglar's wife is named Shirley and she works as a waitress at Gilhooleys, Harry's favorite watering hall and pool parlor. Jerry comes to me. Would it be possible for us to cast his wife Elaine in the part? She would be perfect in the role and besides he was getting very, very LONESOME. I hesitate for a moment. Can she act, I ask. Absolutely, Jerry says. Jerry does not lie. I agree. Fly her in. Elaine flies in leaving the cats in the care of a friend. I meet her on the set. She is a vivacious redhead. She is wearing a skimpy waitress outfit. A one time musical comedy actress, she has a body that won't quit. When she speaks, laughter comes out. She is warm and outgoing and we will learn almost immediately that she can indeed act. We are lucky to have her. Jerry is even luckier. Now he is not so lonesome.

By mid-November it is obvious we are in deep trouble. Jerry is doing all the right stuff, newspaper and radio interviews, but none of it's working. We're not getting a lot of on-air promotion from CBS and what we are getting is aired in all the wrong places. I have felt from the beginning that Kim LeMasters had little interest in seeing us succeed. Maybe because I didn't show him the proper respect, like kissing his ring or worse, more private parts of his anatomy. We had been programmed into the wrong time slot and it was killing us. Remember, too, that it wasn't Kim that green-lighted us, it was Bud Grant and now that Kim was in charge, he undoubtedly had designs on shoving Bud's babies off the schedule to make room for his own brilliant ideas. Maybe I'm wrong about Kim but I don't think so. Neither does Jerry. The problem for someone in Kim's position is to avoid using your position of power to settle scores or inflict punishment. Even though he was President of CBS Entertainment (he'd only been in the job a few months) he still had people to answer to and screwing around with the executive producer of your biggest primetime hit was not the smartest of ploys. As it turned out, Kim "resigned" from his job within a year as CBS sunk lower and lower in the ratings race with NBC and ABC. He went on to a checkerboard career, sometimes producing, sometimes writing, joining and leaving a variety of companies along the way.

In December the axe falls. Cancelled. By now principal photography is done with. Jerry and Elaine are back in New York. I am talking to Kim or the Tower guys by day and to Jerry by night, trying to find a way to salvage one more chance. Back and forth it goes. Finally Kim relents (maybe with a hint from above) and agrees to four additional episodes. And he will give us a new time slot right after the first of the year. Given the reprieve we try to put together some special scripts and I think we succeed.

But in the end it was all for nothing. We got our new time slot. 8:00 on Tuesday evening. We were no more an 8:00 show than we were a 10:00 show. 8:00 was for sitcoms and we got buried again. This time we were gone for good. The year end report card showed "Murder, She Wrote" as the highest rated drama program while "The Law and Harry McGraw" ended up 74th out of 118 shows. I don't think I had ever been so disappointed by anything in my life. I felt as if I had let down Jerry and Barbara and Shea and Juli and Peter because I wasn't good enough at "the game" to make it work. Maybe nobody could have made it work. We'll never know.

However, one good thing did emerge from this heartbreak. A few months later, I got a call from Dick Wolf, the creator of "Law and Order". Dick had been having trouble hanging on to his lead detectives (George Dzundza and Paul Sorvino). He wanted to know what it was like working with Jerry. I told him if he was lucky enough to sign Jerry, he would never regret it. So Jerry signed to play Lenny Briscoe and he lasted for ten years. He got to work in his hometown and Elaine got to stay home with her cats instead of commuting to Universal City. A few years later I spotted a copy of the Inquirer at the checkout stand at the supermarket. Big headline. "Feuding and Backbiting Among Cast Members Threatens Future of Law and Order." Bushwa, says I. I pay my dollar, read the article. A lot of nasty mudslinging and jealousy is going on, but the last paragraph in the story reads something like this: "None of this, however, seems to have involved Jerry Orbach, who is universally liked and respected by everyone connected with the show." And who didn't know that?

Jerry and Elaine kept in touch with Lu and I over the next dozen years. Mostly they'd come to Vegas. Golf at the club with Jerry and dinner for four at one of the 5 star restaurants in town. The one time we visited New York they took us to their favorite restaurant, an Italian joint four blocks from their apartment. Five star? No. But the food sure tasted like it.

The last time I saw Jerry was early 2002. He was on a solo trip to Vegas. After golf, we went to our house off the 10th hole and chatted over a couple of cokes. This was when Jerry told me he'd been diagnosed with prostate cancer. I was taken aback and concerned but I knew that it was a curable form of cancer if caught right away and Jerry gave me the impression that he had just learned of it. Later I was to find out he'd been diagnosed ten years earlier but had done very little about it. He had just started "Law and Order" and there were insurance considerations. In any case he avoided aggressive treatment and now it was too late. He died at Sloan Kettering Hospital in December of 2002, and I felt a part of me had died along with him. Ironically, seven years later, Elaine, who was in the prime of life, died of pneumonia. It reminded Lu and I again that life is short. All too short.

> **24. What was the name of Sidney Lumet's major motion picture about police corruption in which Jerry Orbach appeared as crooked cop, Gus Levy?**

Losses

IT IS THE SECOND WEEK of March. I am not over my disappointment at the McGraw cancellation and I will carry it with me for a long time. Nonetheless, I have work to do. A fifth and perhaps a final season of "Murder, She Wrote" is approaching. We will go out, if that is to be the case, with colors flying. I walk into my office around 9:30. My b.e.a. Sandy looks at me. Her face is drawn. This morning there is no smiling hello.

"Dick Levinson is dead." I am looking at her. I hear the words but they don't register. Dick Levinson what? She repeats it. I shake my head. No, that isn't possible. Lu and I had dinner with Dick and Rosanna three nights ago. He'd quit cigarettes, he looked healthy and the two of them were going on an overseas vacation in less than a week. But it is true. The word has been flying around the studio for an hour. The staff is gathered in my office. Everyone is grieving. I am devastated. I haven't lost a collaborator, I have lost a dear friend. He was 53. I am 52. I scrunch out my poisonous little cigar in an ashtray and head for the parking garage.

Nobody invited me but I drive to the Levinson house. Someone opens the door. I forget who. There are already eight or ten good friends on hand. I search for Rosanna and when I find her we embrace for a long time. I sense she's been crying but she tries not to show it. She is pretending to be strong and doing a good job of it. Most of us know better. I find Bill Link. I embrace him briefly. Bill isn't a hugger. He seems in shock and why shouldn't he be?

I don't remember much about that morning. There was a great deal of silence and very muffled voices, punctuated now and then by the chime of the front doorbell. I learn what happened as much as anyone could be sure of at that early hour. Dick had awakened in the middle of the night with severe chest pains. For whatever reason he did not call 911. Either knowing or fearing he was about to die, he dictated final instructions into a cassette recorder. Exactly what was on the tape I do not know nor would I have ever asked. I do know that the following morning Rosanna found him on the bathroom floor, beyond help.

To this day those who knew him still cannot fathom why he didn't reach out for help. Maybe he was in the ultimate denial. 'I'm feeling rotten but I'm not really going to die. I'll dictate the tape just to be on the safe side.' No one knows. No one will ever know.

At the memorial service Dick Sherman and I were asked to speak. Dick, a hugely talented film composer along with his brother Bob ("Mary Poppins" et al) was one of Dick Levinson's closest friends. I tried to keep it light and upbeat and maybe glean a laugh or two to break the gloom. Dick Sherman followed me and try as he might, he couldn't keep it together. He was in tears and so was everyone else including me. It was a truly awful morning.

For weeks after that, I would be working in my office, half expecting Dick to barrel through the door, a mug of MY coffee in hand. "Fischer! Have you heard about...." And then he would launch into the latest studio-wide gossip, none of which I ever would have known about if not for Dick. Besides being my friend, he was also a mentor. He taught me a lot about the art of screenwriting and particularly the mystery format. He taught me to do better, to not settle for pretty good when excellent was within my grasp. He pretended to be a curmudgeon when he was anything but. He claimed to love gourmet cooking but in truth he was a steak and potatoes kind of guy, at least when he was around me. For a long time I would miss the Valley jokes ("I'd come to visit you, Fischer, but I'm afraid of wild bears and wolves") and the put-downs of my wardrobe (as if he were the ultimate fashion plate.) I loved being the butt of his humor because it told me he thought I belonged and from a man like Dick Levinson, that was the ultimate compliment.

Two years later, in November of 1990, I would lose another good friend. Jon Epstein and I first met when he was producing "Owen Marshall,

Counselor at Law" and we maintained that friendship up until the day he died. We had also worked together on "MacMillan and Wife" which he also produced. Jon had the office in the Producer's Building directly above mine and somewhere in the MSW era Jon's doctor had told him he needed to walk for exercise. He asked me to join him and for over a year we would take a thirty-minute stroll out to the backlot and back, discussing everything under the sun, not necessarily the business. As I mentioned before, Jon threw a dandy party every year and his guest list was awesome. He had been working in television since the early 1960's and it seemed he knew just about everyone.

Twice Jon approached me about working together. The first involved his idea for a series about the juvenile justice system, an area that had not yet been explored on prime time television. One of Jon's friends was a judge in Juvenile Court in Seattle and he was loaded with stories. The idea was solid but one or both of us got sidetracked and we never did make a serious attempt to do anything with the idea. The second was a totally different story. I'll start with a confession. When I was 13 I went to see a movie called "My Dream is Yours" and developed an instant puppy love crush on Doris Day. I went to see all her movies, even the stinkers, I watched her TV series and her specials. Call it a lifelong torch. Well, maybe just a large candle. Well into my 30's and 40's I would still dig out my tape of "Romance on the High Seas" or "On Moonlight Bay". She could act, she could sing and man, was she gorgeous. My wife Lu humored this little eccentricity. If this was to be the extent of my infidelity, she had no problem. Now Jon wanted to produce a television movie (it might even be a series pilot) which would reunite Doris with her old movie costar Rock Hudson. Jon had Rock's permission to explore the notion, I had Jon's blessing to come up with an idea. I developed something that wasn't all that original but perfect for them, the kind of comedy-adventure material that worked well for Bruce Willis and Cybil Shepherd, or Robert Wagner and Stephanie Powers, or Nick and Nora Charles. Sad to say, it never happened. While Doris might have politely told Rock 'nice idea' in passing, when it came right down to it, she wanted no part of any film or TV project. She was happily retired and planned to stay that way. End of story. End of pipe dream.

Well over a hundred people were on hand for the funeral service at Forest Lawn where Jon was to be buried. The first speaker was one of Jon's closest friends and he spoke lovingly and tastefully about Jon's private life. Jon was homosexual and just about everyone knew it although Jon didn't flaunt it and tried hard to make it a non-issue. After this gentleman spoke, Steve Bochco rose to the microphone and paused, looking around with a puzzled look on his face. Finally he said loudly: "Jon Epstein was gay????"

The room exploded with laughter that didn't subside for at least two minutes.

In between the deaths of Dick Levinson and Jon Epstein, I suffered another major loss. Much as I loved both these men, this one was worse. Far worse.

It was early spring of 1987. At four in the morning, the phone rang. I answered it. On the other end of the line was my brother's wife, Geri. She and Geoff had been weekending at the Four Seasons in Montecito. Shortly after one a.m., Geoff had suffered a grand mal seizure. The ambulance had taken him to a hospital in Santa Barbara. Could I come? Lu and I leaped out of bed. Within the hour we were walking into the hospital emergency room where Geri was waiting for us. She was shaken to the core and seemed dazed. She didn't know a lot, not yet. They were doing tests. She can't believe what happened. They were laying in bed, and suddenly Geoff started to shake violently. It came without warning. Never before had he undergone anything like this. What is it, she kept asking. Later she would be asking why. Why Geoff?

The doctors come out and give us the bad news. The x-rays show a tumor in his brain. A star four carcinoma. The doctor explains as gently as he can. It's big, it's ugly, it's in a lousy place and it's inoperable. Later that day Geri takes him home and then calls UCLA Medical Center. There is a neurosurgeon there among the best in the country. She wants Geoff to have the best even in a hopeless cause. Thus begins a year and a half of pain and heartbreak for everyone as my brother refuses to take death for an answer. He fights with every ounce of his strength, submitting himself to all sorts of experimental procedures and all the while, those of us who love him cling to hope when deep down we know there is no hope. In this darkest hour of his life, Geoff shows more courage than I could summon up in a lifetime. I am not a crier but I cry for my brother.

Geoff was a year and a half my junior. We were born into a misbegotten marriage that mercifully ended around the time we were 5 and 3. Although we endured the predictable sibling rivalry, there were patches in our lives when we were the only company the other had. This was particularly true when our mother dragged us to Virginia to live for a year in a tidewater culture that was still fighting the Civil War. Even when back on Long Island, constant moving precluded both of us from establishing relationships with others our age. I was the "brains", the nerdy kid who loved to bury himself in a book and came home with straight A's. Geoff was no student. He was a social butterfly who collected D's and F's the way a squirrel collects acorns. It didn't make sense because he wasn't dumb. He just hated school and didn't care. In my senior year I got the lead in the school play and Geoff, then a freshman, was picked for the smaller part of a photographer. As I said before I was an adequate actor, nothing more, but Geoff was very good at it.

I went off to college and three years later, Geoff enrolled in Sandy Meisner's Neighborhood Playhouse with dreams of becoming an actor. From there he headed to Hollywood where his first experience on a Western series convinced him he should try something else. Universal took him on as a casting director and eventually he rose to head of the department. It was in this period of his life that he got my script for "The Last Child" to the right people and opened the door to my career. Without him there would have been no career.

If Geoff had stopped right there, if he had stayed in casting at Universal, he would have been very successful and very well paid. But Geoff may have decided that scriptwriting might run in the family and that he was capable of much more. One day he handed me a script he had written for a program that was currently on the air. I was delighted to read it and give him my opinion. I just prayed to heaven that it wasn't Godawful. After all I was the brother with the straight A's and the college diploma. Well, I read it and it was very, very good. Good story, good structure and good dialogue. I learned then and there that if you can write, you can write and if you can't, you can't and all the diplomas in the world won't make it so.

Almost immediately, he got assignments for two scripts on a show called "Salvage 1". Following that he started writing for a new series called "Bret Maverick", a follow up to the James Garner version. He also served as producer for a couple of years. When the show was cancelled he moved on to "From Here To Eternity" and then to the James Brolin series "Hotel" where we wrote 10 episodes and was producer in the 85/86 season, After he left "Hotel" he wrote a script for "Highway to Heaven" and then latched onto "Starman" as Executive Story Consultant. When "Starman" was canceled, he and I started to talk about bringing him into the fold on "Murder She Wrote". It never got past the talking stage when the seizure struck him down.

Feeble and unable to speak, his body quit on him on October 4, 1988. A quiet memorial service was held in the Valley for close friends and family. His ashes were interred in a niche at Forest Lawn not far from the resting places of many of the stars he and I had grown up idolizing. Today, as I look back on what has been provided to me and what I have been able to provide for my children and grandchildren, I think of Geoff with great fondness and gratitude. A lot of people have helped me along the way but without Geoff's support on Day One, none of it would have come to pass. Rest in peace, brother.

> **25. In addition to the brilliant "Hill Street Blues" and "NYPD Blue". Steve Bochco also wrote and produced a police series in which the cops would break into song and dance at the slightest provocation.**
> **Do you remember the name of it?**

Can This Be the End of Jessica?

THE THREE BOBS and I go into the fifth season determined to make it the best ever because there is a chance it may be our last. Angie's contract will expire at the end of the season as will mine. Mine is of no consequence. Angie's means everything. Already we are hearing jungle drums telling us that this will be it. Five seasons and goodbye. Peter and Angela do nothing to quell these rumors. Normally when a star's deal is up while appearing in a successful show, all sorts of rumors and speculation abound, mostly ploys to sweeten the next contract. I say normally because in the case of Angela, one can never be sure. There is no doubt she has blossomed in her new found fame. To many she is the First Lady of Television. For all her movie and Broadway notoriety, she has never experienced anything like this. She is a pop culture icon at the age of 64. If she had been able to run for President (she couldn't; she was born British), she would have won in a landslide. She is making a ton of money. Why in the name of St. George would she turn her back on everything she'd just accomplished?

Wet blanket that I am, I can think of two good reasons. One, Angie still harbors a dream of winning an Oscar. If she could just find that one good part in that one good movie, that might do it. Geraldine Page did it for "A Trip to Bountiful". Jessica Tandy likewise for "Driving Miss Daisy". Why not Angela Lansbury? She was at a point in her career where she had enough clout to get her opportunity. As I said, all it would take was that one good part in that one good movie. And second, at heart Angie is a Broadway baby. It's her home. She thrives on an audience. Television has made her wealthy. She probably would never have to work again and still live a marvelous life style. Broadway would be no gamble and she knew all the top composers. They would jump at the chance to work with her. Was

Angie ready to take a walk? I honestly didn't know.

Regardless, Season Five beckoned and we had work to do. First on the agenda was replacing Tom Bosley as the Sheriff of Cabot Cove. Tom, who worked with us without a contract, had just been signed to star in "The Father Brown Mysteries". He felt badly about leaving. He wondered if there was some way he could do both. I think he was half serious. To take his place we brought on board Ron Masak who had just played the police lieutenant in the Harry McGraw pilot. He'd also done Eddie Capra with me and Ellery as well and we were pretty good friends. The idea was to bring in a big city cop who was tired of all the urban mayhem and killings and just wanted to kick back in a sleepy little town where nothing ever happened. As Mort Metzger, Ron stayed with the show until the very end. Like Angie, Ron

Tom Bosley leaves. Ron Masak joins the party and stays for eight years as Sheriff Mort Metzger.

Have no idea what Angie and I find so funny, but I'm pretty sure I'm sober.
That looks like a Dr. Pepper in my hand.

found that people were recognizing him wherever he went. A man who loves the spotlight, he thrived on the celebrity. He also brought to the show a terrific character who could be just as humorous as Tom but also a little more credible as a lawman. Phil Gerson joined us as Story Editor. Stephen Swofford came on board as an assistant to the associate producer, Tony Magro. (Note: Stephen is the son of good friend Ken Swofford. I had known him for years. A very bright young man, he was wasting his time as a restaurant manager. Bob O'Neill and I signed him to help out on post production and to give him a chance to learn the business. Today Stephen is an executive with Disney Studios.)

When a golfer is "in the zone", it means that everything that he knows and has learned and has practiced all come together with seemingly no effort. He is unbeatable. As a group the MSW staff and crew were in a zone. Judging by the material we were amassing this gave signs of being as good or better a season than the previous one. That was saying a lot.

We were getting ready to send assistant director Kevin Cremin to Moscow to shoot some footage. (Yes, it's that old 'photo double' trick again.)

174

"From Russia With Blood" took place in Moscow where Jessica was participating in a writer's conference, all in the spirit of glasnost. When the show airs we again get phone calls wondering where we get the money to send everyone overseas.

"A Little Night Work" involved Jessica in a jewel robbery and murder and introduced our audience to a suave and handsome jewel thief named Dennis Stanton, played by the suave and handsome Australian-born actor, Keith Michel. America knew Keith best as Henry VIII in the BBC miniseries "The Six Wives of Henry VIII" but within a couple of years, they would get to know him a whole lot better on "Murder, She Wrote".

We did an excellent show with Jessica's dead husband being posthumously accused of a twenty year old murder. The cast was terrific and included Efrem Zimbalist, Martin Milner, Richard Roundtree, Jane Greer and Dale Robertson. Dale didn't do many guest shots in those days but he was attracted to the part and the script and the chance to work with Angela. All good. In addition, he had no trouble with the money we were paying him but he didn't like the alphabetic billing. I told his agent it was not negotiable and a deal breaker. The agent suggested Dale would appear but take no billing at all. I couldn't see how that violated policy so we agreed. This is a rarity among actors and almost always occurs when a performer is offered a part he really wants but billing which he believes demeans him. That's why if you watch the Robert Redford baseball classic, "The Natural", you will see no mention of Darren McGavin in the credits even though he had one of the biggest and most pivotal roles in the movie.

For the first time we flirt with the notion of a romance for Jessica even though we had agreed early on that this was slippery territory. We even figured a way to segue from the first Dale Robertson show to put him into another which we had transformed into a sequel. The Robertson character is an old service mate of her husband and while his subtle wooing comes close, in the end Jessica politely discourages him. Good thing. I have trouble visualizing our sleuth globe-hopping into murder after murder with a husband in tow.

We continue to turn out good episodes but the atmosphere is tense. No one knows what the future will bring. Mike Connors is on board as a tough guy writer looking for an old flame played by Elizabeth Ashley. Lucie Arnaz and Patty McCormack appear as two New York detectives named Chadwick and Stacey in a good-natured salute to one of our contemporary rivals and they are hilarious. Glamorous '50's leading lady Jean Peters appears as a Garboesque actress. Even in retirement everybody wants to work with Angela. (Note: Jean is terrified that she did a rotten job and that we will be reshooting with someone else. I tell her she was just terrific and I mean it. Angela seconded my opinion.)

Jean Peters, one of Fox's gorgeous leading ladies from the '50s,
comes out of retirement to play a Garbo-esque recluse

Near the end of the season, perpetual loser-in-love, her nephew Grady finally gets married in an episode that was more comedy than mystery. The victim, Harriet the housekeeper, is played with her usual deftness by Conchata Farrell who basically limns the same character on "Two and a Half Men". Yes, but we had her first.

Our casts continue to excel. Jerry Orbach is back as Harry McGraw and Len Cariou as Michael Haggerty. We also attract Steve Forrest, E.G. Marshall, Michael Learned, Paul Sorvino, Ralph Waite, Dinah Shore, Janice Rule and playing old biddies in a show reminiscent of "Arsenic and Old Lace", Teresa Wright and Joan Leslie.

Unlucky in love, newphew Grady finally gets married to Donna,
played by Michael Horton's real life wife, Debbie Zipp

A few words here about Keith Michel. He is a terrific actor and a charismatic presence whether on film or on stage. I had seen him in the Broadway production of "Irma La Douce" and of course, everyone had seen him as Henry in "The Six Wives of Henry VIII". Even in our first season I was looking for a way to bring Keith onto the show but things always got in the way. But when I came up with the idea for "A Little Night Work", I wrote the part of Dennis Stanton with Keith in mind. We sent him the script, made him an offer and he accepted with delight. But then he suddenly found himself running afoul of U.S. Immigration whose job it is to protect American performers from usurpers from foreign lands. Their power is limited when the performer is a star and we were told that Keith was not a star. What baloney. The assembled power of MCA and Universal came down on the heads of those who were trying to prevent his entry into the country. They should have been warned that Lew Wasserman was not a man to be trifled with. Within 24 hours Keith was on his way to Los Angeles.

Time flies. It is now January, right after the holidays. We have another six or seven episodes to shoot to complete the season and we have the scripts lined up. The City of Los Angeles throws us a huge party on the occasion of our 100th show. Mayor Tom Bradley is supposed to show up but I suspect he is at home watching "Hill Street Blues" and wondering why his own police department isn't that sharp. Congratulations are passed around like chocolate bunnies on Easter morning but all the nice words in the world aren't going to make us feel better if season five is the end of the road.

Angela and Peter are mum. They don't tell and I don't ask. I do know that Universal has made an exceptionally generous offer but that's the extent of it. Mark Rossen has also started negotiations for my new contract should I want one which I am pretty sure I do. Kerry McCluggage has replaced Robert Harris and he's made it clear he wants me to stay. I have only one nagging reservation and it would only come into play if "Murder, She Wrote" was indeed over and done with. When I first signed with Universal they were in the Movie of the Week business and by now they were out of it. They cannot make any money at it or so little profit that it's not worth the effort. As a writer I would like to broaden my output, to write and produce a few two-hour TV movies with different themes, different characters, taking the time to do it right. Series television is a treadmill and once you are on it, there's no way off. Write scripts, rewrite scripts, help edit, make the deadline no matter what. Every week the network has a gaping hole in its schedule which you are under obligation to fill and no excuses will be tolerated. We never really had that problem with any of our series, but overall, that is the nature of the beast and I didn't want to deal with those pressures if I didn't have to. If MSW were to be cancelled, I knew that another series would be right around the corner and having worked under ideal conditions with a hit show and an agreeable and hardworking star like Angie, I wasn't sure I wanted to face the uncertainty and the aggravation of starting again with person or persons unknown.

An idea for a TV movie hit me one evening and I started to noodle with it, even as the season was winding down. If this was to be the end, then so be it. A lot of talented people were involved in the made-for-TV business. Why not me? February came. No word. Then I decided. *Allright, if this is to be the final season, let's go out with a bang and maybe wrap up a few loose ends.* I would write a script that would not only be a solid murder mystery, it would deal with Jessica's relationship with Seth Hazlitt. I put my movie idea on hold and started to write "Mirror, Mirror on the Wall".

Revolving around Eudora McVeigh, for years America's premier female mystery writer, the script would not only deal with a murder but also Jessica's growing preoccupation with her work to the detriment of her relationships with her friends. Eudora's publisher Lew Bracken (Richard Anderson) has told Eudora (Jean Simmons) that her latest manuscript is not up to snuff. It's old fashioned and lacks the vibrancy and modernity of the newer authors like Jessica Fletcher. Bracken is adamant. She'll have to do a lot better or their relationship is over. Eudora, heartbroken, shattered, angry and frustrated, goes home to her apartment. She looks in the mirror on the wall, wondering inwardly if she is still the fairest of them all. She rummages for a map, finds it, opens it to Maine and circles Cabot Cove. She leaves, her face grim with determination.

Eudora shows up at Jessica's doorstep in Cabot Cove carrying a basket of juicy red apples. Jessica, the gracious hostess invites her to stay with her for a day or two. Eudora "reluctantly' agrees. Jessica apologizes in advance if she appears to be a little distracted but she's on deadline for her new book which is almost finished. She's also been shaken by a conversation she had at the opening of the show. Seth Hazlitt has invited her to spend a day aboard his fishing boat the following Saturday and when she put him off, Seth politely laid down the law. She's working too hard, she's neglecting her friends, her whole life is suddenly wrapped up in non-existent characters instead of the real people who love and care for her. If she's not careful she's going to end up alone, a dried up old prune of a woman with nothing but a library of best sellers to keep her warm on a winter's night.

You get the idea. I'll shorthand the rest. A private detective has been murdered and his body dumped in the woods. He's from New York and almost certainly followed someone here to Cabot Cove. But who? Meanwhile Eudora, in the dead of night, has found Jessica's new manuscript and copied all the pages. Jessica sees immediately what has happened. Eudora breaks down in tears, her career in tatters. Jessica commiserates. But meanwhile the town is abuzz with the murder and when Eudora is asked by the press what she thinks might have happened, she finds herself thrust into Jessica's role of solving murders. She takes advantage of it. Maybe THIS is what her career needs and if Jessica can do it, so can she. The last scene of Part One involves Seth who has come to Jessica's kitchen to return a casserole dish. Spotting the apples he takes one and starts to eat it, then doubles over with pain and falls to the floor. Up pops the legend: TO BE CONTINUED.

As Part Two opens Jessica is at the hospital. She realizes now she had been taking Seth for granted all these years and in an instant she may lose him. Luckily the doctors got to him in time. It's poison, all right, but not a heavy dose. He'll be good as new in a day or two but meanwhile Eudora has been arrested for attempted murder and is locked up in the local jail.

The rest of the plot is immaterial. Jessica unmasks the killer. It is not Eudora. Still ashamed by her behavior, she leaves to return to an empty home, her marriage now over and her career in jeopardy. Jessica wishes her well but can't help but realize what an empty life Eudora faces, caused mostly by an almost psychopathic need to work at the exclusion of everything else in life.

In the final scenes we find Jessica in the kitchen at her typewriter banging away. It's Saturday. She stops and starts and stops and starts. Her heart isn't in it. She looks up at the clock, then gets up quickly from her chair, grabs her fishing hat and hurries out the door. At the Cabot Cove wharf she races down toward Seth's fishing boat, still tied up but geared to go. She hops on board even though she's an hour late. As the boat starts to leave the harbor I have the two of them standing side by side next to the cabin. I forget the dialogue but I know there wasn't much of it. However the implication was clear. Jessica was no longer going to take Seth for granted, and all that that entails. From that moment on, her writing was going to take a back seat to her relationship with Seth.

That was the way "Murder, She Wrote" was supposed to go out.

That's the way the script was originally written.

That's not the way it was shot.

Some time after finishing the script and before we all jaunted off to

Mendocino, Jessica signed her new contract. I have no idea what was in it, but I'm sure it was a beaut. Delighted and relieved the staff and crew are grinning from ear to ear. Mark Rossen calls me. Now that Angie is wrapped up, the studio wants to tie up my deal. They make a generous offer. Mark counters. Inside of a week I am also signed. (Note: Mark has pulled a major coup. He has upped my "advance on profits whether or not there are any" by a substantial amount. Since everything is retroactive to the first show five years ago I will get this increase times the 110 episodes we have already aired. I do the math. I am astounded. My tax guy is astounded. My wife takes one look and books us on a two weeks cruise at the end of shooting to unwind. That is why many weeks later I find myself wandering about St. Petersburg, Russia, notepad and pencil in hand, trying to figure out the best way to rehabilitate a jewel thief named Dennis Stanton into a dashing leading man. Lu is less than pleased. She gives me the speech Seth gave Jessica in the last episode. Take time to smell the roses. I say to her, yeah, yeah, yeah. Maybe next year.

26. Filmdom's famous perennial Oscar losers include Peter O'Toole and Richard Burton, often nominated, never a winner. How many times was Angela nominated for an EMMY (never winning)?

a) 10
b) 12
c) 16
d) 18

"Murder, She Wrote" goes to Broadway. Left to right: Lorna Luft, Patrick O'Neal, Robert Morse and Angie.

What About Those Other Nine Hours?

THE FIFTH SEASON wrapped up with a bang. The mood in Mendocino was exhilarating. We were looking forward to several new seasons of "Murder, She Wrote". Ron Masak was regaling us all at dinner with every corny joke he'd ever heard. Bob O'Neill stopped typing his resume. Back at the studio, Van Scoyk and Swanson were diligently trying to develop material for year six. (Because I thought we were through, we didn't have the usual stock-pile of stories and scripts left over.) Donald Ross, who had written several excellent scripts for us in prior seasons joined the staff as the story editor. Meanwhile I had rewritten the end of "Mirror, Mirror" to revert Seth and Jessica's relationship back to platonic. The party atmosphere never waned and Jean Simmons confessed that she had never had a better time on a location shoot in her life. All was right with the world. What did I have to worry about?

As it turned out, plenty.

Angela had signed for a number of seasons but what I didn't know, at least not right away, was the fact that in Year Six she was going to appear in only 13 of the 22 episodes. I have no idea why she wanted this. Perhaps she was tired though I doubt it. She likes work and she is a dynamo. (Note: As I write this she has recently appeared on Broadway at the age of 86. She has also been nominated for two more Tonys and recently she has appeared at the Sydney Opera House in "Driving Miss Daisy" with James Earl Jones.). Possibly she had other things she wanted to explore, a project she had to make room for. Whatever the reason I now had to figure out how to fill those nine other hours and still be able to call it "Murder, She Wrote".

In truth, the solution wasn't that hard. Over five seasons she had worked with dozens of police detectives and others, all of whom had become and remained friends over the years. All we had to do was come up with 9 intriguing, suspenseful, often humorous stories that would capture and keep the attention of the audience even if Jessica herself did not appear. We had no idea whether it would work but we really didn't have a choice.

First, we decided to "bookend" the shows. This meant that Angela as Jessica would appear in an opening scene and through some device (a letter, a phone call, a tape recording) start to recount a wonderful mystery that had been solved by an old friend. The old friend would then carry the load for the hour. At the end of the show, Angela would wrap things up in a short tag scene. This solution made everyone happy. The audience had Jessica on screen if only briefly. We had an easy way to segue into a stand-alone story, and best of all, Angela got paid her entire per-show compensation, even though she needed to spend only a couple of hours shooting her scenes for each show.

Now, about those nine hours.

Surprisingly, the first one came easy. A writer-director named Chuck Bowman had been trying for some time to get me interested in a series idea he had called "Jack and Bill". It was about an ex-basketball player named Bill Boyle who had turned private eye and not a very good one. In the show he dog sits for a friend. When the friend is killed, Bill is stuck with a white curly haired *frou-frou* of a poodle named Jack. Now, the idea of a big burly detective and a dainty white poodle working together was too good to resist. We offer to buy it and put it on MSW as one of our bookends. Chuck agrees, provided he can direct it. No problem, I tell him. I have brought a copy of the script to Mendocino and I hand it to Ken Howard. Would he be interested? He reads it. He loves it. I pencil it in. One down and eight to go.

When last I thought about Dennis Stanton I was strolling around the square outside the Hermitage in St. Petersburg. Dennis was our suave jewel thief in "A Little Night Work" in Season Five. Dennis, played by Keith Michel, was not the killer. In fact he wasn't even much of a jewel thief. It turns out he only stole jewelry insured by one company, the firm that denied him insurance on a technicality as his wife lay dying. Soon thereafter he began his vendetta against the insurers, hoping to put them out of business. At the end of the episode Dennis is helpful in trapping the real killer and the District Attorney declines to press charges. Now it is a year later and I am determined to give Dennis a total rehabilitation. He and Angela worked so well together that I think Dennis can be our suave sophisticated version of "Harry McGraw". We have Jerry to play off of and we have Len Cariou as Michael Haggerty, the British spy. Dennis would complete the triumvirate. So I sit down and write "When the Fat Lady Sings". It takes place in San Francisco. Dennis now works as an insurance investi-

We carry on without Angela in Season Six with Ken Howard as a private eye playing second banana to a poodle named Jack.

gator, putting his larcenous skills to work for the good guys. He and Jessica worked well together and that opened the door for my second Dennis script of the year, "Always a Thief" in which Dennis detected on his own. Another bookend episode. Two down. Seven to go.

For bookend number three, I reach into my trunk. I have been waiting for this moment for thirteen years. I have an absolutely first rate script that might be the crown jewel of the season if we do it right. It is 1947. The Queen Mary is one night out of New York City. Famous mystery writer Lady Abigail Austin (think Agatha Christie) is dining with Simon Brimmer. A murder occurs. When the ship docks Inspector Queen boards to investigate. Ellery will be close behind—Wait a minute. This isn't "Murder, She Wrote". This is an Ellery Queen!

Yes, indeed, it certainly is. As Ellery was winding down in 1975, I wrote this razzle-dazzle script in the hopes of reviving our chances of renewal.

The unit manager tells me, no go. We can't afford it. I visit the Tower and implore Dick Irving, the top budget guy, to reconsider, I make my case. He says no. I say it will save the show. He smiles. NOTHING will save the show, he says. I say, Okay, Dick, but someday I am going to film this script. That's a promise. He just smiles, but I know whereof I speak.

It takes a bit of rewriting. Simon Brimmer is now Edwin Chancellor, host of the cheesy radio show. He's played to a tee by Robert Vaughn. My cop is Lt. Martin McGinn (John Karlen who was Tyne Daley's husband Harvey in 'Cagney and Lacey'). His son Christy (Gary Kroeger from 'Saturday Night Live') is a junior columnist for a New York daily newspaper. He covers the arts and creates the Sunday crossword puzzle because he is very good at puzzles and brain games. He longs to cover a "real" story. The Queen Mary murder may be it. Lady Abigail (a perfect June Havoc) has writer's block. She hasn't written anything decent for a couple of years. She despairs of ever writing again. Nonetheless, Chancellor is trying to get her for his radio show, mostly to cash in on her reputation.

The plot unfolds. Red herrings about. Finally in a gathering of the suspects worthy of Hercule Poirot, pompous Edwin Chancellor unmasks the killer and of course, he is dead wrong as Lady Agatha is quick to point out. She reveals the REAL killer and gets no argument from our hero, Chriaty. But she's wrong, too. Christy was too much a gentleman to dash her new found confidence and so in private he reveals to the authorities the identity of the actual killer. Three logical solutions all based on clues that the audience has seen. And meanwhile, Lady Agatha will remain oblivious, never knowing she had it wrong. Three down. Six to go.

Bob Swanson comes up with a very funny spy adventure that takes place in Sicily and features Michael Haggerty (Len Cariou) posing as a parish priest from Boston. When we film it, Ian Ogilvy, who was delightful and charming in Athens but was, unfortunately, the killer, makes a reappearance as the killer's twin brother. He is a con man going after the fortune owned by Mafia widow Dierdre Hall who has come to Sicily to meet the family but is in reality a CIA agent. Four down, five to go.

Barry Newman signs up to play Lt. Jake Ballinger who runs afoul of the higher ups in the department and is transferred to the local college where he will be forced to teach criminology to a bunch of sloths looking to score an easy A. He scares off most of them but three remain and he uses them and the class as a vehicle to solve the case that got him demoted. Four to go.

By now I am not particularly worried. We will get through the season all right. We have a Michael Haggerty episode set in Athens, and that's right, boys and girls, the second unit comes back with tons of great footage. More envy from our competition. Donald O'Connor plays an old song and dance man starring in a TV special with the singing Haley Sisters (Anne Francis, Connie Stevens, and Elaine Joyce.) We go to Jamaica (actually Griffith Park) for a story of obeah and voodoo intrigue. Angela is reunited with Hurd Hatfield who played Dorian Grey in one of her first movies forty years earlier. In Texas, Jessica's old college friend (Shirley Jones) is about to get married when her homicidal brother (Robert Walker) is released from a mental institution. In Cabot Cove the new priest in town hears the confession of a young woman who has just killed a man and, bound by the seal of the confessional, he doesn't know quite what to do about it.

These are all good scripts so, no, I'm not actually worried but I am troubled. We have some scripts that I consider to be below par. Some of the Cabot Cove material is getting too cute for its own good. Some of the plotting is haphazard, the story lines not very well executed, and they haven't been helped by mediocre direction. In short, even the weakest of them started off with a good premise but they weren't executed as well as they could have been. I really haven't time to run them through my typewriter because I have two scripts in the works already. Think of a youngster in ceramics class making Mom a soup tureen. It's lopsided and not very pretty but it'll stay put in one place and it doesn't leak. We abandon some ideas and start new ones but time pressure is starting to get the best of us. Maybe I am uneasy for no reason. Maybe I am striving for perfection too much of the time. Even the weaker shows (in my opinion) are getting excellent ratings. I tell myself not to worry. But I do worry and one of the manifestations of my angst is a kidney stone attack. I know, there really shouldn't be a correlation but there is. Some people bite their nails. Others flop sweat.

Some get violent indigestion. Me, I get kidney stones. One attack required surgery. Another had me sitting in a hot tub while a machine bombarded me with sound waves. Demerol helps but it is not something I want to endure every few months.

Speaking of those ratings, an interesting phenomenon is developing. I half expected an outpouring of disaffection when we started airing the bookend shows and was ready to respond. *Be grateful,* I would tell them. *13 Jessica shows is a lot better than no Jessica at all.* But a funny thing happened. Not only did we get no letters, our ratings for the bookends were just as good as the ratings for the episodes featuring Angela. Sometimes better. At first I couldn't figure it out. Then someone (it might have been Dick Lindheim) explained to me a few of the givens of series television. Once you've got your audience, you've got it. An occasional weak show won't hurt you. Even two or three. (A seasonful and you are history). As for the bookends, they were all good shows, good stories with good casts. Beyond that, they had Angela's tacit approval since she basically endorsed them by appearing at the beginning of each of them. Eighteen years working at this trade and I am still learning how the business operates.

Meanwhile, the four remaining bookends come easily. Tom Sawyer writes a script that has Grady and his new (pregnant) bride housesitting

Ron Masak (l.), unloads another of his corny jokes. You gotta laugh

Dwayne Hickman, a clueless studio executive in
"Murder According to Maggie," relaxing on the set
with Bob O'Neill who is far from clueless.

Jessica's home while she is in London for a month. Angie has three end-of-a-phone-call scenes. Everything at home is going to hell but Grady and Seth blithely reassure her that all is well (except for the Korean martial arts intruder who just destroyed her dining room, for example). And that's not even the half of it.

"O'Malley's Luck" would star Pat Hingle as Det. Lt. Francis X. O'Malley who comes up against an all powerful real estate mogul (Ron Liebman) who has murdered his wife and made it look like suicide. Or at least that's how it appears. O'Malley is very much like Columbo, shuffling, forgetful, soft spoken, and persistent. We did not see the murder take place and even though we think O'Malley is after the right guy, there's a switch at the end..

We also got another fun script from Bob Van Scoyk called "Goodbye, Charlie". Political pundit Bill Maher starred as a seedy private eye who tries to scam a small town police department so he can collect on an insurance policy on his long-gone Uncle Charlie. Maher proved to be a so-so actor and Anthony Shaw had his hands full dealing with him but the rest of the cast did a bangup job and it turned out well. Funny thing how the most difficult of actors behaved themselves admirably when doing an episode with Angela but reverted to type when on their own. A wonderful testament to the esteem in which Angie was held by her peers.

And finally, we come to Bookend Number Nine. Maggie MacCauley, one of Jessica's former pupils, has become the executive producer of a semi-successful one hour TV action show called "Beat Cop". The shoot-em-up stars hambone Bert Rodgers who has an Olympian ego and a room temperature IQ. He makes Maggie's life hell and if it weren't for all that money, she'd quit. Between being called to the set by her dunderhead leading actor (Tim Thomerson) and being frustrated by her inability to generate a romance with real life detective Vince Palermo (Dennis Arndt), Maggie, played brilliantly by Diana Canova, is at her wit's end. And then murder invades her domain and like Jessica, she is obliged to get involved. We take potshots at the television business and particularly the persona of Bert Rodgers. Some of you may suspect certain parallels between Maggie's fictional travails and my own real ones. I can only say that I admire your perception. This episode was, is, and will always be one of my all time favorites, probably because the subject matter is so close to my heart.

Before I wrap this up, a word about "Jack and Bill". Chuck Bowman came to our first production meeting accompanied by a big strapping doofus who looked very familiar. And he should have. Max Baer Jr. played Jethro Clampett on "The Beverly Hillbillies" for its entire run and I suspect it left him very well off. I recognized right away that Max was no doofus but was in fact a very sharp entrepreneur. He had acquired the rights to the Beverly Hillbillies and was working to raise money to open a Hillbillies casino in Las Vegas. Sawdust on the floor, an oil derrick outside, episodes of the show playing constantly in the recreation rooms. He had it all figured. I believe, and I could be wrong, that Max finally got his dream off the ground in Reno. I sure hope so because Max was one of those people you liked to be around. He talked a blue streak and had an opinion about everything but there wasn't a malicious bone in his body. He appeared in the "Jack and Bill" episode as Jack's owner who is killed and in a later season he would play a state trooper for us.

Me and Angie have serious business to talk over while Sandy Quinn,
my beautiful executive assistant, mugs for the camera.

Off the set we played golf often, sometimes his club, sometimes mine, He was a much better player than me (2 handicap) and I learned a lot from him. With the connivance of Ron Masak, good friend and hustler, the two of us got invited to play as celebrities in a few celebrity golf tournaments though why anyone would consider me a celebrity was beyond me. One particular Saturday all three of us were inked in to play The Roy Rogers Tournament in Apple Valley but Max was nowhere to be found. Seems he was still in bed and he groused loudly when we forced him to stir himself. Well, it turned out to be Max's lucky day. On the third hole, a 171 yard par three from an elevated tee, Max aced it and won himself a brand new Honda Civic courtesy of a local dealer.

After I left MSW, I lost track of Max and it was too bad. You seldom get a chance to meet and know real "characters" and Max was right at the top of my list.

At the end of the season, we have the usual wrap party at one of the sound stages. The food is wonderful, the wine flows forever, there is laughter and self congratulation. Angela is the center of attention as she should be. No one seems to have a care in the world. I join in the merriment but despite the grin on my face, I am troubled. Two phone calls have put me in a quandary. One I received a couple of months ago. The other last week. Both threaten to diminish my wholehearted commitment to "Murder, She Wrote" and both are phone calls I was in no position to ignore.

27. June Havoc, who played
Lady Abigail Austin in "The Grand Old Lady"
is the sister of what famous striptease artist?

Divided Loyalties

ABOUT THAT first phone call in December. We are in the middle of production on our sixth season of "Murder, She Wrote". Peter Falk is on the line. He's in his office having coffee. Do I have a few minutes to chat? For Peter, anything. Ten minutes later I am in Peter's office chewing on a stale donut and sipping inedible coffee while Peter talks urgently with someone in New York. It sounds like a missing persons case and Peter's mother's name is mentioned frequently.

I haven't seen Peter except in passing for fifteen years. After he quit "Columbo" he kept busy making feature films, some of them very good and he was, in all of them, totally captivating. But in the past several years he has returned to Universal and has made maybe a half dozen "new" Columbos. Some have been pretty good, some less so. I suspect why I have been invited but I will wait for Peter to broach the subject.

A year earlier I had been summoned to the Black Tower to meet with Dick Irving. I had no idea why but Dick got right to the point. Peter Falk was up against it and needed a Columbo script right away. Could I find the time to pitch in and accommodate him? My first reaction was, why isn't Peter asking me this himself. My second was, no, I can't. We were just organizing another season of MSW and I was trying to get the McGraw show off the ground at the same time. Much as I loved and respected Peter, it was impossible. With all that was on my plate I didn't have the time and if I tried to squeeze it in, I'd probably make a third rate job of it.

Dick is adamant. He flatters and cajoles and I realize he is under great pressure from Peter. I tell Dick again that it's not possible but I'll take the heat. I look him in the eye and say, 'Offer me double the script fee'. He looks at me suspiciously. I repeat myself. He hesitates, then makes the offer. I give him another flat no. I say to him, now you can go back to Peter and tell him you did your best. You offered me double the money and I still said no. Dick smiled, sort of. It wasn't perfect but I'd given him an out.

But that was then. I continue to chew on the six day old donut, fearing the worst for my digestive system and then Peter hangs up. Before I can ask, he says, 'It's my mother. She's flown the coop'. He explains. His mother lives in a comfortable New York apartment. She has to be at least 75, probably older. She suffers from dementia and has around the clock help. House-keeper, cook, personal attendant. Once in a while she is able to elude her "captors" and starts wandering the streets of New York. Today is such a day. She will be found eventually. Meanwhile Peter stews.

He smiles. 'How do you like those donuts?' I smile back. A little more small talk as he wends his way, Columbo-like, to the point of my visit. 'I need help', he says. 'I need a script. Can you help me out? I'd really appreciate it'. He knows I'm in the middle of writing and producing MSW but he asks anyway. I always wondered why Peter came back to Columbo. God knows he didn't need the money. When the government would run out of cash to send to Upper Lumbago, Peter would call the White House and ask 'How much do you need?' No, it wasn't money but it was the need to work. And more than that, it was the need to work at something he enjoyed and that he could take pride in. For all his carping about "Columbo" and how it had "trapped him" into television and threatened to typecast him, he loved the character and he loved the show and now here he was asking me to help him out. Only this time he was doing it in person.

Like last time, I knew the workload that was coming up and I really felt I didn't have the time to do it. If I were to agree, I couldn't just dash something off and forget about it. I'd have to throw myself into it and I didn't think that would be fair to Angela. So I looked Peter in the eye and leveled with him. I told him the foregoing. I also told him I don't want to slave over a script only to see it rewritten on the set. I respected Peter as a fine actor. I had great reservations about his talents as a writer. Peter shook his head. 'You write the story. We'll go over it together. Then you write the script. We'll do the same. Once we have a shooting script, I won't change a word." He raised his hand like a Boy Scout. I said, I produce it, I pick the director, I do the casting. You get to consult. He nodded. I nodded. Then I told him I 'd had this idea in my drawer for several years and I think it'll make a helluva movie. He's all ears. Tell me about it, he says. I shake my head. It's not formed yet but I can tell you about the first scene. It's at a cemetery. The rain is pelting down. The mourners are grimfaced and you are the grimmest of them all. And I already have a title. It's called "Rest in Peace, Mrs. Columbo" Peter smiled from ear to ear.

True to his word, Peter never changed a word of dialogue. He balked only once, when we suggested casting Helen Shaver as the villainess but that melted away when we showed him some film on her and in the end he was delighted with her. We also had to talk him into accepting Vince McEveety as the director but again, in the end he was more than pleased. From that moment on, Vince became Peter's first choice to direct if he was available. After that Peter was a model of cooperation and decorum. We rushed post production to make a March 31 airdate. The movie was very well received. The ratings were excellent. Peter was delighted and soon was chasing me around, looking for another script and I, like a maiden protecting her virtue, ran away screaming, 'No, no, a thousand times no'. Did I mention that that season Peter won another EMMY as Best Actor in a Series?

So much for phone call number one.

The more recent phone call has come from Jeff Sagansky who has taken over as President of CBS Television. Jeff is an old friend and our relationship goes back to the Eddie Capra days when Jeff was involved in programming at NBC. He invites me to breakfast in Malibu on a Saturday morning. Just to chat and kick around some ideas. I suspect there is more to it than that but one does not slough off a network President. Besides I enjoy breakfast and Jeff is such a nice guy he can't possibly spoil it for me. In addition, if he has an agenda, I have one of my own.

Over french toast and sausage Jeff is a charming guy. He is also a no nonsense straight shooter. He's delighted with "Murder, She Wrote" (naturally) and thinks we got screwed on "The Law and Harry McGraw" though he doesn't say so in so many words. He also tells me the McGraw ship has sailed and I agree. (I also think by now Jerry is tied up with "Law and Or-der".) Finally Jeff gets to the point. He remembers back many years when I was noodling with a series idea I called "Coopersmith". It featured a young rebellious insurance detective, very hip, very mod in dress and outlook, who operated like a much younger Columbo. We would use the open murder format (see the dirty deed done) and then watch as Coppersmith, riding around on his Harley, zeroed in on the perp. The perp, of course, had no idea who or what Coopersmith was until too late. To be honest I hadn't thought about that notion in years but Jeff had it stashed away until the day he needed it. Now he needed it.

I also need something. Some time back I had been fiddling with an idea for a Movie of the Week. Well, I finally wrote it and now it was sitting in a three-ring binder on a shelf in my office and I wanted to make it. It was a good script with a terrific premise. Not a whodunit, but a suspense thriller with plenty of action. I told Jeff about it. He agreed to read it right away and if he liked it, he was sure we could work something out. So there it was.

Beware of poisoned marmalade. Helen Shaver thinks she has Lt. Columbo dead in her sights in "Rest in Peace, Mrs. Columbo." Peter Falk as the lieutenant has other ideas.

Suave and sophisticated ex-jewel thief Dennis Stanton played by Keith Michel (r,) was an elegant counterbalance to Harry McGraw. He appeared in seven episodes, five on his own. That's Ken Swofford as Lt. Catalano on the left.

Tacit agreement to green light my MOW if I would write and produce a pilot for Coopersmith. And that's how it worked out. Later in the year we filmed the pilot. The following spring we were in Texas shooting the MOW.

Meanwhile I had "Murder, She Wrote" to contend with and while my energy level was high, it was not boundless. We needed good scripts and we needed them fast. In the back of my mind I was nagged by some of the duds we turned out in season six and I was resolved not to let it happen again. I had expected Angela to again appear in only 13 episodes leaving us to come up with 9 new bookends. Somewhere along the way, she decided she could handle 17 without a problem leaving me only 5 holes to fill. I knew just how to do it. I hadn't cleaned up Dennis Stanton's image just to see him slink into oblivion. We made a deal with Keith Michel for the five shows and I ended up writing three of them.

Even as I was writing the pilot for "Coopersmith", I was sketching out the hours we were going to need for season seven. I had the three notions for Dennis and two solid ones for Jessica but I was trying to think beyond that. By now we had done 22 shows a year for six years. Do the math. That's 132 hours of storytelling and like most shows that have been on for any length of time, we were starting to trip over our own shoelaces. In great measure I think this was a major reason I had been disappointed in season six, It was getting too easy to fall into the trap of humdrum murder, five or six bland suspects repeating a lot of the things our suspects had been doing over the past six seasons, or using a clue that was dull or far too obvious. Angela could brighten a mediocre script or pedestrian direction with her performance but she couldn't sustain it week after week. When we started out we kept looking for the magic that would make every show a little different, a little more interesting. We needed a hook or a canvas or a twist that would elevate it out of the ordinary, Novelists are lucky in a way. Even if they are prolific they may not write more than fifteen or twenty novels in a lifetime. We had banked those 132 plots and were trying for 22 more and hoping to keep them fresh and exciting. No mean feat although we managed to pull it off.

Arthur Hill returned as Preston Giles, the killer in the pilot. He helps solve Jessica's current case and dies in the process. A bittersweet ending. Vera Miles comes to Jessica and claims that her son was fathered by Jessica's husband Frank many years ago in Korea. Van Johnson appears as an investigative reporter who dies before he can finish his current book about a long-forgotten murder and an unjust verdict. Jessica takes over. A J.B. Fletcher book club is at the core of the trouble when word goes out across the country that J..B. Fletcher is dead. This case of mistaken identity gave us a chance to cast Janet Blair, Margaret O'Brien, Marie Windsor, Betty Garrett, Terry Moore and Jane Withers. What a hoot. And finally, despite the extermination of "The Law and Harry McGraw", Jerry Orbach was back on board pretending to be a Yankee horse breeder when the only thing Harry knows about horses comes from the Racing Form. Famed San Francisco lawyer Melvin Belli joined the cast playing the local judge.

Meanwhile we are putting together material for Keith Michel. There are five episodes and they all work well, and they all feature top notch casts.

Ricardo Montalban as a world famous concert pianist and Patricia Neal as his wife. David Birney as a conman and a forger who "discovers" a lost manuscript by Mark Twain. Susan Blakely as a scheming hussy who has killed her husband and keeps herself busy trying to seduce Dennis. Robert Reed as a sleazy divorce attorney. Vera Miles as a distraught mother. Georgia Brown of "Oliver" fame on Broadway as the tough as nails owner of a comedy club. Grant Shaud from "Murphy Brown" as a shy ventriloquist who can only converse through his dummy. Lyle Waggoner as a Vegas promoter. Even without Angela as bait we still seemed to attract top people to the show.

I have great affection for these five episodes we did with Keith. He proved to be, as I knew he would, a consummate professional and he was perfect in the part. It would have been nice to continue his character in subsequent seasons since we were all getting a real feel for Keith and his character. I also think he could have carried his own spin-off series if I could have persuaded the network to give it a try but after my last experience with Jerry and "Harry" I frankly didn't have the stomach for it.

During this time, Bob O'Neill and I also managed to film the "Coopersmith" pilot. A talented young actor named Grant Show fresh out of "Beverly Hills 90210" proved to be an excellent C.D. Coopersmith, racing around in his leather jacket astride a souped up Harley. He was a rebel with a cause, a sharp inventive insurance investigator who looked and acted like Brando's first cousin in "The Wild One". He had just the right amount of cockiness without being arrogant and a sly sense of humor. Like Columbo he didn't reveal his potent grey matter to the bad guy until it was too late. Up until then he had just seemed like an annoying pest. Nonetheless, the pilot didn't sell. This is not earthshaking news; the majority of pilots don't sell. There is only so much room on a network schedule for new shows and the competition is fierce. Looking back, we did some things right but probably not enough of them.

> **28.** Helen Shaver, who played the vengeful killer in "Rest in Peace, Mrs. Columbo," played Paul Newman's love interest in what Oscar winning film?

To Leave or Not to Leave

IT'S EARLY SPRING of 1991. In a few weeks, we will wrap up principal photography on our seventh season to be followed by the usual gala for cast and crew. Season Eight looms and again, I am not quite sure what form it will take. There will be a season and Angela will participate but for how many episodes, I have no idea.

Meanwhile I am prepping my Movie of the Week which CBS has greenlighted. They are happy with the script. All that remains is to cast our leading man and the final commitment to film will depend on who we sign. This is not unusual. Every network retained star approval of not only series leads but on MOWs as well. After a lot of back and forth and a few anxious moments we get an actor I am thrilled by. Robert Urich IS my main character. CBS agrees. They tell me to go get the best female co-star I can but her part is not a deal breaker. In about six weeks we will be off to Texas to shoot the picture on location. Bob O'Neill has already sent the script to the Texas Film Bureau and they are busy checking out possible locations for our approval when we finally show up.

Meanwhile I have been in constant contact with Tom Hoberman, one of the business's leading entertainment attorneys. An old friend of the boys, he helped structure syndication deals for most or all of the movies of the week that Dick and Bill had written and produced prior to Dick's death. Here's how it worked. CBS puts up a certain amount of money to make the film. They don't care if you make it for less, but if you go over that amount, it comes out of the producer's pocket. Bad weather, illness, a strike. Myriad things can happen to louse up a shooting schedule and I know going in that I will be on the hook if anything goes wrong. On the other hand, Tom Hoberman is busy lining up a syndication deal for me with a company that basically buys the rights to my picture after the network has had its first run and its rerun. Technically, they do not buy the picture, they lease it for a long period of time (in my case, twenty five years). We will split the profits but the key to the deal is that I receive a large sum up front as my advance on those profits. It is a VERY large sum and so I am protected from overages. If I am not budget conscious it will cost me money but I won't be forlornly staring at the world from behind the bars of a debtor's prison. Tom tells me that the casting of Bob Urich makes this a slam dunk deal and he is right. I am starting to get very very excited about going on location. I know it's not a feature film but I don't care. The juices are flowing.

But I am still back in my office at Universal as the season winds down. I get a call from Peter Shaw. He needs a few minutes. Good. We need to talk. Maybe I can get a handle on what is expected for next season. We chat amiably for a few minutes and then Peter gets to the point. Starting this coming season, Angela would like to have input on the stories we develop. I don't say much. I think "I see" was the extent of my response. In general Angela has not been happy with some of the scripts she's been handed. (No kidding. Neither am I). This isn't a dictate, more of a request. I nod. I tell Peter I will give it a great deal of thought. I do not commit. I do not commit because I know this is just the beginning of a whole new dynamic in the producing of the show.

We all know the cliché. If we allow the camel to get his nose under a flap of the tent, pretty soon the rest of the camel is in your lap, taking up most of the space. It is a millimeter's distance between input on stories and script approval. That is something I could not and would not tolerate. "Magnum P.I." has been dead for many years. The beginning of the end came when Tom Selleck demanded and got story and script approval. I know because I got the gory details from people on his production staff. Tom is not a bad guy. In fact he's a very pleasant man to be around but he was also becoming disenchanted with his story lines. Eight years on the air is a lot. Few shows ever get that far and sooner or later, the spark of inventiveness starts to flicker. The problem is, Tom is a busy guy, not only with his acting on the show but outside distractions as well. Public appearances, meetings with agents and managers and developing other projects. A story would be sent over to him and it would sit on his desk unread for days at a time. And while this was going on, script development ground to a halt. When he finally did read something he was obligated to give cogent notes so the writer could proceed to script. When this happens over and over, soon shows are being frantically slapped together and barely making air dates. Usually the quality of the production suffers. When this happens, cancellation ensues. And as for the producers, their jobs have been preempted. Now they just sit and wait for permission to do their jobs.

I could have politely said no to Peter then and there but I knew where Angie was coming from. There were at least six shows that season that didn't live up to my standards and obviously, not to Angie's either. I found myself in a terrible quandary because Angie's request had merely forced me to confront the misgivings I had been having for months. I also knew if I said no, it would change our relationship forever and that the well oiled production machinery we had been operating so smoothly for seven seasons would start to clatter and rattle like an abused Model T. I knew also that if it ever came down to a choice between Angie and me, I lose. They could do without me but not without Angie.

I spent the next two weeks noodling on a scratch pad, trying to come up with exciting new ways to tell a "Murder, She Wrote". After 156 episodes it wasn't easy. I wished Dick Levinson were around to give me some advice though I'm not sure how helpful he would have been. He and Bill had created "Mannix" but hadn't produced it and after a year, the producer, Quinn Martin, had changed the whole premise. And of course we couldn't go by Ellery. Not with a record of 22 and goodbye. This was uncharted territory. The closest thing to "Murder, She Wrote" on television had been "Perry Mason" which ran from 1957 to 1966, nine seasons. I remember watching it toward the end of its run and getting restless because I knew, despite the change of character names and murder weapons and locales, that I had seen all this before. How many shows can you produce in this format without falling all over yourself?

In two weeks I came up with exactly five premises which were notable approaches we had not yet done. One I remember distinctly. Jessica is on a small commuter plane with seven other people. It flies off course in a storm, crashes. One passenger is dead but it wasn't the crash that did him in. He has a knife in his chest. So we not only have a closed environment mystery (one of the people aboard HAS TO BE the killer), we also have a tale of survival under horrendous conditions. It would have made a dandy show. I can't remember the other four but they were pretty good too.

But 5 out of 22 wasn't encouraging and even if my guys came up with another 6 or 7 that were really worth filming, that left a void of maybe 10 episodes where we would be rehashing old material. And what if Angela, for whatever reason, puts the kibosh on one of my favorite stories? What then?

The alternative, of course, was to quit and leave the show to Angela. My producing fees were substantial. I would be giving up a great deal of money. That had to be weighed in. I didn't know what would happen to my staff, the three Bobs in particular. I was pretty sure Angela would bring in her brother Bruce and her stepson David. Maybe they could find writing talent with the fresh eyes that had been eluding me.

I finally decide shortly before the cast party. I don't want to spend the next few years wringing fees out of a show that I cannot help, at least not up to my own standards. "Coopersmith" was an object lesson in what happens when the passion isn't really there. The annals of television are littered with programs that stayed on the air long after they should have departed gracefully. This will not be the case with "Murder, She Wrote". I know the ratings will remain high, that Universal will be minting money, that CBS won't have to worry about a followup show to "60 Minutes" for at least two or three seasons. And I know I won't have to worry about kidney stone attacks. That alone should have made up my mind.

I tell the staff of my decision. Bob O'Neill immediately decides he won't come back. He is 68, still hale and healthy, but it may be time for him to slow down a little and I think he also sees the handwriting on the wall. Bob Swanson asks if I will be upset if he stays on (if asked). I laugh. Of course not. They are going to need Bob and his talent desperately though they may not know it yet. (Ultimately he decides to withdraw but in August he gets a phone call from the Tower prevailing upon him to return to the show which is mired in script problems. He does so and I am grateful. I have been counting on at least three more years on the air and all those royalties. I do not want to see the show sink below the waves after only one more season.)

The word that I am leaving the show gets around and when Bob O'Neill and I announce at the cast party that we are moving on to other things, we get a lot of well wishing but no one seems surprised. No one except for Angela and Peter. But I know Peter was aware of it because Peter made it his business to know everything that was going on. Nonetheless, both he and Angie wish Bob and I good luck. It is a happy and a sad moment all at once. I say goodbye to a lot of people I have worked with over the years and know that I will now see very little of them. That is the nature of the business.

I was wrong about Angie taking control of the show. That won't happen until the Ninth Season. David Moessinger, an experienced show runner takes over as executive producer. He brings his people with him. There are now seven producers turning out the show and they don't have much better luck than I suspect I would have had. Six of the episodes have hooks or premises right out of the first seven seasons. One, a suspected witch in Cabot Cove, is the third with that premise. We did two and that was one too many. Season eight also saw Jessica involved with smuggling informa-tion out of Russia, a story revolving around the adaptation of a Jessica book for the movies, the murder of an MI6 agent, the murder of a jazz legend in New Orleans, and a close Jessica friend murders an abusive husband. All premises we had used before. I know this isn't what David had in mind when he signed on.

But that is all in the future. Tonight, I leave the final wrap party with Lu on my arm, sadness in my heart and Texas on my mind.

> **29. The actor who played "Dorian Gray" in one of Angela's earliest films appeared as a guest star in multiple episodes of "Murder, She Wrote". Do you remember his name?**

Four Weeks in a Texas Town

SPRING IS UPON US and despite what T.S. Eliot may think, April is not the cruelest month. We are in Austin, the capital of Texas, a university town that boasts culture, breeding, great music and friendly people. We have just arrived. We feel right at home. We are staying at a comfortable but not ostentatious hotel abutting the river that forms the western boundary of the city. This will be headquarters for the four weeks we will be shooting the film, not in Austin proper but in the farm areas south of the city. They have set aside rooms for the crew and several conference rooms for support staff. Some of the imported actors like Bob Urich and Markie Post will be staying at one of the fancier hotels downtown. As for Lu and I and Bob O'Neill and Kevin Cremin, we'll be bunking in with the crew. Kevin, who was an assistant director and occasional director on MSW is the line producer on the movie. Bob ONeill is the supervising producer. And our director? Our favorite, the man we always turn to first, Vince McEveety.

The movie we are about to shoot is titled "Dead Aim". It is part thriller, part suspense, part action, and part drama. It is not a whodunit. Bob Urich plays a dirt farmer named Joe Fortier who lives in the middle of nowhere with his two kids, Cindy and Robert. Their house is shabby and could use a paint job as well as some minor repairs, but money is tight. They are scraping along. Markie Post is Sharon, the glamorous wife of the most powerful man in the county, Jimmy Lee Dancey (Michael Beck), who owns everything that isn't nailed down including the county sheriff.

The plot is twisty and turny and mostly suspenseful but pretty easy to follow. In a nutshell, Sharon has seen her husband Jimmy Lee murder his mistress. Jimmy Lee is out to kill her to shut her up. Sharon runs for her life. She hides out in the barn owned by Joe Fortier (Robert Urich) who lives in

Left: Me and Markie Post
Below: Markie and Bob Urich talking though an upcoming scene.

quiet seclusion with his two kids, Cindy (Lauren Stanley) and Robert (Nick Stahl). Joe doesn't like strangers and for good reason. He is hiding from his ex-father in law, a Philadelphia mafioso, who has put a price on his head for running away with his grandchildren. For the kids the entry of Sharon into their lonely family circle is a welcome change and Joe finds himself being attracted to her despite his wariness and mistrust. Meanwhile the local sheriff (James Gammon) is scouring the countryside for her because he is beholden to Jimmy Lee. A crooked Philadelphia police detective (Ken Swofford) has stumbled onto a lead as to Joe's whereabouts and spots him in town. Joe is forced to kill the policeman in self defense and is wounded badly in the shootout. Everything is now falling apart. Joe knows he has to grab the kids and run for it yet again. Sharon is scooped up by the sheriff and turned over to Jimmy Lee. All of this resolves itself in the final fifteen minutes and the ending, if not exactly happy, indicates there is hope for Sharon and Joe and his kids.

Besides the ramshackle farmhouse, the other major locations were the Dancey mansion and the hospital. We were lucky to find just the right house for the estate. It was, in fact, the only one available that matched what I envisioned. The community hospital, used very little at the time, was close by and presented no problem. We were getting very lucky.

We had set aside two days for casting the smaller parts with local talent and the casting director we had retained did an excellent job of bringing top people in to read. We needed a couple of deputies and the doctors and nurses at the hospital. But the two biggest roles we had to cast locally were Bob Urich's kids. In Lauren Stanley we found a natural for Cindy. She had already appeared on national TV in "Lonesome Dove" and she had a nice unspoiled quality about her. Casting Robert proved a little more difficult. We needed a young boy around 10 with the same down to earth non-actor quality and the first day's attempts netted us nothing. On the second day we met Nick Stahl.

Nick was 12 years old, looked younger, but he had a presence and I sat up a little straighter when he entered the room. Despite his youth he could handle a casting session even though his only credit to date was a local mattress commercial. When he read, he read without "acting" and all of us knew we need look no further. Nick's performance was one of the most pleasant surprises for me in making this film. He and his mother lived nearby. As I recall he was an only child and his mother was either widowed or divorced. Nick took every chance he could to hang around the set, toss a football around with the crew (even me) and just enjoy being a kid. A year later he would land the co-starring role with Mel Gibson in "The Man With No Face" which got him not only noticed but also got him terrific notices. He kept working right through the teen years and landed a plum role opposite Sissy Spacek, Tom Wilkinson and Marisa Tomei in "In The Bedroom". Today Nick is working as hard as ever in the Hollywood film community starring or featured in a wide range of motion pictures. It couldn't have happened to a nicer young man.

I'm trying to remember if we had any major glitches in the filming of the movie and I honestly can't think of any. Vince, always the most prepared of directors, had things well in hand all of the time. The weather mainly cooperated and the Film Commission was on hand to smooth out any small problems we might have.

Left: Twelve-year-old Nick Stahl played Bob Urich's son. It was his first film role. A year later Nick was co-starring with Mel Gibson in "The Man with No Face."

Below: Nick Stahl and Bob Urich between shots at the local bus station.

Because we're on location I'm not cooped up somewhere behind a typewriter and so I have more time to hang around the set. I get to know Bob Urich, at least well enough to realize he is one of the good guys in the business. A little more laid back than Jerry but just as genuine. Half kidding he starts batting around the notion of Tom Terrific, Texas Ranger. Half kidding I play along. I don't know where the man gets his stamina. He has just come off a short lived series called "American Dreamer". After this movie he will do three more MOW's, all in a row. Obviously he loves to work and in return the networks love him. I think maybe a series with Bob wouldn't be such a bad idea. He tells me he's really enjoying the role. While contemplating my script he'd been offered one of those Danielle

Steele *papier maché* parts. He just didn't want to do another one. He also said he found a dynamic in my script he could relate to, a sexual heat and energy that he hadn't seen in quite a long while. I laughed. How about Tom Terrific, Texas Ranger with a lot of sexual heat and tension. He laughed. I'm sorry now, looking back, that nothing ever came of that conversation. Bob kept working for many years afterwards. MOWs and series, he was a constant presence on television and in fact at one time held the record for having been the star or a regular on the most television series (15). Sadly he passed away in April of 2002 of cancer. His being made a lot of people happy. His passing caused a great deal of sorrow.

Next to Bob and Nick and the shoot itself, the best thing that happened to us while in Texas was The Coach. In Texas there was only one "Coach" and that was Darrell Royal, the legendary football coach of the University of Texas Longhorns. The moment we arrived in Austin, he and his wife Edith took Lu and I under their wings and made sure we were properly entertained during our visit. Twice Coach was kind enough to take Bob Urich and I out to the exclusive Barton Creek Country Club for a round of golf. We also were invited to a very posh junior league party and Lu was squired around to other events while I was working. But the best of all was our introduction to Willie Nelson. We were, pardon the pun, Hollywood

The ultimate in Texas hospitality. Willie Nelson and pals entertain us at his birthday celebration. A day to remember.

squares and Willie and his band were right at the top of the list of things we liked best. Coach took Lu out to meet Willie and the gang in the famous touring bus (she almost fainted) and he arranged for a bunch of us to play nine holes with Willie at his private golf course near the Perdenales. At the last minute Willie had to beg off, but we did get to attend his birthday party held at the spacious home of a friend. Besides the great outdoor barbecue, Willie and friends spent several hours 'pickin' their best known songs and a lot you never heard of. It was a banner day. I thought hospitality in Lexington during "Black Beauty" was top notch, but it didn't even come close to this. We reciprocated by inviting them all to our raucous wrap party at the end of the shoot. Willie was engaged elsewhere but I'm pretty sure Coach and Edith were on hand. I sure hope so.

When we finally had to pack up and head back to California, the part of Texas we missed most was Coach and Edith and Willie and the warm feeling of hospitality they had shown us.

The movie aired on CBS on Sunday night, September 27, 1991. The title was changed. "Dead Aim" has been used and we can't get the rights. We were re-titled "Stranger at My Door". This, too, had been used before but CBS got the rights for the network showings only. That means when it goes into syndication it will be known as "Dead Run" which had not been taken and for obvious reasons. I have no idea what a dead run is. The ratings were excellent because we had an excellent lead-in in "Murder, She Wrote". The reviews were mainly very good and a couple were five-star.

I look at my calendar. The movie has aired. I have no MSW to worry about, no script in my typewriter and no meetings to attend. Lu and I drive off to Vegas for a week. When I return I will try to figure out what kind of a career I have left, if any.

> **30. In what long-running series did Robert Urich star as a Boston private eye? In what other long-running series did he star as private eye Dan Tanna?**

When Moore is Less

I AM NOW UNEMPLOYED. I no longer have a contract with Universal Studios. I do, however, have a "housekeeping" deal. This means that Universal lets me keep my office in the Producer's Building and they also supply me with a secretary, in this case my b.e.a. Sandy Quinn. The only proviso is they get first shot at any series idea I come up with. Since I have no intention of doing another series, I have no trouble with the arrangement. I turn my attention to ideas for a Movie of the Week. A lot of thoughts come to mind but I'm less than thrilled with most of them. I would prefer not to develop a whodunit but maybe I am kidding myself. Very probably this is how the television community views me. I may not be able to get around it.

I come up with one good idea and take a meeting at CBS with the head honcho for MOW's. This is the guy whose head I went over when I made my deal for "Dead Aim". (Did I tell you I never learned to play the game?) He was peaches and cream all through that process because I had Jeff Sagansky's blessing. Now I am a supplicant. He smiles a lot but I read between his teeth. He is not about to give me the time of day. Did I mention he is not quite 30 years old? I am 57. My hair is just barely starting to turn grey. The lines on my face give me character and stature. Everyone says I am aging gracefully. Maybe so, but all the CBS guy sees is an old fella whose best days are behind him.

I take it to another network. This gentleman is considerably younger than 30 and I am pretty sure he has never seen an episode of MSW. He asks about my credits. I say, "You first." He laughs. He gets it. He smiles a lot and he is unfailingly polite but he speaks a language with which I am not familiar. My idea doesn't have enough "starch" whatever the hell that means. I guess it's film school jargon. I've been getting a lot of that lately. Maybe this young man is right. Maybe even the CBS guy. Maybe my outlook is not as au courant as it could be. I do know that writers who are past the age of 40 have a terrible time getting work. At 50 you are a dinosaur. They won't even give you a meeting. When you near 60 they distribute your picture to the security people in case you try to sneak into the building without an appointment. Guys like Chuck Fries and Len Hill make an excellent living turning out MOWs, but they are salesmen. They know how to put over an idea and get a signature on the dotted line. They are not me. I am quiet, thoughtful, a little shy at times and I have no idea how to promote myself. I slink back to my office and call my agent. Are there any possible assignments around I should know about? Not really, I'm told, unless I'm interested in developing a series. I'm not but even if I were, Universal has first call on my services. I am in a quandary. I start eating chicken salad sandwiches for lunch again. I catch up with "All My Children". Erica is now on her seventh husband and about to jettison him for a younger model. A lot has happened in the past 22 years but Susan Lucci doesn't seem to have aged one whit.

At that moment, my ennui is shattered by a phone call from Charlie Engel who has a project he wants to discuss. He has no ego so he comes to my office, saving me the embarrassment of going up to the twelfth floor of the Tower where people would undoubtedly take pleasure in ogling the moron who walked away from "Murder, She Wrote" and now can't find his way to the men's room. Charlie tells me they have a pay or play deal with Roger Moore and do I possibly have any ideas for a series? Series. There was that word again. On the other hand, what else did I have to do? I told Charlie I'd try to work something up. Interestingly, as a movie buff and trivia nut, I knew two things about Mr. Moore. The first is that he didn't want to do another variation on James Bond. Unfortunately for him, that is exactly what everyone wanted from him. The second was that his favorite movie part was in a film called "Ffolkes" in which he wore a beard and moustache and was sort of crusty and eccentric. That's how I dreamed up "the man in the fat suit".

The series would involve two characters but only one person. One half of this duo is named Thackery Smith. Imagine, if you will, a sort of hybrid between Monty Woolley and Clifton Webb. That would be his professorial personna. With a background set up and validated by MI6, my hero, a mysterious British agent named Bosworth, comes to the USA as a visiting professor at a major University giving two lectures a week. Overweight and out of shape, he harrumphs around the campus, using a cane, walking with a slight limp. His wit is acerbic and offputting. He develops a reputation that precludes his making close friends. A dedicated loner, he wears a suit which is specially padded to add forty pounds to his frame. From his University base in America, he is now invited to various parts of the world as a lecturer. His passport gets him past any border and once in position, he is able to jettison his academic alter ego and perform like, well, say James Bond. He is here, he is there. When the bad guys try to find him, they are totally frustrated. It never occurs to them that he is right under their noses like a modern day Percy Blakeney. It is a compromise that I think Mr. Moore might like because any network would jump at it and Mr. Moore might like doing it for the chance to play this Pimpernel-like spy.

I tell it to Charlie. Charlie likes it and the next thing I know Charlie and I are on a plane to southern France and the small town of Provence where Moore is currently living. We check into a five-star resort hotel where Moore picks us up in his jeep and drives us into the hills to his magnificent villa overlooking the countryside. He is an elegant host. His wife is charming. We are invited to a wonderful lunch. All is well until we finally sit down and start talking about "the fat man". As I suspected, Mr. Moore is unhappy about the super spy aspects of the role but he is captivated by "Thackery Smith". He doesn't say no. He would like to see a script. Not a problem, I say. We fly back to the states and within two weeks I have a pretty good first draft. We ship it off and wait to hear. Ultimately his reaction is not good. I have set the caper in Europe, including Monaco, and for Mr. Moore's taste this comes much too close to Bond. Through Charlie and his agent I get a set of notes. I relocate the action to Australia, set it in and around a cattle ranch but the caper remains much the same. Again a long silence and then comes the word. He is still unhappy.

I take a meeting with Charlie in Tom Thayer's office. Thayer has succeeded Kerry McCluggage as head of the television arm. I have heard via the jungle drums that Thayer has another project up his sleeve for Mr. Moore. I believe it is a sequel of sorts to a Universal series called "The Equalizer" which aired in the '70's and starred Edward Woodward. Moore's agent is also in the room and he tells me Roger is still not happy. Thayer tells me he thinks my script is too linear. I don't know who fed him that line but to me linear means the story has a beginning, a middle and an end. Maybe Thayer knows something about writing television that I don't. Thayer and the agent continue to take amiable potshots at me and my script. Finally I do what they have wanted me to do all along. I have no idea how to accommodate their notes and make the script better since Mr. Moore won't do the spy thing and nobody wants him for anything else. So I tell them my feelings will not be hurt if they want to give it to someone else for a rewrite. In short, I wash my hands of it. They do everything but stand up and dance a jig.

Weeks later I hear that Mr. Moore is getting ready to shoot a pilot for Universal which is a kissing cousin to the old "Equalizer" series. Thayer has slickly removed me from the picture and adroitly convinced Roger Moore that he will be well served by participating in a carbon copy of a Universal series that actually wasn't much good the first time around. In my many years with Universal this is the first time I have heard of a head of TV development acing out one of his producers to feather his own nest, but I suppose it was inevitable. Anyway Thayer has his project and his star and Roger Moore doesn't have to wear the stuffy old fat suit.

Many, many months later Mr. Moore and his "Equalizer" rip-off air in a throwaway time slot. The movie is not a pretty sight. I would tell you the name of it and a few more specifics but I've forgotten it and when I check Moore's filmography, it is not listed. I look everywhere but I can't find it. Happily for him he immediately went on to other things within the year like "The Man Who Wouldn't Die" with Malcolm McDowell, a nice little movie with a twisty plot that got generally favorable reviews.

Despite Mr. Moore, my bombastic hero is not yet dead. Richard

Chamberlain has read the script and he is interested. So am I. You may say that Richard is a far cry from Monty Woolley and Clifton Webb but you would be forgetting that Richard did a lengthy and excellently reviewed stint on Broadway as Professor Henry Higgins. Given his extensive resume and the wildly disparate parts he has played, he is twice the actor Mr. Moore is and beyond that, he is enthused. (And I might add, an excellent judge of material). Richard and I take a meeting at NBC. I make a good pitch. Richard's right with me, echoing the reasons why this would make a highly entertaining series. NBC ponders. They procrastinate. In the end, they pass. I'm not heartbroken but I am disappointed. I liked Richard. We would have had fun together. Thackery and Bosworth are consigned to my trunk.

If I had been sour on series before the backstabbing Thayer incident, now my outlook is absolutely acid. I seriously consider total retirement. I only have one problem. I still love to write. I love to sit at the typewriter and envelop myself in a world totally of my own choosing. I invent people to love, to laugh at, and to despise. However they may squirm, they are at my mercy. I can redeem them or betray them. I can kill them off on a whim or bestow on them the selflessness of a Mother Teresa. Such is the joy and exhilaration I get from sitting down at my typewriter. But if I write a story and then go into the woods and shout it to the tallest branches and there is no one around, have I actually made a sound? I have spent over 20 years entertaining tens of millions of people which is all I ever wanted to do. Can I be content now just to write for an audience of one and be satisfied? I don't know.

> **31. In what well-known TV series did Roger Moore appear in the role of cousin "Beau"?**

Peter Comes Calling...Again

WOULDN'T YOU KNOW, just about the time I am getting ready to move to Las Vegas to become a semi-professional poker player and a halfway decent amateur golfer, I get a phone call from someone who needs a shootable script and he needs it now. You get three guesses. Yes, you've got it. Peter Falk would like to get together whenever I have a chance. I look in my appointment book, sift through my schedule (meetings with agents, power lunches with network executives, a one on one with a United States Senator, two dentist appointments, three massages, eighteen holes with Greg Norman at the country club.) How about an hour from now? I say, because I want to get this meeting out of the way in case any of these other things actually come to pass.

We chat amiably about old times, rehashing the fun we had on "Rest In Peace, Mrs. Columbo." Peter tells me he has an airdate to fill and do I have any ideas in that trunk of mine. Since I have never yet let my mind atrophy, I confess that I had been thinking about an "arena". Basically the "arena" is the background for the episode and primarily the occupation or social status of the murderer. The bigger the better. For several years talk radio had been coming into its own and there was no one bigger or more controversial than Rush Limbaugh so I figure, let's invent an unscrupulous radio talk show host with a huge ego and a dishonest streak a mile wide. Even Rush would admit to a giant ego but the other adjectives are not Rush, just my fictional character whom I have named Fielding Chase. Working with him on his national radio show is his adoptive daughter Victoria. She was born to a woman Fielding had loved in his youth but when the mother died suddenly leaving her daughter an orphan, Fielding stepped in. He has been raising her since she was ten. One thing is certain, he has been keeping her in his shadow for years, running her life from every angle. Victoria is in her mid-twenties and she has written a novel. A Fielding subordinate, Gerry Winters, tells her she must break away from Fielding's stranglehold on her. He has gotten her novel to a prestige publisher. Fielding finds out and calls the publisher, threatening him with adverse commentary on his show. The publisher caves. The deal is off, but Gerry has figured out that Fielding was behind it. Before he can tell Vicky what he knows, Fielding kills him to protect his relationship with his adoptive daughter.

That was all I had. A few characters, a terrific area, an emotional premise different from any that had been used in "Columbo". Peter liked everything about it. All I needed was the killing, the clues and the last act "gotcha" and we were home free. He sent me off to work it out.

Now I have to come up with the hook. How does Fielding kill Gerry and how does Columbo catch him? A few days later I'm lunching with Bob Swanson and I relate my half-story and tell him my problem. Bob tells me he has a clue he's been kicking around for a few months but hasn't been able to tie it to anything. He tells me what it is. I beam. Can I steal it, I ask. He nods his head and gives it to me willingly. Everything falls into place. All I have to do now is put paper into my typewriter and out will come the finished product.(That's right. Typewriter. The same manual typewriter I wrote my first script on. I know there are such things as computers but I have no ambition to explore them. Things mechanical or electronic have an aversion to me and I to them. Progress will have to pass me by, at least for the present.)

I won't bother you with the plot. Bill Shatner is dastardly as Fielding Chase. Molly Hagan was delightful as Victoria and in the end she walks away a free woman even as Chase screams at her to come back. The gotcha clue that Bob Swanson gave me? A dilly. Chase's alibi hinges on the fact that he was on his car phone notifying the police of the murder which he had heard occur on the other end of his cell phone call less than a minute earlier. But Chase lives in a mansion in the Malibu mountains where there is no cell phone service within miles of his house so he couldn't have made the call from his car...and that is his undoing. The resolution was a little more complicated and a lot more fun but it was a satisfying ending and Peter was very happy with it.

I had a good time writing this script. I always do when I write a Columbo. But the morning after it aired, hell broke loose on the Rush Limbaugh radio program. The screams from the faithful ditto heads were many and loud. He had been libeled. He had been slandered. Columbo is nothing but a left wing propaganda show disguised as a murder mystery. Rush took it all in stride but his viewers wouldn't shut up so I mailed Rush an autographed script, explaining why a radio talk show host was chosen as a killer. It was because Rush himself had made it possible. Years earlier we never would have considered the idea. That night on his television show he put up a shot of the autographed script and my note. That seemed to mollify the masses. The subject was closed.

And then came another call from Peter and, you guessed it, he could use another script. I said I'd give it some thought and within a week I had a pretty good notion that I know hadn't been done before. I ambled over to his office and we chatted about it and he liked it as well as I did. So I went ahead and wrote it.

I shouldn't have. This one turned out to be one Columbo too many.

I loved the "hook" and so did Peter. Columbo has a real mind-bender to deal with. Two people die. One is the intended victim. The other is collateral damage who just happens to be a close friend and associate of a Mafia don. Entitled "Strange Bedfellows" the mafioso wants the killer brought to justice as much as Columbo does which brings them together into an odd and almost unspoken alliance.

The setup was simple. Two brothers have inherited a thoroughbred stable from their parents who died in a plane crash. The younger brother is a playboy, gambler, womanizer and cares not a whit for the farm. The older brother, Graham McVeigh, is the worker, ambitious, dedicated and finally has had enough. His brother has to be eliminated and Graham devises an intricate plan to do away with him. First he will disguise himself and go to a pawnshop where he will buy an unregistered pistol.

Right away I know this episode is in deep trouble. I have written the part of Graham for a slim, leading man, urbane, charming, but flawed and decidedly dangerous. Someone like James Spader or James Woods or maybe Jude Law, a young version of Jack Cassidy or Robert Vaughn. The network insists that Peter cast George Wendt in the part. That's right, short stubby roly-poly Norm from "Cheers", that George Wendt who is going to go into that pawn shop in disguise to buy the murder weapon. I envision a makeup job that wouldn't fool Stevie Wonder. My God, did anybody read this script?

That's on the negative side and a big one it is. On the positive side they have hired Rod Steiger to play Vincenzo Fortelli, the Mafia Don, who is livid because one of his closest lieutenants was killed in the aftermath of the murder of Graham McVeigh's brother. Fortelli kidnaps Columbo off the street, treats him to a lavish Italian meal and warns Columbo in no uncertain terms to catch his friend's killer or Fortelli will take matters into his own hands. Peter and Steiger have several scenes together and they are fun to watch. In the final scene Graham is at Fortelli's home. Columbo is there as well. Fortelli knows that Graham killed his friend because Columbo has told him how and why he did it but Columbo has also told him he has no proof, therefore Graham is going to get away with it. Columbo sighs with regret and says sometimes God works in mysterious ways. He gets up to leave. Graham is terrified. Columbo can't leave, he screams. The mobster will kill him. Columbo shakes his head sadly but he has places to go and people to see. He wishes Graham luck as he heads for the door. Hysterical, Graham breaks down and reveals where a vital piece of evidence has been hidden and then we realize that this little one act play has been performed solely for Graham's benefit.

Sounds like fun and it was. At least this one scene was. As for the rest of it, Peter and Vince fiddled and diddled with the structure and the clues to the point where it became incomprehensible nonsense. Peter was no writer and Vince was less so. I sent them a three-page single-spaced letter outlining all the things they were doing wrong but my pleas fell on deaf ears. So I took the only course a self-respecting writer can take in that situation, I take my name off the script and substitute "Lawrence Vail", my official don't-blame-me-for-this-piece-of-crap cop out. The show airs and

A "grieving" Lt. Columbo at the gravesite of his wife in "Rest in Peace, Mrs. Columbo." The funeral was a huge scam perpetrated by Columbo to catch a killer.

it has its moments. The kidnapping of Columbo. The scenes between he and Rod Steiger. But every time George Wendt appears on screen my teeth begin to ache.

A month later I've forgotten all about it. Apparently so has Peter. Years later when I am playing golf on a Saturday morning at the Las Vegas Country Club with my usual group of ganefs and sandbaggers, I notice there is a film crew setting up. I ask what's going on. A Peter Falk movie, I'm told. I go in search of the assistant director and ask where Peter is. He'll be around in about an hour. I give the AD a note to hand to Peter when he arrives. It says: "Feel like playing golf tomorrow morning? Call me." I sign it and leave my phone number. An hour later, Peter calls. Golf? Terrific. What time? The next day Peter plays 18 with me and the gang. Afterwards we gather in the clubroom for lunch. Peter draws a crowd and regales everyone with his favorite stories and I am pleased, mostly because I didn't want our relationship to end on the sour note of that last episode.

June 23, 2011, turned out to be a dark day for not only me but the rest of the world who loved the little cop in the shabby raincoat. Peter died at home at the age of 83 after a long and terrible bout with Alzheimer's Disease. He will continue to live on through his many movies and his 63 Columbo outings. It's not enough. I would love to hear him say, just one more time, "Excuse me, sir, just one more thing." Sadly, there is no longer 'one more thing'.

---

32. What was the name of the episode on The Dick Powell Theater for which Peter Falk won his first EMMY?

    a) The Bachelor Party
    b) Requiem for a Heavyweight
    c) The Catered Affair
    d) The Price of Tomatoes

Fade Out

IT IS A KNOWN FACT that the days and weeks fly by as you get older. The usual landmarks start cramming together as if they had happened yesterday. Our fiftieth anniversary? That was just—uh—last year? Five years ago? Surely you jest. The movie stars I grew up with are dying off. So are some of my favorite authors. Perry Como and Rosemary Clooney have given way to a new breed of singer, probably just as talented, but they sing songs I do not understand. The electronic revolution is washing over the country and I am drowning. I cannot find ribbons for my trusty typewriter. I switch to an electric and jam the keys every time I touch the keyboard. No, I don't need this any more. I really don't.

And so it was final. The move was underway. Our house in Calabasas was on the market and we had already bought a nice two story Georgian on the tenth green of the Las Vegas Country Club. I was looking forward to retirement, sleeping late when I wanted, playing golf, getting hammered in poker tournaments (I wasn't that good but I loved playing). I felt a kind of relief that I wouldn't be waiting for the phone to ring or having to check the overnight ratings or attend some senseless meeting to promote either myself or some new show. Writing? I was done with it.

Finally the move to Nevada is complete. Vegas is our new home. I have converted the smallest upstairs bedroom into an office where I keep my library, my old scripts, and other memorabilia. My typewriter sits on one of the bookcases underneath its dustcover but I seldom take it down to use it. A few letters now and then to friends and the few fans that write. My days are spent with new friends who have nothing to do with the television or movie business. (With one major exception). They are doctors, accountants, businessmen, retired *maître d's* from the big casinos. We play golf, we go out to dinner. We socialize at the club. I play poker.

I learn that down the street, a film legend is living out his years among the photos and treasures of a lifetime. George Sidney is one of the finest directors from the heyday of Hollywood. Among his most famous pictures are "Annie Get Your Gun", "Show Boat", "Anchors Aweigh", "Kiss Me Kate" "Scaramouche". "The Three Musketeers", "The Harvey Girls", "Bye Bye Bird-ie". "Viva Las Vegas" and many many more. George and his wife Corinne take us into their lives and I am over at their house two or three times a week visiting. George takes me upstairs to an expansive room where the walls are covered with hundreds of candid photos that George has taken on the sets of his many productions. Every major star of his era is on display. In all he has over two thousand stashed away in boxes and filing cabinets. He fascinates me with his stories of old Hollywood and his adventures (some unprintable) with the major stars of his day. Over coffee and often something stronger, I learn more about back alley Hollywood from George than from all the gaudy books I keep on my shelves. I am fascinated when he talks about his pain in having to replace Judy Garland on "Annie Get Your Gun". Judy was in the grip of addiction to a wide range of pills and even trying her best, she was not the performer she once was. He never runs out of things to talk about and I never tire of listening.

One of George's dearest friends had been Edward G. Robinson. Near the end, when Robinson was very ill and close to dying, he begged George to marry his widow. Since George was single at the time and had nothing better to do, he did just that. That's what I call a friend. As a keepsake, George gives me a beautiful leather jewelry box that had belonged to Robinson. It is something I continue to treasure.

When Jerry Orbach comes to town, we all go out to dinner. George is a huge fan of "Law and Order". Jerry is in awe of this gentle man who has seen and done it all. George takes Jerry's picture with his wife Elaine. It may be the last picture George ever takes. Frail when we met him, he has declined. On May 5, 2002, he dies in his sleep at the age of 86. My wife Lu is holding his hand when he slips away.

I was very privileged to know this man for many many reasons but chiefly, he showed me that there is life after a career. There are those many years after you have left the sound stages when you can look back and remember the fun days and the not so fun days. All are part of the fabric of who you were in your professional life.

And so I am done with my typewriter.

Well, not exactly. I trade it in for a computer.

> **33.** In what movie did George Sidney direct Gene Kelly and a cartoon mouse named "Jerry" in a dance sequence?

A Guy Named Joe

A NICE PLACE to visit but I wouldn't want to live there.

That's how I have come to feel about Las Vegas. I have good friends here. I play golf on a fun and demanding course, I play poker in various casinos and sometimes win. With a couple of buddies we pony up $1500 each football season to enter the Hilton handicapping contest. Each year we finish in the middle of the pack. One year we win it and split $220, 000 three ways. At the tail end of 1999 I shoot three hole-in-ones on the golf course within a six week period. There aren't enough zeroes in the world to calculate those odds but it happened. Haven't come close to even one since that time.

So I have good memories of Vegas but overall, it is not a wonderful place to live. The summers are much too hot, the winters can be bitingly cold after the sun goes down. The days are all the same and basically I am bored. Lu leaves in June to spend the summers at a rented house on Monterey Bay with the grandchildren. I come up for a few days. It's a wonderful place. Small town. Great weather. I decide I've had enough of Nevada and we buy a house overlooking the water. I'm happier already but good weather doesn't relieve my boredom and I realize I wish I were writing again.

Impossible.

TV is out. The kids running the studios and the networks are barely post-pubescent and I am a fossil. I write a play and I think it's pretty good but I don't know what to do with it except try to shake myself free of my comfortable existence and go out and peddle it. I realize I don't want to do that. I just want to write and I want nothing to do with anything associated with promoting the play or myself.

I toy with the idea of writing a novel but that's a bad idea. I tried it once in my 30s and it was dreadful. I have a knack for scenes and dialogue. The art of prose escapes me. Or so I believed. What I hadn't realized was that my reading had tripled in recent years, now that I had time for it and whether or not I knew it, I was absorbing structure and technique by osmosis from a lot of very good authors.

Because I am a news junkie and still have a few functioning grey cells, I am getting more and more fed up with what's going on in Washington and particularly with Congress which I perceive as a bunch of self-serving elitists with little or no regard for the actual needs of the country. Thoroughly entrenched in office like barnacles on the hull of a dilapidated scow, they need to be removed.

Mad as hell, I'm not going to take it any more and so with great trepidation I sit down and start to write a novel. The premise is simple but revolutionary. A handful of Congressmen and Congresswomen from "safe" districts control the workings of the House of Representatives. Their power far exceeds their tiny little districts. Their actions affect the nation as a whole but the nation as a whole did not elect them. They cannot be ousted by the electoral process, therefore more drastic means are called for. Pretty soon the most egregious of their number are being killed off, one by one, and the country is in a panic. The individual assassins do not run and hide, they surrender meekly to the authorities but have little to say. There is nothing to connect them to one another and how this nationwide cleansing of Congress is being orchestrated remains a mystery.

I have a wonderful time writing it and when I am finished, I read it through and decide it is good. In fact I think it is very good. I let a few people whose opinion I respect read it and they agree. Now what? I could try to find an agent and maybe get it published but here again, I've had my fun. Do I really want to go through all the frustration of "selling" my book and myself? That part of the equation is not fun and so I temporize.

I check around and find that Gorham Printing in Washington state has a good reputation for printing short-run books, what they once called "vanity press" but now call "self-publishing". It is now possible through the internet and particularly through Amazon to publish and market your book on line without having to go through a "traditional" publishing house. I title my novel "The Blood of Tyrants" from a quote by Jefferson and order 500 copies, send some to friends and get the same reaction. They really love it.

Now two things happen. My son Chris jumps in and takes over all the marketing responsibilities for getting the book out into the world and I sit down at my computer (Yes, I'm catching up with the 21st Century) and start to write a follow-up novel which I call "The Terror of Tyrants". It turns out even better than "Blood" and I order 500 copies from Gorham. I get a DBA certificate (Doing Business As) for The Grove Point Press and call myself a publisher. I don't exactly know what I'm doing but I can tell you this. I am no longer bored.

Chris develops a very attractive and informative website to sell the books. We get listed with Amazon, POD as well as Kindle. We start selling books. Eventually we start getting reviews. Almost all are very good. Some are raves. I feel the need to write another one but I've said all I care to say about the state of the union. I search around for something different.

One of my great passions is Hollywood. The other is writing mysteries. I think I can meld the two into one adventurous project. My movie library consists of over 800 VHS tapes and DVD's. I own most of the oldies but goodies. I remember George Sidney's upper floor, walls papered with glossies of old time Hollywood, the golden age of the movies, of iconic stars like Bogart and Cagney, John Wayne and Bette Davis and later on, Brando and Douglas and Clift and Hudson.

I have an idea for a murder mystery that takes place at a third rate Hollywood movie studio in 1947. My hero is a veteran named Joe Bernardi, an ex-war correspondent now working publicity for the studio's cheesy output of B programmers. I have a pretty decent plot loaded with twists and turns, and populated with crooked cops, ambitious starlets, tyrannical directors, egotistical studio executives and on and on. Film noir-ish in style, I can see it all. I have a front row seat at a new movie which is unfolding before my eyes as I write it. I get to a point where I need a scene in the director's office so Joe goes to question him and then I think, wouldn't it be great if Joe barged in and interrupted a meeting with a real actor or actress of the era.

So I put Gail Russell in the scene and she doesn't do much more than say hello and bat her eyes but it inspires me to think beyond this book which I have entitled "Jezebel in Blue Satin".

My trusty guinea pigs read the manuscript. The reaction comes back. It is good. Very good. I was sure it was but fresh unbiased eyes are always better than a biased author's. I begin thinking about a followup and more than that, a lot of followups.

Back to my computer. The year is 1948. I rescue Joe from Trashcan Studios and put him to work at Warner Brothers. Almost immediately he is sent to Tampico, Mexico, to quash a possible scandal. Humphrey Bogart, there filming "Treasure of the Sierra Madre", has been thrown in jail on the heels of a bar fight. It'll be Joe's job to get him out and fend off a nosy press. Instead he gets himself embroiled in the messy murder of a cast member.

1949 rolls around and Joe is publicizing Jimmy Cagney's comeback film for Warner's, "White Heat", when his ex-wife finds herself running from the law, a fugitive with a murder rap hanging over her head.

In 1950 Joe is hot on the trail of a writer who has plagiarized his first novel, even as he's trying to placate Jane Wyman, Gertrude Lawrence and Eleanor Parker, all of whom want Joe's full attention in securing for them an Oscar nomination.

Its 1951. Warners is filming "A Streetcar Named Desire" and America's number one Red-baiting newspaper columnist is coming after Elia Kazan with a vengeance, determined to put him out of business. He never gets a chance. The newspaperman is found murdered and the cops are looking at Kazan with a suspicious eye.

The parade goes on, year after year. 1952 with Ronald Reagan and Doris Day in a baseball movie called "The Winning Team". 1953, Montgomery Clift and Hitchock in Canada shooting "I Confess," 1954. An actor disappears from the set of John Wayne's "The High and the Mighty" and is later found hanging from a lamppost on the backlot. In 1955 it's New York and Joe is working on "Marty" even as he is trying to protect his lady love from a vicious killer who is out to shut her up, permanently.

Upcoming is a murder in Texas on the set of "Giant" with Rock Hudson,

Elizabeth Taylor and James Dean. After that, undercover in Memphis as Joe tries to unearth the perpetrators of an extortion plot against Elvis Presley. And in 1958 Joe finds himself working with Orson Welles to save "A Touch of Evil" before it gets mangled beyond recognition by a bunch of ham-handed film editors.

Bored? Not me. Not on your life. My hero, Joe Bernardi, has become a close personal friend much as Jessica Fletcher was for seven happy years. I may not make much money at this enterprise but I frankly don't care. I'm spending my time doing what I love best and there are damned few of us who can say that.

To quote Lou Gehrig by way of Gary Cooper, "Today I consider myself the luckiest man on the face of the earth."

·········· Trivia Teasers ··········

(How did you do?) 1. d.   2. 37   3. b.

4. Who's Afraid of Virginia Woolf?   5. c.

6. Murder Inc.   7. Sing Sing in Ossining, New York   8. c.

9. National Velvet 10. Finian's Rainbow and Teahouse
of The August Moon.   11. b.   12. Mission: Impossible

13. c.   14. Pocketful of Miracles   15. b.

16. The Outer Limits   17. Birdman of Alcatraz   18. d.

19. Beatrice   20. c.   21. The Rothschilds

22. The four roles Angela played on Broadway for which she
won her four Tonys.   23. Nero Wolfe   24. Prince of the
City   25. Cop Rock   26. d.   27. Gypsy Rose Lee 28. The
Color of Money   29. Hurd Hatfield   30. Spenser for Hire
and Vegas   31. Maverick   32. d.   33. Anchors Aweigh

Dear Reader,

Did you love the quirkiness of Columbo? Did you enjoy sleuthing along with Jessica? Do you enjoy reading murder mysteries? Do you remember the heyday of Hollywood with affection and if not that old, do you enjoy watching the old films on Turner Classic Movies and The Movie Channel? Answer "YES" to any of these questions and I guarantee you will be captivated by Joe Bernardi and his adventures in Tinseltown in an era when the big studios ruled the roost and every starry eyed ingenue from Idaho to Iowa wanted to be another Vivien Leigh. Do yourself a favor and turn the page and introduce yourself to The Hollywood Murder Mysteries, a series of fast-paced page-turning mystery novels which will intrigue and delight you. I guarantee it. And what do I mean by that? I mean that, if you buy an autographed copy of any of the following books direct from The Grove Point Press and you are not completely satisfied, return the book and I will refund your purchase price plus your postage, no questions asked. So far we've turned out a dozen volumes. We hope to create more and believe me, if you folks keep reading them, I'll keep writing them. Many thanks and bless you all.

P.S. Although not autographed, every volume of the Hollywood Murder Mysteries is available from your local bookstore and also on line as a paperback or in the Kindle format from Amazon.com.

TO PURCHASE COPIES OF

Check first with your local book seller. If he is out of stock or is unable to order copies for you, go online to Amazon Books where every volume in the series is available either as a paperback or in the Kindle format.

Alternatively, you may wish to order paperback editions direct from the publisher, The Grove Point Press, P. O. Box 873, Pacific Grove, CA 93950. Each copy purchased directly will be signed by the author and personalized, if desired. If your initial order is for three or more different titles, your price per copy drops to $9.95 and you automatically become a member of the "club." Club members may purchase any or all titles in any quantity, all for the same low price of $9.95 each. In addition, all those ordering direct from the publisher will receive a FREE "Murder, She Wrote" bookmark personally autographed by the author.

Want to know more about
THE HOLLYWOOD MURDER MYSTERIES?
click on
THEGROVEPOINTPRESS.COM

Jezebel in Blue Satin

In this stylish homage to the detective novels of Hollywood's Golden Age, a press agent stumbles across a starlet's dead body and into the seamy world of scheming players and morally bankrupt movie moguls.....An enjoyable fast-paced whodunit from opening act to final curtain.

—Kirkus Reviews

Fans of golden era Hollywood, snappy patter and Raymond Chandler will find much to like in Peter Fischer's murder mystery series, all centered on old school studio flak, Joe Bernardi, a happy-go-lucky war veteran who finds himself immersed in tough situations.....The series fills a niche that's been superseded by explosions and violence in too much of popular culture and even though jt's a world where men are men and women are dames, its glimpses at an era where the facade of glamour and sophistication hid an uglier truth are still fun to revisit.

—2012 San Francisco Book Festival, Honorable Mention

Jezebel in Blue Satin, set in 1947, finds movie studio publicist Joe Bernardi slumming it at a third rate motion picture house running on large egos and little talent. When the ingenue from the film referenced in the title winds up dead, can Joe uncover the killer before he loses his own life? Fischer makes an effortless transition from TV mystery to page turner, breathing new life into the film noir hard boiled detective tropes. Although not a professional sleuth, Joe's evolution from everyman into amateur private eye makes sense; any bad publicity can cost him his job so he has to get to the bottom of things.

—ForeWord Review

We Don't Need No Stinking Badges

A thrilling mystery packed with Hollywood glamour, intrigue and murder, set in 1948 Mexico.....Although the story features many famous faces (Humphrey Bogart, director John Huston, actor Walter Huston and novelist B. Traven, to name a few), the plot smartly focuses on those behind the scenes. The big names aren't used as gimmicks—they're merely planets for the story to rotate around. Joe Bernardi is the star of the show and this fictional tale in a real life setting (the actual set of 'Treasure of the Sierra Madre' was also fraught with problems) works well in Fischer's sure hands....A smart clever Mexican mystery.

—Kirkus Reviews

A former TV writer continues his old-time Hollywood mystery series, seamlessly interweaving fact and fiction in this drama that goes beyond the genre's cliches. "We Don't Need No Stinking Badges" again transports readers to post WWII Tinseltown inhabited by cinema publicist Joe Bernardi... Strong characterization propels this book. Toward the end the crosses and double-crosses become confusing, as seemingly inconsequential things such as a dead woman who was only mentioned in passing in the beginning now become matters on which the whole plot turns (but) such minor hiccups should not deter mystery lovers, Hollywood buffs or anyone who adores a good yarn.

—ForeWord Review

Peter S. Fischer has done it again—he has put me in a time machine and landed me in 1948. He has written a fast paced murder mystery that will have you up into the wee hours reading. If you love old movies, then this is the book for you.

—My Shelf. Com

This is a complex, well-crafted whodunit all on its own. There's plenty of action and adventure woven around the mystery and the characters are fully fashioned. The addition of the period piece of the 1940's filmmaking and the inclusion of big name stars as supporting characters is the whipped cream and cherry on top. It all comes together to make an engaging and fun read.

—Nyssa, Amazon Customer Review

Love Has Nothing to Do With It

Fischer's experience shows in 'Love Has Nothing To Do With It', an homage to film noir and the hard-boiled detective novel. The story is complicated... but Fischer never loses the thread. The story is intricate enough to be intriguing but not baffling....Joe Bernardi's swagger is authentic and entertaining. Overall he is a likable sleuth with the dogged determination to uncover the truth.... While the outcome of the murder is an unknown until the final pages of the current title, we do know that Joe Bernardi will survive at least until 1950, when further adventures await him in the forthcoming 'Everybody Wants an Oscar'.

—Clarion Review

A stylized, suspenseful Hollywood whodunit set in 1949....Goes down smooth for murder-mystery fans and Old Hollywood junkies.

—Kirkus Review

The Hollywood Murder Mysteries just might make a great Hallmark series. Let's give this book: The envelope please: FIVE GOLDEN OSCARS.

—Samfreene, Amazon Customer Review

The writing is fantastic and, for me, the topic was a true escape into our past entertainment world. Expect it to be quite different from today's! But that's why readers will enjoy visiting Hollywood as it was in the past. A marvelous concept that hopefully will continue up into the 60s and beyond. Loved it!

—GABixlerReviews

The Unkindness of Strangers

Winner of the Benjamin Franklin Award
for Best Mystery Book of 2012
by the Independent Book Publisher's Association.

Available from your local bookstore
or online at Amazon.com.
You may also purchase any and all books
in the series direct from the publisher
using the order form at the back of the book.

Book One—1947

JEZEBEL IN BLUE SATIN

WWII is over and Joe Bernardi has just returned home after three years as a war correspondent in Europe. Married in the heat of passion three weeks before he shipped out, he has come home to find his wife Lydia a complete stranger. It's not long before Lydia is off to Reno for a quickie divorce which Joe won't accept. Meanwhile he's been hired as a publicist by third rate movie studio, Continental Pictures. One night he enters a darkened sound stage only to discover the dead body of ambitious, would-be actress Maggie Baumann. When the police investigate, they immediately zero in on Joe as the perp. Short on evidence they attempt to frame him and almost succeed. Who really killed Maggie? Was it the over-the-hill actress 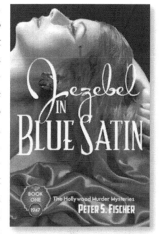 trying for a comeback? Or the talentless director with delusions of grandeur? Or maybe it was the hapless leading man whose career is headed nowhere now that the "real stars" are coming back from the war. There is no shortage of suspects as the story speeds along to its exciting and unexpected conclusion.

Book Two—1948
WE DON'T NEED NO STINKING BADGES

Joe Bernardi is the new guy in Warner Brothers' Press Department so it's no surprise when Joe is given the unenviable task of flying to Tampico, Mexico, to bail Humphrey Bogart out of jail without the world learning about it. When he arrives he discovers that Bogie isn't the problem. So-called accidents are occurring daily on the set, slowing down the filming of "The Treasure of the Sierra Madre" and putting tempers on edge. Everyone knows who's behind the sabotage. It's the local Jefe who has a finger in every illegal pie. But suddenly the intrigue widens and the murder of one of the actors throws the company into turmoil. Day by day, Joe finds himself drawn into a dangerous web of deceit, dupliciity and blackmail that nearly costs him his life.

Book Three—1949
LOVE HAS NOTHING TO DO WITH IT

Joe Bernardi's ex-wife Lydia is in big, big trouble. On a Sunday evening around midnight she is seen running from the plush offices of her one- time lover, Tyler Banks. She disappears into the night leaving Banks behind, dead on the car-  pet with a bullet in his head. Convinced that she is innocent, Joe enlists the help of his pal, lawyer Ray Giordano, and bail bondsman Mick Clausen, to prove Lydia's innocence, even as his assign- ment to publicize Jimmy Cagney's comeback movie for Warner's threatens to take up all of his time. Who really pulled the trigger that night? Was it the millionaire whose influence reached into City Hall? Or the not so grieving widow finally freed from a loveless marriage. Maybe it was the partner who wanted the business all to himself as well as the new widow. And what about the mysterious envelope, the one that disappeared and every- one claims never existed? Is it the key to the killer's identity and what is the secret that has been kept hidden for the past forty years?

Book Four—1950
EVERYBODY WANTS AN OSCAR

After six long years Joe Bernardi's novel is at last finished and has been shipped to a publisher. But even as he awaits news, fingers crossed for luck, things are heating up at the studio. Soon production will begin on Tennessee Williams' "The Glass Menagerie" and Jane Wyman has her sights set on a second consecutive Academy Award. Jack Warner has just signed Gertrude Lawrence for the pivotal role of Amanda and is positive that the Oscar will go to Gertie. And meanwhile Eleanor Parker, who has gotten rave reviews for a prison picture called "Caged" is sure that 1950 is her year to take home the trophy. Faced with three very talented ladies all vying for his best efforts, Joe is resigned to performing a monumental juggling act. Thank God 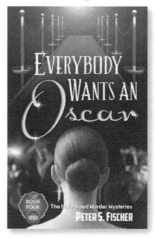 he has nothing else to worry about or at least that was the case until his agent informed him that a screenplay is floating around Hollywood that is a dead ringer for his newly completed novel. Will the ladies be forced to take a back seat as Joe goes after the thief that has stolen his work, his good name and six years of his life?

THE UNKINDNESS OF STRANGERS

Warner Brothers is getting it from all sides and Joe Bernardi seems to be everybody's favorite target. "A Streetcar Named Desire" is unproducible, they say. Too violent, too seedy, too sexy, too controversial and what's worse, it's being directed by that well-known pinko, Elia Kazan. To make matters worse, the country's number one hate monger, newspaper columnist Bryce Tremayne, is coming after Kazan with a vengeance and nothing Joe can do or say will stop him. A vicious expose column is set to run in every Hearst paper in the nation on the upcoming Sunday but a funny thing happens Friday night. Tremayne is found in a compromising condition behind the wheel of his car, a bullet hole between his eyes. Come Sunday and the

scurrilous attack on Kazan does not appear. Rumors fly. Kazan is suspected but he's not the only one with a motive. Consider:

Elvira Tremayne, the unloved widow. Did Tremayne slug her one time too many?

Hubbell Cox, the flunky whose homosexuality made him a target of derision.

Willie Babbitt, the muscle. He does what he's told and what he's told to do is often unpleasant.

Jenny Coughlin, Tremayne's private secretary. But how private and what was her secret agenda?

Jed Tompkins, Elvira's father, a rich Texas cattle baron who had only contempt for his son-in-law.

Boyd Larabee, the bookkeeper, hired by Tompkins to win Cox's confidence and report back anything he's learned.

Annie Petrakis, studio makeup artist. Tremayne destroyed her lover. Has she returned the favor?

Book Six—1952

NICE GUYS FINISH DEAD

Ned Sharkey is a fugitive from mob revenge. For six years he's been successfully hiding out in the Los Angeles area while a $100,000 contract for his demise hangs over his head. But when Warner Brothers begins filming "The Winning Team", the story of Grover Cleveland Alexander, Ned can't resist showing up at the ballpark to reunite with his old pals from the Chicago Cubs of the early 40's who have cameo roles in the film. Big mistake. When Joe Bernardi, Warner Brothers publicity guy, inadvertently sends a press release and a photo of Ned to the Chicago papers, mysterious people from the Windy City suddenly appear and a day later at break of dawn, Ned's body is found sprawled atop the pitcher's mound. It appears that 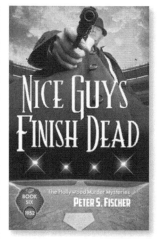 someone is a hundred thousand dollars richer. Or maybe not. Who is the 22 year old kid posing as a 50 year old former hockey star? And what about Gordo Gagliano, a mountain of a man, who is out to find Ned no matter who he has to hurt to succeed? And why did baggy pants comic Fats McCoy jump Ned and try to kill him in the pool parlor? It sure wasn't about money. Joe , riddled with guilt because the photo he sent to the newspapers may have led to Ned's death, finds himself embroiled in a dangerous game of who dun-it that leads from L. A. 's Wrigley Field to an upscale sports bar in Altadena to the posh mansions of Pasadena and finally to the swank clubhouse of Santa Anita racetrack.

Book Seven—1953

PRAY FOR US SINNERS

Joe finds himself in Quebec but it's no vacation. Alfred Hitchcock is shooting a suspenseful thriller called "I Confess" and Montgomery Clift is playing a priest accused of murder. A marriage made in heaven? Hardly. They have been at log-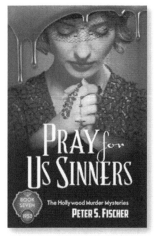
gerheads since Day One and to make matters worse their feud is spilling out into the newspapers. When viva- cious Jeanne d'Arcy, the director of the Quebec Film Commisssion volunteers to help calm the troubled waters, Joe thinks his troubles are over but that was before Jeanne got into a violent spat with a for- mer lover and suddenly found herself under arrest on a charge of first degree murder. Guilty or not guilty? Half the clues say she did it, the other half say she is being brilliantly framed. But by who? Fingers point to the crooked Gonsalvo brothers who have ties to the Buffalo mafia family and when Joe gets too close to the truth, someone tries to shut him up. . . permanently. With the Archbishop threatening to shut down the production in the wake of the scandal, Joe finds himself torn between two loyalties.

Book Eight—1954
HAS ANYBODY HERE SEEN WYCKHAM?

Everything was going smoothly on the set of "The High and the Mighty" until the cast and crew returned from lunch. With one exception. Wiley Wyckham, the bit player sitting in seat 24A on the airliner mockup, is among the missing, and without Wyckham sitting in place, director William Wellman cannot continue filming, A studio wide search is instituted. No Wyckham. A lookalike is hired that night, filming resumes the next day and still no Wyckham. Except that by this time, it's been discovered that Wyckham, a British actor, isn't really Wyckham at all but an imposter who may very well be an agent for the Russian government, The local police call in the FBI. The FBI calls in British counterintelligence. A manhunt for the missing actor ensues and Joe Bernardi, the picture's publicist, is right in the middle of the intrigue. Everyone's upset, especially John Wayne who is furious to learn that a possible Commie spy has been working in a picture he's producing and starring in. And then they find him . It's the dead of night on the Warner Brothers backlot and Wyckham is discovered hanging by his feet from a streetlamp, his body bloodied and tortured and very much dead. and pinned to his shirt is a piece of paper with the inscription "Sic Semper Proditor". (Thus to all traitors). Who was this man who had been posing as an obscure British actor? How did he smuggle himself into the country and what has he been up to? Has he been blackmailing an important higher-up in the film business and did the victim suddenly turn on him? Is the MI6 agent from London really who he says he is and what about the reporter from the London Daily Mail who seems to know all the right questions to ask as well all the right answers.

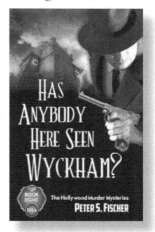

Book Nine—1955
EYEWITNESS TO MURDER

Go to New York? Not on your life. It's a lousy idea for a movie. A two year old black and white television drama? It hasn't got a prayer. This is the age of CinemaScope and VistaVision and stereophonic sound and yes, even 3-D. Burt Lancaster and Harold Hecht must be out of their minds to think they can make a hit movie out of "Marty". But then Joe Bernardi gets word that the love of his life, Bunny Lesher, is in New York and in trouble and so Joe changes his mind. He flies east to talk with the movie company and also to find Bunny and dig her out of whatever jam she's in. He finds that "Marty" is doing just fine but Bunny's jam is a lot bigger than he bargained for. She's being held by the police as an eyewitness to a brutal murder of a close

friend in a lower Manhattan police station. Only a jammed pistol saved Bunny from being the killer's second victim and now she's in mortal danger because she knows what the man looks like and he's dead set on shutting her up. Permanently. Crooked lawyers, sleazy con artists and scheming businessmen cross Joe's path, determined to keep him from the truth and when the trail leads to the sports car racing circuit at Lime Rock in Connecticut, it's Joe who becomes the killer's prime target.

$12.95
Available December 2013

Book Ten—1956
A DEADLY SHOOT IN TEXAS

Joe Bernardi's in Marfa, Texas, and he's not happy. The tarantulas are big enough to carry off the cattle , the wind's strong enough to blow Marfa into New Mexico, and the temperature would make the Congo seem chilly. A few miles out of town Warner Brothers is shooting Edna Ferber's "Giant" with a cast that includes Rock Hudson, Elizabeth Taylor and James Dean and Jack Warner is paying through the nose for Joe's expertise as a publicist. After two days in Marfa Joe finds himself in a lonely cantina around midnight, tossing back a few cold ones, and being seduced by a gorgeous student young enough to be his daughter. The flirtation goes nowhere but the next morning little Miss Coed is found dead . And there's a problem. The coroner says she died between eight and nine o'clock. Not so fast, says Joe, who saw her alive as late as one a.,m. When he points this out to the County Sheriff, all hell breaks loose and Joe becomes the target of some pretty ornery people. Like the Coroner and the Sheriff as well as the most powerful rancher in the county, his arrogant no-good son and his two flunkies, a crooked lawyer and a grieving father looking for justice or revenge, Either one will do. Will Joe expose the murderer before the murderer turns Joe into Texas road kill? Tune in.

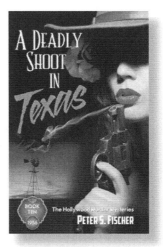

$12.95
Available 2014

ORDER FORM

To
THE GROVE POINT PRESS
P. O. Box 873
Pacific Grove, CA 93950

GROVE
POINT
P R E S S

☐ Please send the volume(s), checked below at $12.95 each. I understand each copy will be signed personally by the author. Also include my FREE "Murder, She Wrote" keepsake bookmark, also autographed by the author.

☐ Please send the volumes checked below (three or more) at the low price of $9.95 each. I understand this entitles me to any and all future purchases at this same low price. I also understand that each volume will be personally signed by the author. Also include my FREE "Murder, She Wrote" keepsake bookmark, also autographed by the author.

TITLE	QTY	PRICE
Jezebel in Blue Satin		
We Don't Need No Stinking Badges		
Love Has Nothing to Do With It		
Everybody Wants An Oscar		
The Unkindess of Strangers		
Nice Guys Finish Dead		
Pray For Us Sinners		
Has Anybody Here Seen Wyckham?		
Eyewitness to Murder *(available Dec. 2013)*		
A Deadly Shoot in Texas *(available March 2014)*		
Shipping and Handling: Add $1.50 per book, (max. charge $6.00)		
TOTAL		

Name: _____

Address: _____

_____

City: _____ State: _____ Zip: _____

☐ **Check**   ☐ **Credit Card:** __Master Card __Visa __Discover

Card number: _____

Exp. date: _____ CSV: _____

ORDER FORM

To
THE GROVE POINT PRESS
P. O. Box 873
Pacific Grove, CA 93950

GROVE POINT
P R E S S

☐ Please send the volume(s), checked below at $12.95 each. I understand each copy will be signed personally by the author. Also include my FREE "Murder, She Wrote" keepsake bookmark, also autographed by the author.

☐ Please send the volumes checked below (three or more) at the low price of $9.95 each. I understand this entitles me to any and all future purchases at this same low price. I also understand that each volume will be personally signed by the author. Also include my FREE "Murder, She Wrote" keepsake bookmark, also autographed by the author.

TITLE	QTY	PRICE
Jezebel in Blue Satin		
We Don't Need No Stinking Badges		
Love Has Nothing to Do With It		
Everybody Wants An Oscar		
The Unkindess of Strangers		
Nice Guys Finish Dead		
Pray For Us Sinners		
Has Anybody Here Seen Wyckham?		
Eyewitness to Murder *(available Dec. 2013)*		
A Deadly Shoot in Texas *(available March 2014)*		
Shipping and Handling: Add $1.50 per book, (max. charge $6.00)		
	TOTAL	

Name: _____

Address: _____

_____

City: _____ **State:** _____ **Zip:** _____

☐ **Check**   ☐ **Credit Card:** __**Master Card** __**Visa** __**Discover**

   Card number: _____

   Exp. date: _____ **CSV:** _____

ORDER FORM

To
THE GROVE POINT PRESS
P. O. Box 873
Pacific Grove, CA 93950

☐ Please send the volume(s), checked below at $12.95 each. I understand each copy will be signed personally by the author. Also include my FREE "Murder, She Wrote" keepsake bookmark, also autographed by the author.

☐ Please send the volumes checked below (three or more) at the low price of $9.95 each. I understand this entitles me to any and all future purchases at this same low price. I also understand that each volume will be personally signed by the author. Also include my FREE "Murder, She Wrote" keepsake bookmark, also autographed by the author.

TITLE	QTY	PRICE
Jezebel in Blue Satin		
We Don't Need No Stinking Badges		
Love Has Nothing to Do With It		
Everybody Wants An Oscar		
The Unkindess of Strangers		
Nice Guys Finish Dead		
Pray For Us Sinners		
Has Anybody Here Seen Wyckham?		
Eyewitness to Murder *(available Dec. 2013)*		
A Deadly Shoot in Texas *(available March 2014)*		
Shipping and Handling: Add $1.50 per book, (max. charge $6.00)		
	TOTAL	

Name: _____

Address: _____

_____

City: _____ State: _____ Zip: _____

☐ **Check**   ☐ **Credit Card:** __Master Card __Visa __Discover

Card number: _____

Exp. date: _____ CSV: _____